SIXTEEN YEARS OF TRAVEL IN SCOTLAND, IRELAND, ENGLAND, AND WALES

By

Bob Jones ©

DEDICATION

Without the steadfast encouragement and support from my lovely best friend and wife, Anne, this book as well as the three other travel guides we've published would never have been written.   Her contribution to this and the other books can never be acknowledged enough.

TABLE OF CONTENTS

A Preface

The golf round at West Linton Golf Course in West Lothian was our second round in Scotland. We'd played with a local member, a retired civil servant from Edinburgh, who kept saying, "Oh, no!" at my wayward shots. He was very pleasant, despite reminding me constantly that I wasn't playing up to even my low standards. After saying good-bye to our playing companion, Anne and I asked in the pro shop if there was a good pub nearby. The recommendation was the Golden Arms in the small village of West Linton. The hunting lodge-styled Golden Arms was the third Scottish pub we'd visited in the two days we'd been in Scotland and we were getting used to the pub dogs which seemed to be a fixture. Anne had a Guinness--real Guinness, not the canned imitation we get in the states--and I, as the driver challenging a right-hand drive car on the left side of the road, had coke. We shared a bag of potato chips (we'd learn later that they are called "crisps" in the British Isles). Two pub dogs came over to our table and sat quietly watching us eat the potato chips. When offered, neither dog refused chips and they were very polite about taking them without nipping our fingers. One wall had a working fireplace taking the chill off the early fall day and book shelves filled with old tomes. In a corner sat a well-used upright piano with a sign on it: "Feel free to play me!" Between sips of her Guinness, Anne said to me, "We ought to write about this--the golf, the pubs, the dogs."

Thus was born our first book, or at least the germ of our first book. It took us five years to complete *Scotland's Hidden Gems: Golf Courses and Pubs* (now revised as *Golf in Scotland: The*

Hidden Gems), which covers 110 of the lesser known Scottish golf courses, more than 80 pubs, and a whole bunch of tourist attractions. That was just the start. We now have three golf/pub guide books on the market. In the past sixteen years we've played almost 1000 rounds of golf on more than 400 golf courses in Scotland, Ireland, England, and Wales. We've eaten at about 300 pubs, restaurants, and tearooms, and visited literally hundreds of cultural and historic attractions and a few that were nothing more than tourist traps. For more than two years I wrote a column for *Historic Scotland Magazine* presenting the American tourist's view of historic properties. I've submitted several travel-related or history-related articles to various magazines, and even had a few accepted. My files are filled with more than 35,000 images of castles, great houses, cairns, standing stones, and magnificent scenery. We've stayed for almost a cumulative year and a half in one B&B in Scotland, where we've become so much a part of the family that we are expected to be there for birthdays (important days to the Scots) and graduations. In our twenty-seven trips to Scotland, four to Ireland, four to England, and three to Wales--that's 40 months in Scotland, four months in Ireland, and two months in England and Wales give or take a jet-lagged day or four--we've accumulated enough miles that three of the trips have been free, except for the taxes and fees you pay to fly for free.

In all these trips we've gathered numerous stories in our daily journals about places and people, some of which appear in our travel guides. Many more, though, have been waiting for this book to see the light of print. Some of the vignettes in this book are informational. Many are humorous, at least I hope they are. Some are poignant or painful. At least one is nothing less than pure rant. Most of the characters in these stories are quaint or interesting, but a couple of villains do make appearances.

The purpose to this writing? These stories strive for no higher purpose than to entertain and enlighten. I sincerely hope they, in some small measure, accomplish that goal. Please, enjoy!

Anne the Navigator

CHAPTER 1: It's Never the Wrong Side Unless Someone Is Coming at You

One of the questions I am often asked is, "How hard is it driving on the wrong side of the road?" The answer I give is that driving on the left side is not the wrong side, just the other side. In truth, I haven't had much difficulty driving a right-hand drive auto on the left side of the road, especially after the first couple of years. I now have driven about 80,000 miles on the left side of narrow, narrow roads with only a couple of minor scrapes to hang around my neck.

It is driving on the other side, the roads, and the cars, that have generated many of our stories--humorous and scary. Other stories have been generated by the difficulties in getting to the small roads—air travel. I remember a time when we used to dress in suit and tie to get on a plane. Now we wish we could wear a suit of armor, but those difficulties lead to some entertaining stories, and I'll start there.

Why Air Canada Is Not My Favorite

Our first few times flying Air Canada were good, but our fall 2002 trip was our last on that airline. If anything could go wrong it did and yet there were a few good things that happened as well.

On our day of departure our early morning flight from Portland to Vancouver was canceled and we were rebooked on a flight several hours later. Suddenly we had gone from 4 hours layover in Toronto to only 45 minutes which worried both of us and rightly so. When we got to Vancouver we were directed through Canadian Customs--a 40 minute line. As we got to the Customs officer he told us we could have gone through a much shorter (15 minute) line for passengers with connecting flights. As we left Customs we wanted to get a bite of lunch, but one look at the security line gave us pause. We asked an agent about the long security lines. She asked us our destination and we told her Glasgow, Scotland. "You'll need to be in the international line I'm afraid." Thirty minutes later we got to where security checks our tickets and the attendant says, "You're going to Toronto; you need to be in domestic security," and pointed us to a very short line. By this time we are close to our 1:30 flight time for Toronto so headed straight to the gate. The gate was empty. We finally found someone who told us the flight had been delayed until 2:30. Now we knew there is no way we'd make our connection from Toronto to Glasgow.

When the gate opened we asked an agent about our missed connections. He said that not only would we miss the Glasgow connection, but that there wouldn't be another flight to Glasgow from Toronto until the next day at 9:30 PM. Anne was near tears and I don't blame her. We had booked our flights six months early and had planned golf and meeting our friend Marcia in Ayr. Now it looked like we'd miss it all. We were resigned to it; it didn't seem like there was anything else we could do.

On our flight from Vancouver to Toronto I asked the purser about our missed connections. He said he'd do some checking for us. Before we got off the plane in Toronto the purser told us he'd arranged for us to catch a midnight flight to London and then a hop on British Airways to Glasgow. We'd get to Glasgow about 3:30 PM instead of the 9:30 AM of our original schedule, but at least we'd be in Scotland on the correct day. The relief was evident on our faces.

Then he told us about the problems we'd face in Toronto. First, we had only two hours to make our flight which was departing from a different terminal. We'd have to get our luggage, change our tickets, and recheck our baggage. The airlines had a special cart ready to pick us up and take us to pick up our luggage. The trouble was that it was now 10:45 PM and the luggage office closed at 10:00. It took another fifteen minutes for someone to come and find our bags so we could be taken to the next terminal. We got reticketed and bags rechecked with about ten minutes to spare.

After all these hassles the last two legs of the trip were fairly smooth. Even negotiating Heathrow in London wasn't much problem. Perhaps the only highlight of the day was while we waiting in Heathrow for our British Airways flight to Glasgow a lady overhead Anne and I worrying about whether the B&B would hold our room. She turned to us and said, "Don't worry, dearies, I used to run a B&B and you could always stay at my farm--here's my address and phone." Such kindness from a complete stranger is one of the reasons we love Scotland.

In the end we got our car, made it to the B&B within a few minutes of our friend Marcia, and had a lovely dinner in the pub across the street--although both Anne and I did keep falling asleep over our meal. The main lesson we took away from the experience is that now we always leave our first full day in Scotland unbooked of any important activities in case we get hung up in travels. Oh, yes, and we don't fly Air Canada anymore.

Pay for Economy Plus Seats and Get Less

In late August of 2012 we took a new routing to Edinburgh. The flight was booked through Delta Airlines but flying a KLM, the Dutch airline, plane and partnered with Alaska Airlines. The flight plan called for an early morning flight from Portland to Vancouver,

BC, then after a four and a half hour layover on to Amsterdam then to Edinburgh.

I knew we were in trouble when I tried to check-in online the day before our flight. The Delta check-in site routed me to KLM, whose plane we'd be flying in. I checked in on the KLM flights (Vancouver to Amsterdam and Amsterdam to Edinburgh) and even purchased Economy Comfort seats for $185 extra a ticket--more leg room, two seats in a row instead of three, but our flight from Portland to Vancouver appeared nowhere. When I tried to get boarding passes for that flight specifically I was directed to Alaska Airlines. On the Alaska site I input all our details and was told we couldn't check-in online and had to go to the Alaska counter on the day of our flight. The problem was I had no documents from Alaska/ Horizon, only from Delta. At the airport I was first told I had to go Delta since that's where we got our tickets. After standing in the Delta line for twenty minutes a clerk told me I'd have to go back to Alaska to check-in. After twenty minutes in that line a different Alaska clerk checked us in without further complication.

The 4:30 layover in Vancouver isn't bad---interesting shopping, nice eateries, and comfortable seating areas. It is, though, quite a long layover.

From Vancouver to Amsterdam we were flying on an older Boing 777 configured 3-3-3. We had paid for the better seats, Economy Comfort, and had selected the row of two seats (instead of three) by the bulkhead. Economy Comfort on this plane was the most uncomfortable seats we've ever had--seats so narrow I had to literally squeeze my hips down against each arm rest to even get in, trays that wouldn't come down (pushed against our bellies, one attendant even suggested she'd bring our food on a tray we could hold to eat from), seats with one inch of foam padding (within minutes my legs were going to sleep), but plenty of leg room. I complained strongly! An attendant gave me an extra pillow to sit on, but that just made the seat tighter and the tray fit even less. This was unacceptable, especially for $185 a seat extra. To her credit, an attendant did get a fellow in a row by himself to trade for our two seats. It solved our problem, but he didn't get a good deal and seemed uncomfortable most of the time--if the drinks hadn't have been free I would have bought him one, or several. To top it off we got bad food (worse than usual), bad movies, no air, too hot, I ended up with a minor reflux attack. All in all, one of our worst trips.

On most of our other trips we've had good experiences with Economy Comfort. This trip, though, it was the most expensive and we were really paying for Economy Minus.

The Emergency Exit Row Nursery

On the long flights from Portland to Scotland or returning, we are always on the lookout for ways to make the trip a little more comfortable. Now we buy the Economy Extra Comfort seats on the Delta/KLM flight we take from Portland to Amsterdam (the extra four inches between seat rows does make a difference), but before Extra Comfort we'd try to get exit row seats for that little extra room. The last time we did that, though, cured us of taking exit row seats near the galley. With a little standing room by the galley and some extra room in front of our seats, our galley exit row turned into a nursery. On this flight there were several families with young children and they sought whatever extra room they could find to let the children move a bit or to have some pacing room for bouncing babies in their arms. Once our little extra room sanctuary was discovered by one mom others soon latched onto it as well. It took only an hour or so into our flight for our extra room to turn into the economy class nursery. All through the flight we had front row seats to watch the show, Moms with Kids on Planes. Our Bose Noise Reduction Headphones is what kept us sane--thank you Bose!

Let the Glasses Speak

Early in our fall flight to Scotland in 2010, I was busy reading when a male flight attendant stopped to ask me a question, probably whether I wanted peanuts or pretzels. I was so engrossed (or so close to falling asleep) that he startled me. I looked up, took off my glasses which I wear all the time, and answered him. He gave me a quizzical look and said, "Do you have to take your glasses off to talk?" I hadn't even noticed that I had done that. I put my glasses back on and we both laughed. For the rest of the trip each time he talked to me I took my glasses off to answer. I should have just let the glasses do the talking.

We Don't Lose Luggage Often, but When We Do...

On our spring 2014 trip to Scotland we were late getting out of the Portland airport--luggage from no-shows had to be off loaded and delayed our flight 35 minutes. The delay meant that we barely had an hour in Amsterdam's Schiphol airport to make our flight to Edinburgh. We practically had to run from one end of the airport to the other to catch our flight. Without legs our luggage couldn't make it and missed the connection. When we arrived in Edinburgh we found that no luggage from the Portland flight to Amsterdam made the connection.

It took KLM the rest of the day to track our three bags. That evening (Wednesday) we got an email from KLM saying they turned our luggage over to a courier at 7:30 PM. Our bags didn't get to us that night. Thursday morning we got a call from the courier that they had just received our luggage and would get the bags to us in Crieff between three and four PM. Our luggage arrived at 4:45. The courier blamed KLM for the delay and KLM blamed the courier.

In the meantime, we were without clothes or essential toiletries. KLM said they'd compensate us for essentials and to just buy what we needed and send them the receipts. Anne and I did a mini shopping spree: underwear, shirts, socks, sweaters, toiletries. I contacted KLM about reimbursement and gave them amounts, but before I could send them receipts they emailed that a check was already on its way to our home. We were duly impressed. And, yes, when we got home there were two checks waiting for us, but they were made out in British Pounds. It took several weeks to get our bank to finally cash the checks and deposit the money to our account.

Shame on KLM for losing our luggage. Kudos to KLM for compensating us so quickly.

Driving on the Other Side

Being ambidextrous helps with driving a right-hand drive car (the steering wheel is on the right side, you shift with the left hand, and, yes, the clutch is on the same side as in our cars) when your forty-some year driving career has been in a left-hand drive. The first time, though, was traumatic. Even after doing a few practice laps of the rental car parking lot, I was ill prepared for the first two traffic circles we had to negotiate to get out of the Glasgow airport. I pulled out into traffic slowly and had to go around one traffic circle twice before figuring out which exit to take. I know that whole trip I was the typical, slow, excessively cautious tourist driver.

Anne, the wonderful navigator she is, had one difficulty. In the traffic circles, which replace our stop-signed intersections, you drive around clockwise with all the exits leaving on the left. It's like driving clockwise around the hub of a wagon wheel where each of the spokes is an exit road. Her trouble was she kept telling me to take the next right--that's the way it looked to her on the map. There are no right turns off a traffic circle in the British Isles; they're all lefts. We finally figured out that she needed to tell me to take the second or third exit and forget about left or right, which was all right with her since she doesn't know her right from her left.

My most dramatic impressions of driving the first year come from the drive from Crieff to Kenmore in central Scotland. The road is fairly narrow, although at the time it seemed infinitesimally small. Add to the narrowness a bush-covered rock wall on my left side for five miles. In that five mile stretch we meet two buses and one lorry (truck). Anne was flinching every few seconds as the bushes slapped at her side of the car. I drive that section of road now hardly slowing down, but will still come close to the bushes if a bus or a lorry is taking more than their share of the road, as they usually do.

Single-track roads present special challenges. Many of the roads in the far northwest corner of Scotland and on the west coast of Ireland are big enough for one vehicle at a time. The better of these roads have pullouts or wide areas meant as passing places about every half mile or so. We soon learned that there is an etiquette to driving in these single-track areas. When approaching another vehicle head on, the driver closest to a passing place pulls into the middle of the passing place if it's on the left or stops across from the middle if it's on the right. The approaching vehicle then goes by if the passing place is on the left or around through the passing place if its on the right. It may sound complicated, but works brilliantly when you know the system. The first few times I would be nervous about whether I was doing it correctly. Now, like most locals, I can time my approach so that we both hit the passing place at about the same time and neither of us has to slow much at all. Anne, though, still shuts her eyes until we're by the other car.

The biggest challenge I now face concerning driving on the left is coming home and driving on our side. In the British Isles I concentrate on my driving because I know it's not my natural side. When I get home the tendency is to put my driving on automatic pilot, and not concentrate the way I should. On the other side, I have hardly ever found myself driving in the wrong lane, but I have caught myself several times pulling out into the wrong lane at home. Luckily, no one else has caught me doing it by hitting me head on in their lane.

Driving the Ring of Kerry

Ireland's Ring of Kerry, from Killarney through Glenbeigh, Cahersiveen, Valencia Island, Waterville, Kenmare and back to Killarney, is one of the "must take" driving tours in the country. The scenery around the peninsula is breathtaking--vistas along Dingle Bay and Ballinskelligs Bay, out to Skellig Michael (a pair of small islands), and along the Kenmare River. Attractions abound--the Peat Bog Village, the Skellig Michael Visitor's Centre, Staigue Fort. Overriding all the features and the beauty are the BUSES! Seemingly hundreds of large, aggressive tour buses! If you're not careful, all of them will be coming for you.

We'd read several Ireland guide books and all agreed: drive around the Ring clockwise so that you won't have to eat the exhaust of dozens of oversized tour coaches. We were so lucky that our B&B hosts at Abbey House in Kenmare suggested we follow the buses instead of meeting the buses. As locals they know better than the best guide book writers who are most probably visitors.

Driving the Ring counterclockwise, with the buses, meant several things. Yes, we did have to breathe a little exhaust, but the tour buses pull off enough so that we could get by them relatively easily. It also meant that at the Kerry Peat Bog Village we got the reduced tour price of admission because the ticket seller thought we were part of the tour--a € saved is an extra half of Guinness. Next, either way you go around the Ring, you lose the coaches at Valencia Island because they can't cross the bridge. Most important, however, is the fact that on the narrow (almost single-track) ring road you won't meet a bus that takes up three-quarters of the road coming at you around a blind corner with a 300-foot drop-off on your side. We've seen buses clip the mirrors off autos as they passed and keep on going. We also watched as a particularly large coach keep right on coming as two autos backed into a side ditch to get out of the way around one corner in the Killarney Park part of the road. The tourists on the bus had quite astonished looks on their faces as they passed the screaming drivers--the ones who had followed the tour book advice.

The exception to the follow-the-buses advice is if you plan to be out at Waterville or Valencia Island before noon and come back the same way. It takes the tour buses until noon to get that far out on the Ring Road. Anyway you go, the Ring of Kerry is a lovely, difficult drive well worth you time, but a great deal less frightening if you follow the buses.

GPS

We have good maps. We buy new maps every couple of years. Yet, we find that a GPS like we have at home is useful in our overseas travels. The final straw in our map-orienteering-camel's back was a trip back to Crieff from some southern golf in Stranraer and Portpatrick.

As we were coming into the metro Glasgow area on the A74 we looked for our junction with the M73. About a mile from our junction was a big sign which said, "Motor-way Closed." We passed the closed junction and Anne tried desperately to figure out where to go next when we ran out of A74. The main road ended and dumped us unceremoniously into a suburb of Glasgow. Anne tried to find us on her map, while I didn't help matters by saying in a cartoonish manner, "Which way do we go? Which way do we go?" Actually, it was a more panicky, "Quick! Tell me where to go!"

"I don't know what to tell you because I don't know where we are," was Anne's matter of fact statement.

For me, a person with so little sense of direction I can get lost in a phone booth, that was not what I wanted to hear. So, I did what any self-respecting male would do (despite the stereotypical characterizations to the contrary), I pulled into a petrol station to fill up. My thinking was very logical. I'd fill up with fuel in case I had to drive around lost all night, and I'd send navigator Anne in to ask for directions. What Anne found out in the station store/office was not at all helpful. No one seemed to know how to get where we wanted to go on the M73 if the M73 was closed. Finally, a woman paying for her petrol came to our rescue and said she was heading the way we wanted to go and we could follow her to the M9 from which we could find our way.

We thanked her and took off for the ride of our lives. As helpful as the lady was, she wasn't the easiest to follow. After driving down back streets and alleys, having to run red lights to stay with her, she did drive past an open entrance to M73 which Anne recognized. We waved to our guide and headed for home. As a result of our detour we increased our resolve to bring a GPS with us to Scotland.

We have used our new GPS well in the last few trips. It has really helped us find some of the out-of-the-way courses we've wanted to play, but a GPS does have its limits. For example, we used our GPS to find Tudor House, our B&B in Shrewsbury, England. At least it helped us get close to the B&B. The directions from the GPS kept taking us around a one-way grid and saying we were at our destination as we passed a sidewalk leading to a church. Finally, I parked and walked back to the sidewalk. Sure enough, it was a small street and it led to the 15th century house hidden in an alley. The GPS just couldn't tell us what we needed to know. Even worse on that trip was using the GPS to find the massive Durham Cathedral in Durham, England. We could see the cathedral, it's hard to miss, but our directions from the GPS first took us past the cathedral to a Sainsbury store (like a large grocery/ department store). On our second pass, we again could see the cathedral off to our right, but the GPS street directions led us to a petrol station and said, "You have arrived." We shut off the GPS and went in to the station to ask for directions the old fashioned way. What we learned was that the GPS was being asked to do an impossible task--to find a cathedral on an island with no public road over to it. The GPS must have been just as frustrated as we were. In another case we missed a GPS direction when trying to find Ratho Park Golf Course. The GPS kept trying to get us to turn around at crossover points on the divided highway we were driving. The trouble was that all the crossovers had been barricaded--a fact the GPS didn't know.

With all these examples of GPS problems, our GPS has been a savior at times. As we were leaving Baberton GC near Edinburgh which had been easy to find, our playing partner mentioned that we couldn't go back the same way we'd come. We turned on our GPS, trusted her directions (we program our GPS with a female voice), and went straight home.

Maps are good, but a new GPS can be better. Can be. If you let it. We turned on the GPS one morning to help us find The Duke's Golf Course on Fife, down a tricky bit of small road. The GPS would start up, locate us, and then stick at "calculating 44%." Anne tried everything she could think of and anything I could think of. After shutting it off and restarting the GPS, we got up to "calculating 48%" before it stuck. Anne tried one last time: "In point four miles enter a roundabout and take the third exit." Wow! We had her back and working. I asked Anne what she had done. She said she'd removed a paper clip she had put on the antenna before we'd left that morning. The metal clip must have been creating interference or blocking full reception. Poor Lizzie (yes, we've named our female-voiced GPS) had been struggling all day to help us and was thankful to be free.

Lizzie does take directions well. Going into the downtown shopping area of Aberdeen from well out in the country, we programmed her for "Town Center." She took us past the shopping district and down a side street. In the middle of a block of derelict office buildings she deposited us saying, "You have arrived." She had brought us to the geographic center of Aberdeen, instead of the heart of town. Be careful what you ask for.

GPSs can be very helpful, if you let them.

Does GPS Stand for Great Personal Satan?

I've written about GPS problems before--taking us into the geographical center of a city instead of city center, not able to find major attraction like Durham Cathedral--so it is perhaps not surprising that even with newer GPS devices we still have concerns. In the spring of 2013 we had problems with a brand new Garmin GPS system. On the good side it got us to the B&B in Bude, Cornwall, with no problems. It also did a good job of directing us to the back parking area for the B&B in Tavistock. But on the bad side we have several examples.

First, trying to get to Cheddar Gorge was a major fiasco. Coming from the north we could see on the map that the Gorge was on the southeast side of Bristol and the motorway went around the city to the west. But that's not where the GPS took us. She (the bitch) took us off the motorway and directly into the heart of Bristol. Bristol's a major city! By the time we realized she was going to take us through the downtown section we were lost enough that we had to give her her head. Through the shopping district, through about three small neighborhoods, through a suburb village and out into the country we went. And then to Cheddar Gorge. It had taken us 40 minutes to go where the motorway would have taken us in ten. When we left we found out the entrance to the Gorge was about five minutes off the M.

Next, at Penzance she took us off the coast road and up through the town's one-way grid and got us near our B&B destination which was only one block off the coast highway we'd left. Not only was the routing terrible, the GPS directed us into a city garden--literally into the garden--and said, "You have arrived." We had to get a gardener to help us get out and back to city streets.

Third, the GPS said in her supercilious voice that we should leave the M before Taunton to get to the Greyhound Inn in the village of Staple Fitzpaine. Onto a series of small roads and through numerous small hamlets we went to get to Staple Fitzpaine the back way. The next morning our hosts directed us straight down the road to the motorway--a five minute journey. At this point I checked all the settings on the GPS again to make sure we were being directed the quickest route.

Finally, when heading to Tynemouth on the south side of Newcastle, we turned off the GPS when we saw that she was going to take us off the main highway (A1) and onto back roads through village after village and the heart of Newcastle to get to our B&B which was on the A1.

When we got home from the trip I sent the GPS unit back to Garmin. They called and said that even the technicians couldn't get it to work correctly. So far the newest one has been better; although she did take us a rather circuitous route to one golf course on Fife the next trip.

Mirror, Mirror, on the Rock Wall

Ireland is notorious for narrow, winding roads in not very good condition. On our first trip I found out how narrow the roads really were.

We were touring the Connemara area in the west of Ireland, having an enjoyable drive looking for sites and photo opportunities. Since I had driven two trips before in Scotland, I felt fairly confident in my ability to negotiate the roads on the other side. We came to a bridge, about 100 yards long with stone walls on both sides. The road indicated that the lanes narrowed, but I didn't interpret that to mean the bridge was single lane. Mistake! A small pickup was already part way through the bridge when I started across thinking it would be a tight squeeze, but still thinking I had room. The closer we got to meeting the less room I could see I had. The pickup crept past me, the driver glaring at me all the while. I moved as far to the left as I could when...crunch!...my left side mirror caught the stone wall and popped in.

On the other side of the bridge I pulled off to look at the damage. The mirror was the break away kind and had simply turned in. There were several dirty scrapes on the edge of the mirror, but they weren't very noticeable. I had been lucky. My misjudgment had cost me some embarrassment, but nothing more severe than a bruised ego.

Pay the Price

The UK tax system is quite different from ours. Great Britain has a VAT (Value Added Tax), like a national sales tax on produced goods, and heavy, heavy petrol (gasoline) taxes which are used to pay for government services like schools, roads, and medical care. The system makes our gas taxes seem paltry. We've paid as little as £.78 a litre and as much as £1.06 a litre--that's between about $6.50 and $9.00 a gallon when you factor in the exchange rate. Those figures pale in comparison to the price we paid in Durness in the far northwest corner of Scotland.

We've visited Durness a couple of times to play the wonderful 9-hole Durness Golf Course and to enjoy the scenery along the mostly single-track road you drive to get to Durness. On one particular fall Sunday in 2008, we had played golf, had a sinful cup of hot chocolate, and were ready for a drive along the top of Scotland. Before we left Durness I asked about petrol and found out that the only place to get petrol in town was closed on Sunday. About half way along the route from Durness to Bettyhill, I started paying attention to our dropping petrol gauge. At our lunch stop at the Tongue Hotel I asked about the possibility of filling up. The response I got, with a chuckle, was that there was none available on Sunday in Tongue and probably not in Rae or Thorso. The whole of the north of Scotland had closed pumps on Sunday. After lunch we traveled as far as we dare and then headed back to our B&B in Durness. With less than a quarter of a tank for our trip to Dornoch on Monday, we knew we'd be staying in Durness until the pumps opened up about 10:00.

Just as the station owner opened, we pulled up to the station's single pump. After picking my jaw up off the floorboards, I ask for 40 litres (less than ten gallons). I paid the bill of £75 and we were on our way. It didn't take me too long to figure that at an exchange rate of $2.05 to £1, my petrol had cost me over $150.00 or about $14.00 a gallon! Lesson learned. Be sure to fill up before heading into the back country in the north of Scotland or be prepared to pay, pay, pay the price.

Peebles' Parking

Our first B&B in Scotland, Carl and Kathryn Lane's Lindores House in Peebles, is in a great location on the main road through the village and only a few blocks from the shopping area. The neighborhood, we have since learned, is very typical of Scottish village neighborhoods. The streets are narrow with not much off street parking. Houses which do have garages have small, single car garages. After moving our suitcases into our room, Carl suggested we move our car into the garage. We went out to the car and Carl opened the small garage and pulled his car through into a back parking spot. I pulled our small five-door rented Vauxhall off the street and toward the garage. I stopped abruptly. As small as my car was I just couldn't imagine being able to shoehorn it into this tiny garage, especially since I had only been driving right-hand drive cars for a couple of hours. Carl saw my look of panic and suggested that he pull it in for me. He took my place behind the wheel and without hesitation drove straight into the garage with at least millimeters to spare on both sides. For the rest of that trip Carl pulled the car in for me, although the last morning of our stay I did pull it out of the garage without tearing the building down or even scraping the Vauxhall label off the sides of the car.

The next year I impressed Carl when on our first night at Lindores I drove the car into the garage with only slight trepidation. A couple of thousand miles experience on the other side the year before made much difference in my confidence.

Petrol Strike

Peebles was the first village we stayed in on our first visit to Scotland in September 2000. We stayed with Kathryn and Carl Lane at their lovely Lindores House B&B [see B&B Chapter for more information about Lindores House]. Our trip started out wonderfully with great golf, fun pubs and dining, and interesting attractions including a real Highland Games on our first day. Then disaster hit as a nationwide petrol (gasoline) strike. The news was filled with images of Tony Blair trying to keep the country calm as station after station shut down its pumps due to the lack of fuel. The news was also filled with images of angry truckers refusing to deliver petrol because of the high taxes they had to pay. The only two stations in Peebles hung up signs saying, "No Petrol," and we had only three-quarters of our first tank left and 20 days remaining on our trip.

All kinds of thoughts went through our minds including turning in the car and continuing our Scotland stay as a train trip, or using all our petrol and flying back early. In the end we decided to extend our stay locally, see what we could with the limited petrol we had, and hope that the Petrol strike could be settled.

We played golf at the local courses a couple of times, hit all the attractions within short driving distance, arranged with Carl and Kathryn to stay an extra day at Lindores, and constantly watched the petrol gauge. We did have our only negative pub experience in Scotland (in all 27 trips) because of the strike. After golf at West Linton we were seated having a beer in the Golden Arms when a local trucker, unable to get fuel and so fueling up on local ale, started getting louder and louder about how this problem was all caused by the Americans who were controlling Blair. As he started getting off his stool his friends grabbed him and hustled him out of the pub with profound apologies to us, "He's normally not like this."

As our tank got emptier and decision day got closer, we implemented our final plan. Carl believed that the strike was mostly English media hype and that we'd find petrol when we headed north. He also arranged for us to get ten gallons under the table from his neighbor, a station owner. We said our good-byes and headed north to the M9, a major north-south motor-way, with the plan to find petrol soon or take the turnoff toward Glasgow and end our trip. At the Kinross exit on the M9 we finally saw a major petrol station with all pumps working. We filled up there and although the news kept touting that the nation's pumps were closed, we never had trouble filling up again. Carl was correct, the strike and petrol crisis had been a phantom crisis blown way out of proportion by English media hype, an occurrence we've seen repeated many times in our other trips.

Rip-off Car Rentals

Renting a vehicle is problematic, especially in a foreign country. We've had success in Scotland renting from Arnold Clark, the UK's major car dealer. Having rented enough and for long enough periods that we are now preferred customers, we get some really sweet deals. In Ireland, however, we can't use that resource. Instead we rented from Rip-off Rentals.

The company we have used is Thrifty of Ireland, but I believe the same thing could happen when renting from most agencies in Ireland or even in the UK. So be warned.

Our first experience in Ireland renting a car opened our eyes. Driving conditions in Ireland and poor drivers have forced most credit card companies to refuse to insure drivers who pay by credit card, a service they perform in other countries including the UK. Drivers in Ireland have a reputation for being the worst drivers in Europe, and from the death tolls posted at Black Spots (notoriously dangerous spots of roadway) I'd say the reputation is deserved. Next, when we returned our car after our first trip we watched the person turning in his car ahead of us get charged €200 extra for scraped wheels (probably from hitting curbs). We were fine that first trip, but it persuaded me to take out full CDW, Collision Damage Waiver, which covers the complete car completely.

At the end of our next trip to Ireland I was especially thankful for the full CDW coverage. It had cost me an extra €5 a day, but was well worth it. We turned our car back to Rip-off Rentals (aka Thrifty of Ireland). I knew we'd done absolutely no damage to the car, so I wasn't worried when the agent wanted to go out to check the car over. He looked high and low, carefully at each wheel and tire, under the front and rear bumpers, rubbed every spot that could possibly be a scratch, wrote several notes on his paper, and then gave me the bad news. A puncture of the metalwork under the front bumper, scrapes to two of the wheels, excessive sidewall damage to one of the tires, and several small scratches at various places. The damage amounted to several hundred euros in repairs, but he'd be willing to settle for €200 cash to call the whole thing even. I smiled and said, "Read the contract. We took out the full CDW, so I don't believe I owe a thing."

He looked at the paper and then at me, then he tore up his damage survey and wished us good journey home. If we hadn't taken out the full CDW or hadn't understood what it meant, he could have pocketed a cool couple of bills and no one, not the customer nor the company, would have been the wiser. It's a good scam, but being wise to it we continued to rent from Rip-off Rentals (they did have the best prices on good cars) until they went out of business in 2008. Renter Beware!

Street Crossing Guard

Anne and I were looking for lunch in the Irish village of Slain. A stop into a small local grocer and a quick question gave us a good lead on lunch. The Old Postie, a coffee shop/tearoom occupying the old village post office, sounded like our cup of tea. We got directions and set out on foot to cross the N2, the main road through the village.

At the corner was a crosswalk, but no signal. We waited and watched the traffic whiz by. The N2 is the main road from Dublin toward Newgrange, one of Ireland's most popular tourist attractions. Each time we thought there was a lull one direction, the traffic would pick up from the other. We must have stood there for three or four minutes waiting for someone to stop or the flow of traffic to be interrupted. Just when we were about to give up in exasperation two elderly locals (elderly to us, anyway) came up behind us and without hesitation one said, "Come on, dearies, they won't hit you." Both continued to step out into the flow of traffic. With screeching tires the sea of cars parted and the ladies walked boldly across the road, with us sheepishly in tow.

When we reached the other side, the ladies bid us a good afternoon and continued their jaunt. We figuratively dusted ourselves off, not knowing quite what had hits us, and continued down the block to The Old Postie.

We might have starved to death if it hadn't been for the good graces of two matronly Irish ladies who took pity on a couple of visitors and played street crossing guard.

We Almost Bit the Dust

I have driven more than 80,000 miles on the "other side" since 2000 and I feel comfortable behind the left-hand drive wheel. I do not drive like a tourist, but I'm not exactly a native driver either. When golf courses tell me it will take me "x" amount to get to them, I ask how long it would take them to get from where I am to them. I then split the difference between the two times and am usually just about right. I feel confident about my driving now on the other side. That's where the problem came.

On this particular day, Anne and I were driving from Crieff in central Scotland down the Glendevon Road to our golf date in Dunfermline. It's a road I'd driven many times before. As we came to the crossing of our road, the A823 and the A92, we stopped at the stop sign--it's unusual that a major crossing isn't a roundabout. I looked both ways and then started to pull out. Zoom! A small sports car came from the right at about a hundred, and I barely had time to stop. Anne and I both sat for a second thinking about how close we'd come to becoming a serious statistic and news article. I realized that although I had looked both ways, I had looked first right and then left before I started to pull out, the way I would have at home. That is a major no-no; a real tourist blunder! If I had first looked left and then right, I would have seen the sports car coming from the right before I pulled out. We continued on to our golf, shaken, but not stirred.

The lesson for me was that I am a tourist driver on the "other side" and always will be. I must remember that the complacent become the statistics.

We Missed the Turn

Heading to the West Linton Golf Course we took the M9 motor-way through Stirling toward Edinburgh. Rain was pelting the car and the wipers going full speed were barely keeping up. There would be no golf this day, but we had promised to deliver a copy of *Scotland's Hidden Gems* to the golf manager at West Linton. Anne and I were having great fun ticking off things we could do with a non-golf day, when she suddenly yelled, "That was our turn!" We had missed the turn off the M9 to the M9 and were now on the M80 heading to Glasgow, the opposite direction we wanted to go. Yes, it's one of those uniquely Scottish motor-way things--you sometimes have to turn off the road you're on to stay on the road you're on, and if you don't turn off you find yourself on a different road.

Anne quickly grabbed the map and started scurrying to find a place to turn around or an alternate route. What she found was that there are no turnoffs for about 10 miles, and at that point we'd be able to junction with the M878, which would take us from the M80 Glasgow bound to the M9 heading to Edinburgh. The junction came just as we hit a major construction zone, but the junction was still open. Twenty minutes later we were back on the M9. We paid careful attention to the rest of our route to West Linton GC. We also vowed to pay more attention even when we thought we knew the route. We didn't want to miss that turn from the M9 to the M9 again.

A week later we were heading back to Edinburgh, this time for a night at the airport Hilton Hotel in preparation for our flight home. M9 through Stirling. Great discussion about what we were going to do for the afternoon in Edinburgh, what shops we wanted to visit, which pubs, what for dinner... "Wait! We missed it again!" shouted Anne. This time she noticed just as we entered the major construction zone. "Get over, get over! There's our exit," she said just as we passed the M878 cutoff. Back to the map. Five miles of construction later we finally found a place to turn around and go the other direction on the motor-way so we could find our cross road, the M878. It was only a 35 minute diversion.

Could it be we're too old to learn? I'd rather believe even after 41 years together we just enjoy our conversations so much we sometimes can't concentrate on other things.

The Easy Drive Around Loch Earn---Are You Kidding Me?

We've driven around Loch Earn at the edge of the Highlands several times--it's very near St Fillans GC where we're members and the drive is usually fairly photogenic. One spring, after a round of golf, since the weather was exceptionally good we decided to take the drive on the south road around the loch to the village of Lochearnhead. The road is single-track but it's usually not too busy. Wrong! We didn't expect the throngs who were out on the loch in the nice weather. Twice I had to back up because of meeting traffic coming the other way and a couple of times others had to back up. We actually saw people who had set up their picnics in auto passing places (widened spots for passing). This was one of the hardest single-track drives I've done--all because of good weather in Scotland.

The Trip to Harburn Golf Club or Round and Round We go and Where We Stop Nobody Knows

We had a tee time at 11:30 for Harburn Golf Club in West Lothian southwest of Edinburgh. The trip from Crieff we figured rightly at an hour and fifteen, so we planned to leave for golf at 9:45 to give us time to check-in and get our kit together. We were going to Harburn to take them a copy of *Hidden Gems II* and to play the course a second time. From Crieff to get to Harburn GC we caught the M9 (motorway) at Greenloaning and headed down through Stirling to where the M9 turns off onto the M9 (it's a Scottish road thing, see the "Missed Turn" story). Then at Exit 4, the Linlithgow exit, the adventure began. As we came off the M9 we reached the first roundabout (traffic circle) on our way to the hinterlands of West Lothian and the village of West Calder. From that circle we faced twelve more roundabouts in about nine miles--at Loan, two more between there and Westfield, three more to Windeknowe, a double circle to get under the M8, one at East Whitburn, one at Blackburn, another at Addiewell, and a final one at the village of West Calder. At the run up to each roundabout Lizzie, our GPS, would say, "In point four miles enter the roundabout and take the third exit to A801...In point four miles enter the roundabout and take the fourth exit to A801...Continue 2.2 miles, then enter roundabout and take the first exit to A801..." and so on.

After a nice round of golf in the dry (already unusual for this particular trip) at Harburn we retraced our twelve roundabout trip from Harburn GC to the M9. Immediately, Lizzie began, "In point four miles enter the roundabout..." Oh, well, you get the idea. On the homebound trip we did add a side trip into the Stirling Sainsbury store (large grocery).   That only added eight more mini-roundabouts. This kind of travel gives new meaning to the phrase, "We played 'round about Harburn."

This Car Has No Reverse

It was our first trip to Scotland--in fact, it was our first trip out of the country. We landed in Glasgow after a frightful trip through Heathrow Airport in London where we got on a bus and actually drove under the airport, down narrow passage ways, on the wrong side of the road.   Once in Glasgow we spent that afternoon wandering the shopping area of downtown Glasgow figuring it would be best not to drive in our jet lag addled condition; it was difficult enough catching a bus from our airport hotel to downtown and back.

Feeling refreshed after a night's sleep we tackled the car rental agency in the morning. A small Vauxhall Astra station wagon was our wheels for the three week trip (we were picking up a friend and traveling with her for a few days so we needed the larger car, besides we had all our luggage and two large golf bags). In the Avis parking lot I tried to get used to shifting gears with my left hand by driving around the lot several times. Once I thought I had mastered the shifting, or least was accomplished enough to only grind the gears every third shift or so, we drove back to our hotel to pick up our luggage--a tricky task since I had to negotiate two roundabouts which I did by going around one of them twice.   I pulled into a parking spot in front of the hotel and we went in to get our luggage which was being held in the lobby.   We loaded the car and then discovered that this particular model had no reverse gear. "R" was marked on the shift nob, but all the pushing or pulling or twisting wouldn't get the car into reverse. Of course, no manual was in the globe box. We finally called Avis and they found a manual and read me the part that said, "Push the button on the back of the shifter to engage reverse." We found the button and the car immediately fell easily into reverse. As I backed carefully out of my parking space I realized driving in Scotland was going to be quite the adventure.

Stop the Alarm!

We loved the Toyota Prius we got as a rental from Arnold Clark Car Rental in the spring of 2012--it was comfortable, easy to drive, and quite economical. It did come with a major problem as we found out a week into our trip. At Huntingtower Castle the car alarm went off as we toured the castle--we heard it and then it shut off. I went out to the castle parking lot to check it out. Everything seemed okay. As I walked away the alarm started again. I shut it off by unlocking the car, opening the door, and starting the engine. We didn't have any problem the rest of the evening--it never went off at the B&B.

The next day we were scheduled to play at Carnoustie GC, one of the major golf venues in the world. We parked in the main clubhouse lot to check-in with the pro shop. No alarm problems. We drove over to the lot for the course we were playing and unloaded our golf gear. No alarm problems. We walked over to the starter's office and met with the club manager and our alarm went off. I walked back to the car, shut it off and checked that everything was set the way it should be, and walked back to the starter. The alarm went off again. Colin McLeod, the golf manager, asked for the keys and said he'd take care of our car. We heard the alarm once again as we headed down the first fairway.

We heard the alarm again as we came up the 18th. McLeod and his staff had moved the car from the parking lot to in front of their office. Every ten to fifteen minutes the alarm would sound and a secretary would come out to unlock and re-lock the car which would shut off the alarm. Colin had even called Arnold Clark Rental main office in London, but they didn't have any answers. We thanked Colin and the secretaries and apologized for the trouble we had caused.

Back in Crieff at the B&B I called the rental company repair number and a mechanic was sent out to deal with the alarm. He did everything he could to set off the alarm--we rocked the car, popped the bonnet, simulated breaking in through a window--nothing would trigger the alarm. His conclusion was that the alarm sensor was completely defective and he had no idea what it would do next. This was not good news since the next day we were leaving for the far north of Scotland for two weeks.

I called Arnold Clark Rental and made arrangements to exchange the car up north if the alarm started again, but said that I'd keep the car even if the alarm wasn't functioning.

The alarm never sounded the whole rest of the trip. But when I turned the car into the rental branch at Edinburgh Airport they had already heard about the car from the London office.

To continue the story, the next spring we again showed up at Carnoustie to give them our newest book and play the course again. Colin met us outside his office and only half jokingly said, "If you have car alarm problems you can just turn around right now." We assured him that we'd had no problems with this trip's car. He then took us to meet his staff. He introduced us by saying, "This is Bob and Anne Jones from the States. And if that doesn't mean anything to you just think back to "Beep! Beep! Beep!' every ten minutes." Almost together the secretaries went, "Ahhh!"

We enjoyed our round and the alarm never went off once. I thought it might be fun to hit the Panic Button and set the alarm off just once, but wiser heads prevailed--Anne said she'd walk home if I did that.

This Time It Wasn't the Alarm

We've had problems with our rental car alarms [see the previous story], but this time the problem wasn't with the alarm. This trip we seemed to have lost the ability to lock the car boot (trunk) on our rental Toyota. We first noticed the problem when I parked the car near our B&B in Dumfries in the south of Scotland. We had parked, walked around the corner, checked in at Ferintosh House B&B, and were going back to the car to get our suitcases. I walked up to the car and opened the car boot without hitting the unlock button on the car key. That was bothersome, but it seemed to work okay as we left the car. The next morning I tried several times and each time was the same--lock the car, try the back door to make sure it was locked, pop open the boot without unlocking it. We tried double-locking the car but nothing worked.

Now we were worried that we were going to be at risk (golf clubs, clothes, books, camera gear all with an unlockable boot). After golf, as the rain was pouring down, we drove past an Arnold Clark car dealer. I turned around and drove back hoping they could help. The dealer wasn't a rental dealer and was selling VW and

Vauxhaul not Toyota. A mechanic came out in the rain and played with the lock and key and got the same results--lock the car and pop open the unlocked boot.   Finally, he got an idea. He locked the car, gave me the key, and told me to walk about twenty feet away. He then tried to open the boot--it wouldn't open.

It had been opening because I was within range and the car recognized the key in my pocket. Nothing about that had been in the manual, both of us had checked. Problem solved. The car had been locked all the time--until I walked up to it. It seems I was the key to the mystery.

Some Trips Just End Up Being Slow

Ever have one of those days that just seem to drag by? You know, those days when no matter how hard you try you just can't speed up? We've had a few examples of those days. In September of 2014 we had a really slow trip from Crieff to Crail near St Andrews.   Normally we can make it in an hour and fifteen, but not this day.   Before we got to to Cupar about two-thirds of the way to Crail we ended up behind two extremely large farm implements (balers, I think) with escort cars. On the highway the speed (I use the term loosely) was about 15 miles an hour.   In the village of Cupar the tractors and all the following cars were creeping along at five miles an hour. The Agricultural implements were so large that they had to ignore traffic lights (there are a couple in Cupar) to make it through town.   Anne the navigator desperately poured over the map to find an alternate route. A little more than half way through town Anne had me take a side street which lead to some some roads we could take across Fife. Even the small farm roads were much quicker.

Another time we were taking the same route from Crieff to Crail and ran into similar problems. Cupar is such a bottleneck, tight shopping district with parking on both sides of the street, and again we got behind a large farm implement. This time it took 40 minutes to go a mile and a half through town because of the farm traffic and normal Saturday shopper traffic. The town's signal system just can't handle the crowds--besides two traffic lights there are several pedestrian signals where a walker would press the crossing signal, traffic would stop until they crossed, two cars would move on, and another walker would hit the signal. We've got to find a way to get around Cupar.

Sometimes the slowness comes in clumps. In the spring of 2011 on our trips in Scotland and England we noticed slow happened behind red cars. It seemed that every queue we ended up in was lead by a red car or truck. We don't know what it was with red cars that trip, but white-silver-black-blue-orange vehicles all went fast. On one stretch we followed a slow red VW GTI, a car I know is fast (we've owned three different red ones and a Lamborghini orange one) going 15 miles under the speed limit. Never did fathom why red was the slow color that trip.

While in the UK I know I don't drive as fast as a native, but I don't drive like a normal tourist either. I really notice those slow days.

You Won't Believe What Happened Right in Front of Us

In our travels we've seen several road accidents or at least the aftermath of the accidents. In Ireland we were almost late for a tee time at the Dooks GC near Killarney when we came upon a motorcycle accident (learned later that the cyclist had died) and in the North Berwick area of Scotland (East Lothians) we had to wait as they cleared the debris from a car/motorcycle accident (non-fatal).   But in the spring of 2013 we witnessed our first motor accident right in front of us. As we were returning to our Crieff B&B home after golf we got stopped in a traffic snarl going through the shopping area of the village.   Parked cars on the road and a construction project had reduced the main road to just one lane. The path was very tight for a large blue double-deck bus. As the driver inched his way through the constriction a parked car pulled out of its parking spot straight into the middle of the big blue double-deck bus. How the driver (or anyone) could miss seeing the big blue double-deck bus right beside her was beyond belief.   The driver of the car was a woman (probably early thirties).   The accident put a large dent in the bus and took off a good portion of the car's left front. The accident also completely blocked all traffic both ways. We watched the maneuver as if in slow motion directly in front of us.   Took about fifteen minutes to get traffic (one-way) flowing again. We figured we didn't need to register as witnesses to the accident, after all the bus was full of witnesses who watched in shock as the lady rammed the bus.

Driving Mistake

To get from Kirkwall where we were staying to Stromness GC where we were to play meant that we had to get to the south side of town when we were coming from the north. Anne saw a route on our map that went straight through the heart of town—one road, no turns. As we approached the shopping area, the two-way street got narrower and narrower. It was like driving down a small pedestrian mall, only with two-way traffic. To pass cars coming from the other direction, I practically had to pull into a store to make room. At one point a delivery truck was leading us and the whole line of traffic (from both ways) had to stop as he made his deliveries. Anne found the "Back Road" (that's its official name) for the way back. Narrowest town road I've ever driven.

Wrong Side

As we were driving back to Crieff from golf at Dragon's Tooth GC near Glencoe, we drove through Bridge of Orchy. Going through town a girl driving pulled out from a pub into the wrong lane and came right at us. Everyone in town was going slowly, but she kept on coming at us. I started honking at her. She's practically stopped now, still in my lane. People outside the pub were yelling at her and I was still honking. Suddenly, she seemed to wake up and realized she wasn't in Kansas anymore. She sharply pulled over to her side and off the road almost into the pub. All I could say was, "Tourist!"

Stuck on Isle Arran in More Ways than One

Isle Arran is one of our favorite haunts in Scotland. Called Scotland in Miniature because it has a little bit of everything Scotland is famous for, Isle Arran has much to attract and interest the visitor. Brodick Castle is one of Scotland's better castles for touring and has a wonderful set of gardens. Goatfell Peak and surrounding hills offer a variety of hill walking and climbing. Some magnificent ancient stone sites, such as Machrie Moor stones and Auchtagallon stone circle, are intriguing. The ocean and fantastic beaches abound. And, of course, Arran has seven interesting golf

courses including the great course, Shishkine Golf and Tennis Club. Isle Arran would be a great place to get stuck, but not the way were.

On our last day of a three day stay on Arran we drove completely around the island's perimeter, only about 60 miles, killing the morning until our 12:00 ferry back to the mainland. On the northeast side of the island, near Corrie GC, we pulled off the road onto a grassy area which led down to a small beach. We got out of the car and wandered for a few minutes around a small hamlet taking pictures. We got back into the car and tried to back up onto the road, but got nowhere. I had pulled onto the grass bonnet (nose) first. When I tried to back up the front wheels just spun on the grass and the car slipped a little further down the hill toward the beach. Only two attempts told me I was losing ground. I got out wondering what I'd do next when a local from across the street came to our rescue. He directed me to pull a little left and forward to a flatter area and then back up and keep going. It worked. We thanked him and I said this must not have been the first time this had happened. He said, "Oh. About twice a week is all."

We hurried into Brodick, Arran's main village, to catch the ferry to Ardrossan only to find out that we were stuck again. The ferry would be late and no one knew when it would get in that day, if at all. The problem was that the Ardrossan port was closed because the port authorities had found an unexploded ordinance (a World War II mine) in the harbour. Ferries couldn't leave or dock until the mine had been cleared. We wandered around the village for about three hours before a signal came saying the ferry would run, but not to Ardrossan. A ferry had been sent from Gouroch much further up the Clyde to pick up the Brodick passengers and autos and deliver them to Gouroch. We caught the ferry and while heading to the mainland tried to figure out how to get from there to our B&B in Crieff. But that's another story.

Shiskine Golf Club's Fifth Green

CHAPTER 2: Golf, More Golf, and Sometimes Too Much Golf

Golf is one of the most important reasons we first traveled to Scotland, though once we got there we discovered there was much more to the country. Golf is still one of the reasons we keep visiting the British Isles. The courses--such as St Fillans, Carne, Enniscrone, Narin and Portnoo, Royal Dornoch, Crail Balcombie, Shiskine, Ashburnham, Royal Porthcawl--draw us back. It was at Shiskine Golf and Tennis Club that I played a whole round under par for the first time [Okay, it was the only time.], even though it was only one under. It was at Boat of Garten in the Highlands that I played so badly that after the tenth hole I left my clubs in my bag and just walked a few holes with Anne. I still love that course.

The golf courses of Scotland, Ireland, and Wales have been the scene of some of our most treasured memories, even though there are a few scores I'd rather forget. We met some great people and shared our experiences with Scottish and American friends. These are just a few of our memorable experiences, starting with the people of the golf courses and then moving on to the game itself.

GOLF: The People

Best Friends

We joined St Fillans Golf Club in Perthshire, Scotland, because we love the course, got a good deal as International Members, and so we could enter Open competitions at other clubs (a great way to visit other golf clubs cheaply). On a day we have nothing else planned, we often end up at our course for a quick nine or a full round.

One day as we played our first nine, we caught up with a couple of local gentlemen. After following them for a couple of holes, we began to pay more attention to the interaction going on before us. It seemed that the two were having some kind of disagreement, which by the sixth hole almost turned into fisticuffs.

They called us through at that hole and as I passed one of them he said, "That #%^*?! has been messing me up all morning. He's such a screw up!" To which the other shouted, "Don't listen to that bastard, he lies about everything!" "Oh, I do not, you're the &*^#!$ who lies." The language wasn't as polite as I'm making it and there were several Scottish phrases I'm not sure I could translate. The volume got even louder as we quickly moved on to the next hole. The argument continued as we got out of sight.

On our second round we passed the two who were playing an adjacent hole. They greeted us like we were long lost friends, asked us how our round was going, and wished us good day. They walked on as if they were best buds.

At the end our round over a tea in the course lounge, we asked Gordon, the course manager, about the two and their behavior. He said not to worry about it. They had that kind of tiff about every other week, but they really were best friends.

Fighting Off the Ladies

At Castle Bar Golf Course in the west of Ireland we had a tee time all arranged. We showed up in plenty of time, got our clubs and gear together, and waited for our slot at the first tee. As our tee time arrived a group of three women came up and said they were a foursome playing a competition and wanted to play ahead of us. I pointed out that this was our prearranged time, that we were only two, that we'd be faster, and that their fourth wasn't even there yet. The one pushy lady ignored me and got up on the tee box. I said, "Look, we're only guests of your club president here to write about the course for the American audience, but you go right ahead." The two other ladies pulled the pushy one back and told us to please go ahead. The pushy lady got pushed back. We never did see them the rest of the day.

Our score that day: Visitors 1, Pushy Lady Member 0.

The First Birdie in Scotland

The wives, Anne and Helen, were visiting Blair Castle while Grady Morgan and I played a quick round at Blair Atholl Golf Club's nine-hole course. Blair Atholl is typical of Scotland's village tracks-- holes which fit the contour of the land and sometimes means they're a little quirky. The two of us were having at least as good a time as we figured the ladies were, and when we came to the par four sixth hole, which is overlooked from the clubhouse lounge patio, Grady's first shot left him with a nine-iron shot to the green. He stuffed one in close and members at the patio railing gave some polite golf claps. When Grady reached the green, he tapped in for his three on the par four and said triumphantly, "My first birdie in Scotland!"

One of the members hearing that said, "Laddie, we have a tradition here in Scotland that whenever a player gets his first birdie he buys drinks for the club." To which all the other members cheered and hooted. Grady would have bought a round, too, except that he had no money since Helen had taken the credit card.

Quick thinking Scots almost had a free round.

Flying Low

Our home course, Arrowhead Country Club in Molalla, has the small Mulino airport next door. As we play the course all manner of single and twin engine aircraft and various helicopters will be taking off and landing. I find the planes an interesting diversion, especially at times of bad golf, but many of the members view the air traffic as a distraction to curse. I tell them they should try golf in the UK.

Particularly in Scotland, but in Wales as well, we've watched plenty of low flying aircraft. Not the little piper cub or bonanza-style prop planes. Oh no. We mean NATO jet fighters or fighter bombers. Several courses, including Royal Dornoch, Nairn, Tain,

North Wales, and the St Andrews courses, are in the flight path of fighter bombers heading out to sea to do practice bombing runs. At Moray Old Golf Club on the Morayshire coast in northern Scotland, the takeoff and landing paths are directly over a couple of holes. The NATO Tornadoes coming in were close enough I got a picture where I can almost see the pilot's face. On one hole I had a ball knocked out of the air by jet backwash.

The most exciting (I use that word cautiously) examples of jet encounters were in Scotland. One day while playing at St Fillans

Golf Club, where we are members, we were waiting to tee off at the elevated third hole. Suddenly the ground rumbled and a jet roared not more than 100 feet over our heads. It was so loud and so startling that Anne literally fell to the ground. Even on the low level runs through the hills they are supposed to stay at least 500 feet off the deck, but obviously they don't always. On another occasion we were driving south on the motor-way by Moffat, the A74(M), when a jet came around a hill and flew straight at us at what seemed to be 100 feet above the motor-way. It's hard to duck when driving at 60 miles per hour. In southern Scotland I was visiting Cairn Holy chambered cairns high in the Dumfries and Galloway hills working on an article about Historic Scotland sites with views when a fighter flew below my position on its twisty path through the hills.

Perhaps the most dramatic instance was on 9.12.2001, the day after the attack on New York. Everyone was already on edge about the terrorist attacks. We were in the Tourist Information Centre in Killin, a pleasant Highland village, when the peace was shattered by two fighter jets screaming by at low level and at what seemed to be full throttle. One lady in the shop screamed, "Oh, my God!" Everyone in buildings ran out to see who knew what.

It was just a practice run, but then they say that timing is everything.

Golf at the Small Courses

We tend to get one of two reactions when we show up for an arranged round at a village course. First, we often get treated as celebrities with club managers greeting us and arranging for us to play with local dignitaries (club secretaries, captains, presidents, historians, etc.). In many cases, lunch or dinner will be set up for us after our round. The second reaction we get is that they don't seem to know what to do with us. At Fort William GC, on Scotland's west, they told us to go play and when we came into the clubhouse after our round grilled us about how we liked the course. The club captain did buy us a drink, but we had to ask for maps and a club history which had been promised to us. Macroom GC in Ireland was another example of what-do-we-do-with-the-writers. We arrived plenty ahead of our scheduled time as we do most of the time, but the secretary in the office didn't know what to do with us. Yes, she had us on the tee sheet. Yes, the golf was complimentary.

But she kept asking what else was she supposed to do. We kept saying that we were fine, but she was beside herself that there was no one for us to play with. We finally headed to the first tee and left her sputtering about what else, what else. Obviously, we prefer the first response of being treated as celebrities.

While we've never been treated like rock stars, we have received some rather grand receptions. At Rush GC, a fine 9-hole track near Dublin, we were met by the entire club's executive committee dressed in suits and dresses. In our golf attire we felt distinctly underdressed, even though we were there to play golf. When we played Ennis GC in western Ireland it was arranged that we would play in a two-ball competition with the men's club captain and the ladies' club captain as our partners. After the competitive round, where Anne and I were the stones around the necks of our partners, we were paraded into the club's dining room to meet a large portion of the club's members. I guess that's almost like being a rock star. At Torvean GC in Inverness the club president, men's club captain, and pro were our welcoming committee. Niddry Castle GC near Edinburgh invited the club historian to meet us for lunch after golf--we got some wonderful stories from that visit. It's not just the small courses that treat us well. At Gleneagles we were guided around the Queen's course by the resort's Head Teaching Pro, John Murray, and the St Andrews Links Trust arranged for us to play with both PR directors and then had lunch arranged for us after. Yes, indeed, we do prefer the second approach.

GORP

In the States many golf courses, particularly the more upscale and expensive resort courses, will have refreshment carts patrolling the course offering drink, snacks, and more drinks to parched or hungry golfers. On the courses in the UK and Ireland you'll be lucky to find a drinking fountain. At Pitlochry GC in Scotland, the only drinking water on the course comes out of a pipe sticking out of the side of a ditch. The water is clean, pure, and delicious even if the facility is a tad rustic. What this all means is that we've learned to bring with us whatever we want to have on the course.

In Scotland, Wales, and Ireland, where we've played our most golf, we will often carry a light lunch of local cheese, bread, and water--we don't carry any wine, although I have been known to have a flask of single malt in my golf bag, for medicinal purposes, of course. We also usually stick in some kind of snacks or nibbles for quick energy. This brings me to the subject of this commentary: GORP. GORP or Good Old Raisins and Peanuts (actually raisins, peanuts, and M&Ms) is a left over from backpacking and sled dog racing days. The combination is high energy, easy to carry, and satisfying. We build batches of it, bag it in handy sizes, vacuum seal it, and take it in our luggage on our trips (M&Ms are sometimes difficult to find when traveling). There's usually a bag of GORP in one of our golf bags on a course.

At Gleneagles Kings in Perthshire we were playing with our Merlindale B&B friends John and Jacky Clifford one year. At about the 13th hole I was feeling particularly down, having been beaten up fairly badly by the first twelve holes. I reached into Anne's golf bag for the GORP and stuffed a handful into my mouth. John watched me and said, "What's that?" I told him about GORP and offered he and Jacky some. They thought it was "brilliant" (their word) and wanted some more. Ever since, whenever we play with them, they can't wait for the GORP to come out. When playing the Crieff Ferntower course (their home club), we always have a GORP stop at the tenth tee. When we leave for home, any remaining GORP stays with John and Jacky and is put to good use.

In Ireland at one of our favorite courses, *Ceann Sibeal* (Dingle) Golf Links, we stopped at the tee of the eighth hole on a round to let a couple of local ladies play through. Anne and I aren't slow players by any means, but we do like to take photos and enjoy the scenery especially on such a picturesque course. The ladies hadn't yet had to wait, but we could see that they were catching up. So we stopped, pulled out the GORP, and waved them through. One of the ladies, seeing us dig our hands into the bag of goodies, said, "Is it snack time? Aren't you going to offer us some?" "Of course," I replied and held out the open bag of GORP. Each of the ladies took some and asked about it. We told them what it was, which started a whole conversation and we joined them for the finish of the round.

GORP--convenient energy snack and conversation starter.

Hole-in-One and Drinks

In the Peterhead GC clubhouse after a wet round, as we enjoyed a dram of Scotland's finest thoughtfully provided by a gentleman playing ahead of us who had scored an ace (a hole-in-one), we were told an interesting story. One day when the members knew some Americans were playing, one of them took four drams of whisky to the 18th green and waited for the Americans to come in. He told them it was a Peterhead custom to meet their American friends on the last hole with a dram. It isn't, by the way, but he said that when the Americans left the clubhouse later they and most of the members were all blotto! Not only that, but the Americans had bought all the drinks, except for the first four.

Playing with a Laird

In the spring of 2007 we arranged to play golf at The Montgomery Course at Kinross Golf Club not far from Perth, Scotland. We didn't know if anyone would play with us or not--often

clubs try to get us guides, but it's difficult to match schedules. This day we arrived for tee off time, checked in at the golf shop, and headed out to the first tee. Before we teed off a gentleman walked up and introduced himself as Jamie Montgomery. I recognized the name and knew he was the owner of the course. This day we had a special guide.

As we played I talked to Jamie about the history of the course, which used be called the Blue but is now The Montgomery (there's also The Bruce course which used to be the Red). I asked if Jamie's family name and the course's name had any relation. He confirmed what I thought, that the course is named for his family which has owned the land for several hundred years. He explained that his father, the current Earl of Kinross, owns the land of the courses, the Kinross House (castle), and most of Loch Leven which includes the island housing Loch Leven Castle where Mary Queen of Scots was at one time imprisoned (which she had been at seemingly most of castles in Scotland). Jamie then informed us that he would be the next Earl of Kinross. We were getting bogies beside an Earl-to-be.

Jamie is very comfortable with his position as Laird of the ancient estate which we learned had been in the family since the 1200s. He talked about the social responsibilities he owes to "his people" and the respect he feels he's due by "his people" for the things he does for them. Never, though, was he condescending toward the people living on or off his estate. To him it's just a fact of life that he's the Laird and they're the subjects.

Playing The Montgomery Course with "The Montgomery" proved a very interesting and enlightening round. Oh, the course is very good as well.

Playing with Royalty

To research golf courses for our tour books we usually write ahead to the course manager or club secretary and request a tee time. We also ask if there is someone we could play with who knows the history of the course and maybe some interesting stories about the course or club. About half the time arrangements have worked out for us to play with guides--club officers, managers, historians, or long time club members. At St Andrews New and Jubilee courses we played with the two St Andrews Links

Trust, the organization that manages all the St Andrews courses, Public Relations directors. As we played the New Course at St Andrews (built in 1894, but compared to the Old Course it is new), Michael Woodcock related an event that had occurred the week before. American money mogul Donald Trump (the closest we come to American royalty) had appeared one day with his full entourage and was getting set to do a press conference on the Old Course's famous eighteenth hole Swilcan Bridge to announce his plans for a new Trump golf venture to be built on Scotland's east coast north of Cruden Bay. Michael said it was his duty to go out and tell Trump to take his press conference someplace else--in other words, he got to say to Donald Trump, "You're Fired!"

Our brush with royalty was on Fife when we played Charleton Golf and Country Club. I sent our usual email asking to play the course to include it in our next book. The reply I got threw me a little. We were invited to play the course by the owner who signed the email Baron St Clare Bonde. A Baron! My first problem was how do I address my email reply? What do you call a Baron? We finally decided to address it simply "Dear Baron St Clare Bonde." With arrangements made, we arrived early for our scheduled round at Charleton G & CC. We sat in the clubhouse lounge having a cup a coffee because the barkeep said that St Clare would be a tad late. Now we at least knew how to address the baron, St Clare. St Clare is a gracious host and a competent player. He told us the history of the course as we played the front nine. The course is a project in conjunction with the local Council to help provide jobs for locals and promote tourism to the area. St Clare told us an interesting story about the opening of the course. He had wanted Sir Sean Connery to open the course and saw him at a Royal and Ancient Golf Club of St Andrews function, both he and Connery are members of the R&A. The baron went up to Sir Sean and introduced himself cleverly he thought, "I'm Bonde, St Clare Bonde." The baron said Connery was not amused. Eventually, though, it was arranged for Connery to play the opening round at the course, except that near the appointed time Connery had to be away on a scheduled movie shoot. St Clare had to resort to plan B--George H.W. Bush, who had just ended his term as President came over and played that first round.

The baron talked about "his people," not in a pejorative sense, but with a sense of responsibility. St Clare explained that he was a Scottish Baron from his mother's side (the Sinclairs) and a

Norwegian Baron from his father's side--he could have listed his name as Baron Baron St Clare Bonde. On his estate he had the golf course, an equestrian centre, a working farm, and a pheasant hunting farm. I asked St Clare about his name. Was he related to the Sinclairs of Caithness, early great landowners in Scotland's north? He said that was his family. Then I asked if he was related to the Sinclairs of Rosslyn Chapel (the chapel made more famous by Dan Brown's book *The Da Vinci Code*). Again, he said that was his family and that he was the trustee of the chapel.

After our round and lunch in the clubhouse, St Clare invited us up to his house for a quick tour. We had seen the manor house (small castle) from the course and were excited about the opportunity to get up close and personal. St Clare took us for a tour of the lower floor which included the grand hallway, the dining room, library, and several sitting rooms. He introduced us to his lovely wife, showed us portraits of his ancestral family, and family crests. Our overall impression of Baron St Clare Bonde is that he is just a regular fellow, the kind of person you'd love to pair with on a golf course.

Our brush with royalty on the golf courses has been both fun and enlightening. Those with royal connections and usually royal-sized bank accounts seem to us to be some of the nicest, least pretentious people we've ever met. Let me play with royalty anytime. Charles, want a round?

Stolen Golf Shoes

Auchterarder Golf Course east of the Gleneagles Resort is a fine, mature Scottish parkland course. Uncomplicated, yet challenging, it's a good venue for a competition. I had played the course enough to feel comfortable entering a Senior Gents Open and I talked our B&B host and friend, John Clifford, into entering with me. We hoped to play together or at least at nearly the same time, but that was not to be. Auchterarder scheduled us an hour apart with me teeing off at 10:15 and John at 11:30. I drove over for my tee time and John's wife, Jacky, and Anne dropped John off for his. John and I would ride home together.

On the day of the open I had no illusions of doing well in the tournament and I played down to my expectations. It was an enjoyable round, though, with Clarence from Kurriemuir GC on the edge of the Highlands. After my less than stellar performance I bought Clarence and I drinks in the clubhouse lounge, chatted with my fellow competitors, and waited for John to finish his round. I was the hit of the lounge having come the furtherest to enter--my 6000 mile journey won the prize while a golfer from 65 miles away was second--no contest!

John came in with stories of equalling my poor showing and with a splitting headache. John said he'd pop into the gents' locker room for his shoes and we'd be off for home. Without changing into his street shoes, he grabbed the shoes and I loaded his clubs into the back of my rental and off for home we headed. Back at the B&B

John went in for a lie down while I unloaded his clubs, trolley, and shoes. For the rest of the day we both tried to forget how poorly we'd played.

Fast forward to the next morning. After breakfast Jacky comes into the kitchen and says, "Whose shoes are these?"

"Those are John's shoes I brought in from the car yesterday," I said.

"They most certainly are not. These are size eight and John wears a twelve."

"Well," I replied, "those are the ones John brought from Auchterarder clubhouse."

It then hit us what John had done. With a pounding head and in a hurry to leave the scene of his criminally poor golf, John had taken someone else's shoes from the locker room and brought them home. At about that time John came into the room and we all burst out laughing hysterically. Through our sobs of laughter we explained to John what he had done. John was mortified, but joined our laughter as we imagined some poor golfer coming in from his round, searching the gents' locker room for his shoes, and then saying, "Ach! Who the hell took mae shoes!"

John tried to bribe each of us into returning the shoes for him, but no one would bail him out. Later that day he drove over to Auchterarder, retrieved his shoes (which no one had taken), returned the pair he'd stolen and left a sleeve of new balls in each shoe as an apology. We never did hear if the shoes got back to their rightful owner, but we will certainly remember the day John stole a pair of shoes he couldn't wear.

Golf with Frank; an Unexpected Pleasure

The story of playing golf with Frank at Balfron Golf Club in the Trossachs near Loch Lomand begins with leaving Crieff in bright sun and only scattered clouds. By the time I reached Stirling, 22 miles away, the clouds were increasing. At Buchlyvie (I'll give you the pronunciation later) the rain started in earnest and by the time I reach Balfron GC four miles further on it was a mix of rain and hail. I sat in the car for five minutes until the rain let up a bit. Putting on my rain gear and taking five clubs out of my bag so I could carry, I started up the hill to the clubhouse where I was to deliver a copy of *Hidden Gems II* to the club manager and then play the course for a

second time. Brian wasn't in the clubhouse or anywhere around, but Frank was. Frank directed me into
the small members area and I put the book on Brian's desk. Then it was time to decide whether to play in the still dripping rain or bag it and drive back to Crieff. Frank was considering the same decision. Finally, I said I'd give it a go and Frank asked, "Fancy a playing partner?" It seems he too had decided to risk the iffy weather. Together we headed to the first tee.

Let me tell you about Frank. Seventy-years old, he had worked for 44 years on electrical power lines all over Scotland. He'd been a member of this club for ten years and kept saying he wasn't a very good golfer. He was actually quite decent, probably an 18 or 20 handicap

and he played strictly by the rules. He had what he described as a "shinty swing"-- shinty being an ancient Scottish team game played with a hockey-type stick and ball. Shinty is thought to be the foundation game of both Irish Hurling and North American Ice Hockey. Frank's shinty swing was with wide stance and hands slightly apart. It wasn't a classic golf swing, but it was effective for hitting the ball a good distance although his short range accuracy wasn't sharp. Frank made a good playing partner as he helped me play my way around the course I'd only played once before. What made Frank most interesting though was his manner of speech. He had a way of slurring and mumbling that made me think he might be from Yorkshire and a familiar laugh, a sort of "ha,ha,he,he,he," that took me a few holes to place. Frank's speech pattern and laugh was that of the character Jim Trotter from The *Vicker of Dibley*

British TV show. Once I realized that, I kept waiting for Frank to say, "No, no, no, no...yes."

Frank congratulated me for winning our match on the 13th hole, even though I hadn't known we were playing a match. We finished our round in the dry--it had been spitting rain most of the way around--and in only three hours and five minutes. We'd been moving so fast up and down the hills of Balfron GC that I'd barely had time to grab a handful of peanuts on the 16th. Frank introduced me around to the members getting ready to go out, wished me a good rest of my trip, and then invited me come to the course and play again as his guest.

On the drive back to Crieff I realized that my round with Frank is a perfect example of why we spend so much time in Scotland. Oh, yes, and Buchlyvie is pronounced "buck'-lee-aye."

Owen Morgan, Forecaddie Extraordinaire

When we arranged to play the new Machrihanish Dunes GC on Scotland's Kintyre Peninsula we also arranged for a guide or fore caddie to take us around. We had heard that it was advisable to have a guide or caddy the first couple of times around this tricky course--and we would certainly give that advice to anyone planning to play there. Our fore caddy for the day was Welshman Owen Morgan (a more Welsh name there could never be)--he doesn't carry our clubs, but does guide and advise, and spot for us.

Owen is a great guide--he gave us good direction about where to hit, very little about where NOT to hit, and had wonderful stories. He is a retired Royal Navy meteorologist who caddies four or five days a week and plays on Saturdays and Sundays. He's a member of both Machrihanish and Dunaverty golf clubs, two more great courses in the area.

One of the stories Owen told us was about a group of Japanese golfers who had come to play the new Dunes course. They went out for their round sans caddy and after five hours hadn't returned. Owen and a couple of others went out to look for the lost group. He found them in a section of the course where several greens and flags were visible. They were just playing back and forth across the area from flag to flag, not sure where they were going, but having fun anyway. When he pointed them in the right direction they happily finished the course. It had taken seven hours!

Owen was definitely worth the £35 plus £25 tip we gave him. When we played a second time (about a year later) we again asked to hire Owen, but he was having a birthday party at the course and would be leading his own group.   Dean, the young fore caddy we did hire, was very good, but we missed the chance to get more of Owen's stories.

Michael Dooley Stories

We first visited *Teach an Phiobaire* (The House of the Piper) B&B in Tralee, Ireland, in the spring of 2002. The B&B was fantastic (it closed in 2011) and the hosts Patricia and Michael Dooley friendly and fascinating. Michael was a world renown uilleann pipe (small Irish bagpipe) maker and musician (pipes and guitar). Michael was also a golfer and storyteller.   In the two times we stayed at the B&B we got some great golf stories from Michael.

The first story is about a golf tournament that a friend got him to enter as a partner. When Michael arrived at the Ballybunion golf course he discovered that the tournament was for Catholic priests. So as to not disappoint his friend, Michael became Father Dooley. The pair of faux priests ended up winning the competition and had to give speeches. Michael said he was never so thankful for the Irish gift of gab as he was on that day.

Another time the same friend invited Michael to play with him at Tralee GC. After making sure it wasn't a competition Michael agreed. When the two got to the course they found that their tee time had been given to an American visitor. The two were a bit pissed at the club for giving away their spot until the American visitor, professional golfer Tom Watson winner of four British Opens, apologized for usurping their tee time and invited them to walk along with his group. Michael said Watson was fantastic to watch and made their day special. The next week Watson won his fifth and last British Open.

The last story tells about a day Michael was walking in town when a limo pulled up beside him. The window rolled down and the occupant leaned out and asked if Michael knew the way to Tralee Golf Course. Michael looked at the person and said, "Are you....oh, never mind. I'll direct you to the course." It was Tiger Woods! Tiger asked him to get in and direct the driver to Tralee GC. Michael said they had a pleasant conversation as he directed the driver to the course about fifteen minutes out of town.

When they got to the course, Tiger thanked Michael and the limo driver took him back to town.

We did see Michael one more time. One night at home we put on a video called "Historic  Pubs of Dublin." There in a scene of a session in Dublin's Temple Bar was Michael Dooley playing guitar. At the B&Bs, whether in Ireland or Scotland, you never know what kinds of entertaining stories you'll get.

Royal Dornoch and the American Ladies

Anne and I arrived at Royal Dornoch GC for our 11:00 tee time only to find that the course was very crowded and play was slow. We'd be a half hour late getting off the first tee. We were very understanding--we ought to be since the round was free to us.

We followed a foursome (two couples) off the first tee and caught up with them on the second tee. After visiting with the two couples from Maine for a couple of minutes they teed off and again we followed. This was the pattern on a very slow day--play a hole, wait on the next tee box, play a hole, wait... We quickly became friends with the couples from Maine since we had plenty of time to visit on each tee box. At one point the two ladies asked Anne where the toilets were on this course. Anne chuckled and said, "In the clubhouse. There are no toilets on the course." Anne said the ladies' faces dropped a little when she said that.

After our round we met up with the Americans in the clubhouse lounge for drinks. The ladies told us their story. It seems that on about the fourteenth hole the ladies could wait no longer. They said they hunted out what they thought was a safe hidden spot behind thick gorse bushes, dropped their pants, and squatted. In the middle of relieving themselves a golfer, male of course, walked around the edge of gorse looking for his golf ball and instead found the ladies. One of them told us, "We were in the middle of our business and all we could do is look up and smile sheepishly." Ah, golf in the highlands.

The most recent time we played Royal Dornoch we learned that they have now built a half-way house between the 10th and 11th holes which has a snack bar and toilets. No more gorse bush adventures for the ladies now.

Sneaking onto the Golf Courses

People will do anything to save a buck, bob, quid, or pound. That includes sneaking onto golf courses without paying. We've had a couple of encounters with these sneaky duffers. In 2004 we played the second course at Montrose on Scotland's east coast. It's a relatively easy track being a relief course for the Championship Montrose GC and not very expensive. It was quite a surprise when several holes away from the clubhouse three people walked off the road with their clubs, threw down balls, and started playing in front of us. We'd never seen that before. Several holes later the threesome found an easy egress and left.

A year later at Moray Old GC in Lossiemouth on the Morayshire coast of Scotland we had a similar situation. On the third hole we saw a man park his car by the side of the road next to the course and walk onto the course and start playing behind us. He seemed to be in a hurry and was pushing us until on the seventh hole he disappeared. He could have left and walked back to his car, gotten kicked off the course, or just hoppe over to some other hole, but we didn't see him again.

There are other, more sophisticated ways of sneaking onto a golf course. A Scottish friend of ours said he could get us onto a major golf course for £25 each when the normal price is £150. We said sure, set it up. When the appointed day came we went over to the course and our friend paid the starter £100 "under the table" for the four of us. We were put into the queue as the Thompson foursome and the starter said when they check us at the turn we had to be the Thompsons.   None of us played well, we were all nervous about being caught as phony Thompsons. At the turn we did everything we could to avoid the attention of the marshals (After all, don't outlaws usually avoid marshals?).

I don't know how the people at Montrose or the guy at at Moray could do it. Our one experience with sneaking onto a course was enough to cure me.

The German Golfer

Anne and I were getting ready to check in at the Crieff Dornock course for a quick nine holes when a German drove his large Mercedes sedan past the parking lot, up the footpath, and parked amongst the rental trolleys in front of the golf shop. He was mobility challenged but wanted to rent clubs and a motorized buggy so he could play the front nine today and the back nine tomorrow when he wanted. He obviously had money and was used to getting his way.

Hazel, the clerk in the golf shop, handled him very kindly while making sure she was in charge. First, she explained that it was not appropriate to drive up the footpath to park at the golf shop, and that there were designated handicapped parking spots in the lot. Second, she explained that the course was nine holes out and nine holes back. There was no way he could play just nine, unless he wanted to follow Anne and me on the wee course.

At this point she told me to just take the trolleys and forget about green fees for being so patient. Then she went on to number three with the German...

Scottish Golf Starters

We've met some friendly and engaging starters (a course marshal whose job it is to make sure golfers start at the proper times) of Scottish golf courses. There was one starter at Cruden Bay GC near Aberdeen who granted me a "breakfast ball" (mulligan) when I duffed one off the first tee. We also remember fondly the starter at Grantown-on-Spey GC one year who made us a half hour late for our tee time because we had such a fun conversation with him in the golf shop. But in the fall of 2013 we had two unique starters on courses in two days.

First, at Alford GC in Deeside east of Aberdeen we met a starter who couldn't understand that we had complimentary golf arranged. He knew he was supposed to collect green fees from visitors and we wouldn't pay--we had an email from the club secretary granting us courtesy of the course. That was a concept he couldn't fathom. Finally, I told him to check with the secretary whose office was next door to the shop. He looked at my email from the secretary again and thought better of asking. Then, when Anne got her golf buggy (riding cart in America) he couldn't understand that she knew how to drive it. He kept trying to explain everything multiple times even though Anne was telling him she'd driven buggies hundreds of times. He finally left us at the first tee and walked away muttering. Obviously, he was at the top of his food chain as a starter.

The next day at Tarland GC, a lovely nine-hole heathland track, we met the gentleman (I use the term loosely) starter at the lounge bar where we checked in for golf. We got a surprise since we don't often meet zombies as golf starters. He was tall and older and absolutely expressionless. He talked in monotone grunts and couldn't understand simple concepts like we had a letter from the club secretary granting us free golf. Our first zombie experience in Scotland.

Golf starters are usually interesting people who like interacting with visiting golfers. These two were unique!

GOLF: The Game

Small Island Golf

We emailed ahead to the secretary at Isle of Harris Golf Club and were granted courtesy of the course (free golf). When we got to the course we discovered it's really an honesty box course with a small clubhouse built into a dune. Nobody came to meet us—after seeing how rural the course is, I could see that I shouldn't have expected a reception.

We didn't see any trolleys (eventually, we spotted them at the side of the building), but I decided to cut my clubs down to seven, empty my golf bag, and carry my clubs. It felt like it fit the course to play that way. The wind was 20-25 miles per hour and it was about 6°C (about 42°F). The course is very interesting with

some fun shots—several blind. Anne walked along and took notes and photos. With a little help (a mulligan or two) I played fairly well. I'd rate the course up with other interesting 9-hole links or seaside courses, such as St Medan, Connemarra Isles, Cruit Island, and Durness.

The most entertaining aspect of the course was that the flag was out of the hole and laying on the green at eight of the nine greens. The only reason the flag was still in the hole at the the 9th was because that green was surrounded by tall dunes which blocked the wind from blowing the flag out.

Playing golf at the grand course, like Glenaeagles and Kingsbarns, is a fun experience, but playing at the out-of-the-way local courses takes me back to the way golf was meant to be played —basically you and the golf ball against the elements.

A Booking for Golf at Cullen GC

I had several times tried to arrange a round of golf at Cullen GC on the Morayshire coast in exchange for a copy of our golf book which includes the course. I sent at least three emails to the club secretary at Cullen, but I didn't get any response. We took Cullen GC off our itinerary for this year.

As we were having breakfast on a fine Sunday morning at the Cullen Hotel, we could see that the golf course across the road was practically empty. the weather was lovely and the course looked in great condition, so we decided to try to get in a round anyway, even if we had to pay. After breakfast we packed the car and drove to the course. Nobody was there—not in the office and not in the bar. The club had some trolleys in by the office, so Anne left a note and we took two trolleys and headed out to play. The course is a fun and tricky course with a number of tough par threes.

When we finished our round, we returned the trolleys and went into the bar to settle up for our round. We met Sandy who has been at the club for 24 years, though she isn't a golfer. I told her about our trouble getting any communication back from the secretary. She said she wasn't surprise and made some comment about having to do everything herself. When I told her that we had wanted to exchange one of our books for a round of golf, she said, "No problem, I'll do that if you've got a book for us." I went right out to the car and got a golf book for the club and a book of our stories for her. Sandy said she'd give the golf book to the secretary "when she was ready," but that she would certainly keep the story book for herself. I'm certainly glad we said something to the person who really runs the place.

The First Tee Prayer

This adaption of the Lord's Prayer was found on the wall in a golf course toilet in Boulder City--I did get strange looks standing at a urinal writing:

> Our Father who art in Augusta
>   Nicklaus be thy name,
> Our Kingdom come thy will be done
> On greens as it is on fairways.
> Give us this day our share of birdies
>   and forgive us our gimmies
>   as we forgive those who gimmie against us.
> Lead us not into the deep rough
>   and deliver us from sand traps
> For we drive for power and
>   putt for glory forever and ever.
> Amen.

Golfers' Serenity Prayer (from the Rough)

Lord give me grace to visualize the shot Tiger would make from this rough;

Give me the knowledge of my own game to recognize the shot I can make;

And Lord grant me the wisdom not to try Tiger's shot anyway.

A Golfing Village

At Elie GC in Scotland there is a pub across the street from one of the early holes. It's call The 19th Hole and is a good place for a drink or a meal. There may be other courses with pubs just off the course, but in Wales there's a course with not only a pub, but a whole village in the middle of it.

We played the seaside Nefyn (NEFV-in) and District Golf Club on a glorious day with no clouds and no wind. While talking to the pro shop manager, he said we needed to plan to stop after the 15th and drop in at the Ty Coch Inn. We most of the time stop in the clubhouse lounge after a round, but we were being told to stop in the middle of our round for a drink.

Before teeing it up on the 16th hole we walked down the hundred yards from the course to the smallest official village in Wales, Porthdinllean (PORT-thin-cleen). The village is made up of a couple of houses and the Ty Coch Inn, a 200-year-old public house. Easily accessible from the 12th green or the 16th tee, Ty Coch is a popular stop for golfers playing the Old Course at Nefyn and District. The Ty Coch Inn has been a bar since 1795. We had a drink at the outside picnic tables along with the foursome who played in front of us. Since they were having lunch, when we finished our drinks we started back up to the course. As we passed the foursome Anne jokingly said, "Hope you don't mind if we play through." They laughed and told us to go right ahead. Back up at the 16th tee, we waited for an opening and got back into the rotation of play.

It's the only golf course we know of with a village, complete with fantastic pub, in the middle of it.

Another unique feature of golf in the British Isles is playing from one village to another in one round. We first saw this while playing on the Morayshire coast of Scotland. As we finished the seventh hole at Strathlene Buckie GC we realized that we'd played to the next village. Just off the eighth tee was the village of Portessie. We'd played from one village all the way to the next-- from Buckie to Portessie. We saw this feature again when we played Inverallochy GC on the north Aberdeenshire coast, where we started in Inverallochy and turned back at the neighboring village of St Combs.

All these examples give new meaning to the phrase "a golfing village."

Birdie in the Clubhouse

Strathtay Golf Club is an interesting course in Perthshire with some very unique golf holes. Located between Aberfeldy and Pitlochry on a lovely small Highland road, the 9-hole track is very rustic. The clubhouse consists of a small club room, a gents' and a ladies' locker room, and small kitchen.

The beautiful fall day we played we were the only players at the course. No one was about the clubhouse, so we found the honesty box, filled out a ticket, and dropped our money in the box. After we finished the third hole, a worker came running over to us and asked would I help him get a bird out of the clubhouse. I said, "Of course," and we traipsed over to the clubhouse not far from the green. Fluttering in the kitchen was a barn swallow who'd gotten in through an open door, but couldn't find the door again to leave. The birds were just returning to the area on a migration pattern and this one was obviously wanting to join its mates. While the worker tried to guide the bird with a broom, I went directly to the task of grabbing the little guy. Between the broom and my arm waving I was able to trap the frightened bird against a window pane.

Anne screamed, "Don't let him bite you!"

I looked down at the three inch long bird with its quarter inch beak and said, "I don't think that will be a problem."

After a quick examination, with the bird looking none the worse for the experience, I walked to the door and threw the bird into the air. He (or she) took off like, well, a freed swallow. The worker thanked us and went back to work. Anne and I went over to the fourth tee to continue our round. It was my only birdie of the day. The phrase, "A bird in the hand is worth..." comes to mind, but I have yet to come up with a satisfactory ending to the phrase which fits this story.

The Courses that Turned Us Away

For our first travel book, *Scotland's Hidden Gems: Golf, Pubs, and Attractions* (2005), we didn't ask for any concessions from courses. Until the book was published and we could show that ours was a serious (albeit small) endeavor, we paid for everything. After that first book, we've felt justified seeking complementary golf when visiting a course to write about it for our books. Several times courses have not responded to my email requests. In the case of Brodick GC on Isle Arran we found out that the club secretary left and took the club's email address with him. A couple of times courses would respond with a we don't do that, but in most of those cases I've been able to negotiate at least a special rate for our visit. Not so with two particular courses.

I could keep the course names a secret, but why the hell should I. In Ireland we had arranged to play Bearna Golf Course outside of Galway on Sunday, May 7, 2006. Our tee time was for 11:00 and I had an email from the secretary, Anna, confirming our visit. We showed up and went up to the golf shop to check in. The man at the till greeted us and found our tee time, and then said, "That will be €80." I responded that I believed the golf was complimentary. He said, "Yes, and that will be €80." I was beginning to get a little frustrated and said, "No, it's supposed to be free," and I showed him the email from Anna. His response threw me, "It doesn't say free, only complimentary. That will be €80." At this point I asked if Anna was in. He said that she was on vacation and "that'll be €80 if you want to play." I made one last attempt, "Look, Anna arranged the golf to be free because I'm going to write about the course for our guide book." His comeback was unfathomable, "Anna is only the club secretary and has no authority here and she didn't say free, she said complimentary. Besides, we don't need any writers telling people about our course." In a huff, Anne and I walked out, snuck out on the course to take a look at it and take a few pictures. On Monday I called Anna, who wasn't on vacation and was very sorry for the misunderstanding. The gentleman (sort of) whom I had met was a temporary starter who should have never questioned that the golf was free, and would I please consider a return visit. I do hope the worker got fired, he was the rudest Irishman we've ever met.

The other incident happened in Wales at Borth GC on the west coast. It too centered on the definition of "complimentary." This time we showed up for our 11:20 tee time with our email in hand which said they would be glad to have us play and review their course. My response on the email thanked them "for the courtesy of the course they granted us with complimentary golf." This time I was talking to the lady who had arranged the golf and she said, "That will be £50." Pretty much déjà vu all over again (thanks Yogi). "Yes, it's complimentary, but it's not free. £50 please." At least we got a "please" here. That course didn't get written up in our book.

Don't Rush Me

One thing that Anne and I both hate is to be rushed on the golf course. We are not slow players; on our home course we are considered the fastest couple in our club. We've been trained to play Scottish golf where a round should not take over three and a half hours, not the four and a half to five hour rounds typical on American courses. Being quick players, it's even more bothersome to be pushed. A couple of instances stand out in our minds.

At the Dooks GC in Ireland we arrived later than we meant for an 11:00 tee time because of a dying deer on the road causing a traffic jam. We still got to the first tee ten minutes ahead of our scheduled time. A tour group of American players were milling around the first tee--they had been told they couldn't tee off until the writers were off the tee. The group was noisy and obnoxious having to wait for a duffer and a woman, but we both had good drives anyway. The group had acted as if they owned the course; of course, for the money they were probably paying for their tour, they were probably making a good down payment. It's easy to see why American golfers don't have a good reputation overseas. Although we felt rushed getting off the tee, we never did see the Americans again, except when I helped one of them find the correct tee box.

Twice in Wales we had rushed rounds. The first instance was at Royal St David's GC in Harlech and it was our choice. We arrived at the tee box and had the choice to rush our prep and get out ahead of a group of Germans or take our time and play behind them. We rushed and after a couple of hurried shots, played the rest of the round with nobody pushing us. The second instance wasn't our choice or our fault. We arrived at Tenby GC in southern Wales an hour ahead of our scheduled tee time of 1:00, only to find out that our playing partners expected us at 11:00. The problem was that the course manager told us one time (we had the email confirmation) and his members a different time. Because they had been waiting for more than an hour we felt that we had to hurry to get on the course. Neither Anne nor I ever did get our timing slowed down the whole round. Golf is a game of rhythm, so I don't know what game we played that day.

A different type of rushed golf occurred at Luffness New GC in East Lothian, Scotland. We started to head to the first tee for our scheduled start when a group of five elderly members (older than us) rushed out to get ahead of the visitors. It fit with the attitude of the whole club: only the male members are important, women and visitors are given little consideration. Anne and I were a bit put out to have to follow a fivesome of old farts who stole our tee time. We got our surprise when after the first hole we couldn't keep up with the geezers. They left us in the dust (or sand, since it's a links course). At first we tried hard to push them, but soon realized that we were lucky they weren't following and pushing us.

Golf is meant to be played quickly, but it's never fun to be pushed or to have to push others.

I Can't Believe They'd Do That

At one time golf was almost exclusively a man's game. Women came to golf kicking and screaming...at the men. Rosie the Riveter played an important role in opening up the game of golf to women. With all the men gone to war and the women at home doing the traditional man's work, golf courses became more accepting of the women. For some places, though, tradition dies hard.

Luffness New is a venerable bastion of the male golfing society. The course is an interesting links design well worth playing, but the club is an example of the old, stuffy Scottish chauvinist attitude. We had golf arranged, but I couldn't go into the bar to check in because I wasn't wearing a coat and tie. They checked me in through a side door to the bar. The club secretary, a woman no less, was willing to meet me in the foyer and tell me about the course. She was not, however, willing to let Anne, a lady, into the clubhouse through the main entrance where the secretary's office was. Anne had to stand outside in the cold wind while the secretary and I talked in the warm entry way. Anne could go into the lady's locker room, a closet-sized room with small bench, through the women's toilet from the outside. The club was eager to have us write about their course, but made us pay for a course guide and the club's history--items most other courses will give us. When we played, the course had no tee boxes for ladies--Anne was told to tee off from somewhere in front of the men's tees. The score card had no handicap or distances for lady players.

After golf, as I reviewed the club literature bought by me from the secretary, I came across two interesting comments. First, the course says, "Guests will be put at ease by the quiet friendliness of the members." The friendliness was so quiet Anne never heard it. Second, "Where wives play for free." Of course, who'd pay for that kind of treatment?

The Luffness New course is high quality and fun to play, but the club's attitude left much to be desired -- such as 100 years of progress!

"If There's Nae Wind, There's Nae Golf"

The Scottish saying about "no wind means no golf" is especially true on the links courses. Many of the links golf courses in Scotland, Ireland, and Wales are designed with coastal winds in mind. Other than sand bunkers, many links courses are fairly defenseless--not much water, very few trees, mostly flat. It is the wind that creates much of the challenge on courses like Fraserburgh, Old Moray, Wick, Peterhead, Royal Aberdeen, Elie, Crail Balcombie, Machrihanish, Durness, Royal Porthcawl, Carne, Tralee, and the St Andrews courses.

Anne and I have been lucky enough once to play the fantastic Moray Old with no wind. When we played a second time with winds between 10 and 20 miles per hour, we were playing a different course. Some courses we've seen only in the wind. Both times we played the wonderful nine-holer at Durness, we played in heavy wind. I can't imagine how it would play in the calm. In the almost 1000 rounds of golf we've played in the British Isles there have been some memorable wind rounds.

Our first experience with extreme wind, not just the ordinary zephyrs, but real wind, was at Rae GC on the north coast of Scotland. The wind was strong when we started the round, maybe 20 miles per hour steady. By the time we reached the ninth hole the wind was howling at 30 plus. We got blown off the course at the 14th. Gusts over 50 miles per hour meant we couldn't keep the balls still on the tees or on the quick greens. We walked in cursing the tail end of the hurricane that had hit us. On our first visit to Ballybunion in Ireland we had a similar experience, only this time they wouldn't even let us on the course because of the 60 miles per hour gales. Bracing against the back of the clubhouse I was able to get one decent picture, but camera shake ruined a dozen more.

We recently played the Struie Course at Royal Dornoch in high winds. Gale winds were blowing a steady 30 miles per hour with gusts to about 50 and the sun was shining brightly. We played the entire round in those conditions which made for entertaining golf; not good golf, but highly entertaining. The first half of the course played into the wind. I was lucky to get a good drive out to 125 yards (normal for me is 200-220 yards), with 100 yard drives more common, unless I sliced even a little. With a slice I'd get a drive 100 yards out and 100 yards to the right. Anne, who plays a lower shot, was driving almost as far as was I. At the tenth we turned back so the wind was helping. My, how it helped! The tenth at Struie is a 341 yard fairly straight hole with a large mound blocking the left side of the green and heavy rough right. I drove straight and long. We watched the ball skirt past the left mound. We found my ball about ten yards over the green; it had been right in line with the pin. 355 yards! My next drive was about 320 yards. Anne was now hitting 200-220 yards--some of her longest drives ever. The second half made the struggles of the first half worth it.

We were scheduled to play Tralee GC, an Arnold Palmer design on the southwest coast of Ireland, at 10 o'clock on one of our Ireland trips. We arrived in a heavy rain and watched the tour group of Americans set to go out in front of us suiting up for the rain--rain covers on golf bags, rain pants, rain coats, rain gloves, rain hats. We talked to the club manager who agreed that under these conditions we couldn't do the writing and photo work we needed to write up the course. Since drier conditions were expected in the afternoon (we are dubious of forecasts), he suggested we come back and tee off at 2:00. By the time we got back to the course the weather had indeed changed. The sun was out, the rain was gone, but the wind was up, 30-40 miles per hour. We played the fantastic course, or rather got beat up by the fantastic course. I'd take the wind any day over coming in looking like the bedraggled tour group who came in from the morning round. When we were getting ready to go out in the wind, they were taking off rain suits which hadn't kept them dry and packing up to head to an afternoon round in Killarney.

After our last trip to Scotland, where we'd played Struie, I played at our home course on a day with a slight breeze of maybe 10 miles per hour. I played through a gent on the 7th hole who commented, "It's rather windy today, isn't it." I replied, "This isn't wind. Two weeks ago I played Dornoch Struie and the wind.........."

Lost Golf Balls

In World War II a lost playable golf ball was worthy of an hour's search or more. For us, a lost ball is worth a couple of minutes, maybe. There are times, though, when a lost golf ball does create an interesting story.

The golf course manager at St Fillans Golf Club in Perthshire, Scotland, told us about the time he put up a sign near the golf check-in counter. The sign said, "Lost Golf Ball. White. If found please turn in to the clubhouse." Gordon said that in one week golfers turned in 23 balls!

There is a saying in golf that a good way to meet new people is pick up a stray golf ball . . . while it's still rolling. Anne knows this first hand. At Royal Dornoch Golf Club in the north of Scotland one day Anne found a ball just laying on a path between gorse bushes. She looked around, but nobody was in sight. She picked up the ball and was just about to hold it up to show it to me when a gentleman came around the edge of the gorse and said, "Lassie, I believe that's mine." Anne jumped and dropped the ball and then began to profusely apologize. The local told her not to be bothered, "It's only a golf ball. The course has thousands of them." He then told her about a dog trained to find golf balls that in one day found over 200 on the course.

At Narin and Portnoo GC in County Donegal, Ireland, I lost several golf balls in one round. That by itself is not unusual--I can lose balls on any course. What was unusual was that I lost all the balls on good shots in the fairways. We played on an early spring day and the course hadn't been mowed very recently. The fairways were blanketed with small white daisies. I thought it was especially picturesque until I hit a drive into the middle of the fairway and couldn't find my white ball in the sea of white daisies. Hole after hole the same thing happened: hit in the middle, lose the ball. The only balls I didn't lose were ones that missed the fairway and ended up in the rough where there weren't any daisies. That's the only round I can remember where I was glad to miss the fairway.

I had an unusual encounter with a lost ball at St Deiniol Golf Course in Bangor, Wales. On this course the first hole is really tough and I lost a ball in heavy rough on my second shot. Several holes later I teed off on a blind hole (I couldn't see where the ball landed). As I approached my ball I saw two of them and I hadn't even had a nip from my flask, yet. Both were my golf balls and had my mark on them. While I pondered this conundrum a golfer approached from the adjacent hole asking if I'd seen his ball. I told him that I found two of mine, but no others. He then told me that he was playing with a ball he'd found on the first hole and did I want it back. I said, "Finders keepers," and we both played on. Later in the clubhouse he told me that he lost the ball a couple of holes from where I'd met him. Some golf balls just want to be lost.

Some want to be found. We played Leadhills GC, the highest nine-hole course in the UK, on a squally spring day. We were the only people on the course--literally. No one else was about, not on the course nor in the clubhouse. We had left our fees in the honesty box at the small clubhouse and played. As we played we saw only sheep and rabbits, both of whom claim the course as theirs. When we finished the ninth and walked over to the car, there was a fairly new golf ball sitting up prettily on the car's wind screen (windshield) wiper blade. Some golf balls don't want to be lost.

Stuck between a Rock and a Hard Place

A few years ago we were invited to play a new course in the Borders area of Scotland. The MacDonald Cardrona Hotel Golf and Country Club was just opening up when we visited. The course was open, but the "clubhouse" was just a remodeled small railway station and the hotel was only a plan. As writers, the manager offered us a buggy (gas cart) for our round. We usually prefer to walk, but he was persuasive and we were tired from a long trip. The cart was fun until after the eleventh hole.

As we approached the twelfth tee, the path we were on went around the tee box to the right. It looked a little tight, but we saw no other path for the buggy. As I eased the buggy past the back tee, the tee box got higher on the left and the bushes got closer on the right. I could see the path open up beyond the members tee, but I never made it that far. Crunch! The buggy was scraping the rocks on both sides. When I tried backing up I only succeeded in wedging the buggy tighter between the rock walls. We were stuck fast! We pushed and pulled and lifted to no avail. I had wedged the buggy tighter than the lid on a new jar of pickles.

We unloaded our clubs from the back of the buggy and walked back to the clubhouse. On the way back I'm trying to figure out how to tell the manager that I've basically lost his buggy. He was very kind about the problem and tried to make us feel better by saying they planned to put up a sign directing buggies a different way and it wasn't our fault. As true as all that may be, it's still my most embarrassing moment on a golf course--pardon me, I've jammed your buggy between a rock and a hard place and left it to rot!

Tidal Flood Golf

Garmouth and Kingston Golf Club along the Spey River on the Morayshire coast has a special feature we didn't find out about until the ninth hole. The first eight holes are pleasant parkland holes--not much challenge, easy walking, stress-free golf. The ninth is the first of the links holes and we could see quite a bit of water to the right and left on the hole. We each hit (I hit two because it looked like my first might have found some of the water) and had to walk down to the eleventh tee to cross a bridge over a large burn. We should have suspected something because the bridge on our hole was washed out. As we got out to the fairway of the ninth we saw that there was much more water than we'd thought. All three balls had found watery graves. As we stood in the middle of the fairway planning to drop a ball and play on, I looked more carefully at the water on the right. It was expanding quite rapidly. Clearly, it would have covered our escape route in short order. The green at nine was still visible, but the tee box for ten was by now an island

and the path from nine to ten was under water. We hastily retreated to the tee on eleven.

After talking to locals we discovered that they usually check the tide table and avoid playing at high tide. If a couple of holes are inaccessible, they simply repeat a couple that are playable.

We not only picked high tide for our time to play, but autumnal high tide (the year's highest). We played twelve down to a hundred yards out from the green, which was almost an island. We played most of a couple of other holes, but only half of fourteen and seventeen.

The story of almost being stranded on the island ninth fairway was the best part of golf at Garmouth.

You Play the Front and I'll Play the Back

In Ireland, more often than in Scotland, nine-hole courses expect players to go for a full round of eighteen holes. They make no concessions for only playing nine--golfers pay for eighteen holes whether they play the full round or not. On our schedule we often don't have time to play a full round and have to decide whether to pay for more than we get or to skip that course which may mean skipping golf that day.

At Mulranny GC west of Westport almost to Achill Island, we stopped at the course to try to get in nine holes before sightseeing on the island. We saw the sign indicating an eighteen-hole (all-day) price only. We told the golf manager we were writing and wanted to play a quick nine to get a feel for the course. He said that it would be fine and asked for the full price. I explained we couldn't do a full round and still hit the sites we needed to write about. He said that he understood, but that their all-day price was the only price they would offer. We thanked him and said that we'd skip his course. We drove on to Achill Island, Ireland's largest island, where we discovered Achill Island GC, a sheep pasture track in a beautiful setting next to the sea and edged by mountains. At this course the manager indicated that he too had an all-day price, but that he's be glad to cut it in half for a quick nine holes. Smart business.

We think that a nine-hole course with only an eighteen-hole (or all day) price doesn't make good business sense. The course will get some who will pay for what they don't get, but more will be like us and find somewhere else. Either take some of my money or get none of it.

We have handled the Mulrannys of the golf world in several ways. At Kildare GC, even though they only had an eighteen-hole price, the golf manager said he's always willing to negotiate. At Tarbat GC near Tain, one of the few nine-hole Scottish courses without a nine-hole price, we traded a copy of our book for a quick round each. Our most unique approach, though, was at Swinford GC in Ireland. There was a sign above the honesty box at the course which said, "No Concessions for Nine Holes." We decided since there were two of us, we really were one player playing eighteen--Anne was playing the front nine and I was playing the back or second nine. It was just that we were each playing our nines at the same time!

A Quick Scottish Golf Round

In late September we had a round booked on one of Scotland's highest 18-hole courses, Braemar GC. The village is home to Braemar Castle and hosts the Queen's Highland Games in early September since the Queen's Scottish home, Balmoral Castle, is only a few miles away. Nestled down at the base of tall mountains (tall for Scotland), at an elevation of about 1200 feet Braemar GC is closed all winter by snow.

We had a scheduled tee time of 1:00, but arrived to find out the secretary had forgotten there was a medal (a competition) scheduled for that same time. We'd either have to get ready 15 minutes early or wait until almost 2:00 to get out. We hurried our prep and got up on the tee with about two minutes to spare. Competitions usually play fairly slowly and we always play quickly, so we thought there'd be no problem staying ahead of the medal. What we didn't know was that "Rabbit" McDuff's group was the first group off the tee in the medal. He was renown as the fastest player in the Highlands. His group was practically running between shots and the match was alternate shot, meaning only two of the four players were hitting at a time not all four. We did eighteen holes on a tough Highland course in two hours and forty minutes and finished two holes ahead of Rabbit's group, who finished three holes ahead of the next of the medal groups. Both our scores were within our handicap range--fast is not bad!

The Golf Hole that Isn't

A couple of years ago Anne and I were watching the Golf Channel, as always, when a particular commercial caught our attention. The commercial for ??? (who remembers what commercials advertise) showed a golfer traveling in Scotland from course to course looking for the perfect place to play on a rainy day. Finally, he stops at one clubhouse, grabs his clubs, and the next scene shows him teeing off over the sea to a distant green. Having played now more than 245 courses in Scotland we were intrigued to see if we could recognize the course he chose. The green and surroundings looked familiar, but something wasn't quite right. With the help of Anne's photographic memory for every golf hole she's ever played, we finally figured it out. The green is the 13th at The Glen in North Berwick in East Lothian. The 136-yard par three actually has a blind tee shot over a cliff edge down to a green backed by the North Sea. What the commercial showed was a golfer teeing off from the fairway of the 14th fairway back across the sea to the 13th green. It makes an interesting hole the way the commercial played it, but we think the real hole is more unique. We've seen lots of over-the-sea shots--Machrihanish, Durness, Cruit Island, Connemara Isles, St Andrews Castle--but very few blind drives with the sea behind. Thank you commercial producer for giving us an interesting puzzle. By the way, we are still trying to figure out which clubhouse the golfer stops at--it's not the clubhouse at The Glen.

Lahinch in the Rain

We arrived in the Irish coastal village of Lahinch a little after noon. The weather was iffy, but golfable--cool, windy, with a threat of showers. Since this was our only day in Lahinch and our only chance to play the famous course, we asked in the pro shop about a chance to play. The famous Old Course was fully booked, but the shop attendant said the Castle Course, a strong track in its own right, had tee times available and was half the price of the Old Course---only €50. We've played many second courses--Royal Dornoch's Struie course, St Andrews' New and Jubilee courses, the Queen's course at Gleneagles, Carnoustie"s Burnside course, the Kintyre course at Turnberry--and always thought them as interesting and challenging. Our decision made, we paid our fees, gathered our kit, and headed to the first tee.

As we played the first hole we took notice of several local groups playing ahead of us, all moving quickly. Quick play helps make a good round. On the second hole the weather turned nasty-- the wind picked up, gusting to 40 or 50 miles per hour, and a heavy squall settled in. We quickly put up umbrellas and facing them into the wind, huddled behind our bags to ride out the squall with only our legs getting soaked. Five minutes of heavy wind and downpour drained the squall. As the rain ended and the wind calmed down to 30 we put down our umbrellas. The golf course was empty. Empty! All the other groups had gone in. We had never considered quitting--not for €50 each. Later we learned that locals pay only €5 per round. With only a fiver at stake I might have walked off as well (I'm sure Anne would have).

We continued our round having a classy course to ourselves. The wind and sun dried our pants by the sixth hole. On the eighteenth we could see a few groups had come back out onto the course. Being a local may have some advantages, but being a visitor, even in extreme squalls, is not so bad either.

This Story Might Ring a Bell, or Two

At the lovely Brechin GC in the Scottish Highlands we ran into a problem. On the tee box of one hole was a sign: "Don't Tee Off Until You Hear the Bell." We had seen nobody on the course in front of us. We heard no bell. We waited. And we waited. And we waited. We were running out of daylight and, as much as we try to always follow local rules, we had to tee off without hearing a bell. When we got over the hill there was the bell. Nobody was playing behind us, but I had Anne go over and ring the bell so that whomever would follow us could be sure the bell was rung. At times we just marvel at how confusing local rules can be.

Another course, Lochmaben in the south of Scotland, had an interesting local rule about a bell. The tee box of one hole was sited right next to the local cemetery. On the cemetery wall was a sign: "Please Ring Bell upon Passing." I wondered aloud to our group about how many deceased had actually rung the bell upon passing. If our golf round had been a Twilight Zone episode the bell would have rung by itself as we stood on the tee box.

Rain Check at Muckhart Golf Club

Muckhart Golf Club in central Scotland has three nine-hole layouts. We booked in for eighteen holes, paid our fee in cash, collected our gear and headed out on our first nine. Muckhart isn't a very hilly course but the track we were playing had one hole which went up quite a bit and then the next hole came back down. We had teed off and were walking down the gravel path when Anne slipped on the pebbly path and fell hard landing on her knee and hand in the gravel. The damage was significant enough for us to skip the last hole and call it a day. Sorry to say this but Anne falling isn't unique enough to make an interesting story--there are similar events in Stonehaven, Edinburgh, and Forrester Park GC to name a few. What happened next makes the story.

While Anne put our golf kit into the car I went into the Muckhart pro shop to see about getting some money back for the second nine we'd paid for and hadn't played. The young lad in the shop (I refuse to call him an assistant) said it would be no problem and started to write me out a "Rain Check" for our next nine holes. I stopped him and said, "Look, we'd love to play the next nine, but our flight back to the States is in two days and today we are moving to Edinburgh. We can't really use a rain check." He said, "No problem." and continued writing out the rain check. I told him we had paid him cash only an hour and a half ago and asked him, "Why can't you just give us cash back." "This is as good as cash," he said pointing to the rain check. "For someone from Scotland it might be, but we're from America." "That's okay, just use it at a course in America." At that point I walked out without picking up the rain check. I could hear him call after me, "You forgot your rain check." We drove away.

Golf and the World at War:
Effects of World War I and II on Golf in Scotland and Wales, originally published in *Highlander Magazine*

War and golf in Scotland and Wales are not inextricably linked, but their paths have crossed several times. One of the earliest records of "gowf" was King James II of Scotland's decree in 1457 to ban the game, so that soldiers and nobles would spend more time practicing archery to better defend the homeland against English invasion. James III and IV persuaded their parliaments to affirm the ban.

Though the ban was unenforceable, the most important connections were forged during the two World Wars, 1914-19 and 1939-45. These were times of extreme crisis in which the game of golf was but one of the victims. Golf courses suffered the ravages of war through damage to the land and club finances. At the same time, golfers incurred losses to their own games.

My wife Anne and I first became aware of the golf-war relationship as we played courses with village or parish monuments to those lost in the War-to-End-All-War (though names of locals who gave their lives in other wars have been added to many of the monuments). Maybole Golf Club in Ayrshire has such a monument beside the sixth green. Also in Ayrshire, Turnberry displays a monument just to the right of the twelfth hole. While other courses, such as Anstruther on Fife and Bucky Strathlene on the Moray coast, have monuments near greens or tees, Abernethy GC in the Scottish Highlands has a monument in play on the eighth hole. Knowledgeable golfers aim to the left of the monument to find the fairway on this blind par four. We've seen a different kind of monument to war in use at Elie GC on Fife. The starter's office includes a periscope from a late-1930s vintage submarine. The scope is used to check that the landing area is clear for the blind drive on the first. Whereas monuments, whether in play or not, are reminders of war and the casualties of war, golf courses themselves were casualties.

During both world wars, the MOD (Ministry of Defense) needed golf course land for its own purposes. In 1914 the Old Birnam and Dunkeld course along Scotland's Tay River was dug up in practice trench digging exercises. The course didn't reopen in its new location until 1927. At Tenby GC in southwest Wales the defense demands started early. The MOD made a compulsory buy of four holes of land for a training facility early in the century, and then demanded a further two holes in World War I. The course never did get any of the land back, and today Tenby still has a target range next to several of the beginning holes. Local defense volunteer forces used Southerndown GC in southern Wales for training and gunnery practice during the Great War. The west end of North Berwick West GC, an Open qualifying venue when the Open is at Muirfield, was used for RAF (Royal Air Force) target practice, and weapons pits and defensive bunkers were built on the sea edge of the course.

In World War II Aberdour GC on Fife became home to Heavy "A" Batteries, while nearby Balbirnie Park GC and Edinburgh's Baberton GC were both heavily damaged by placement of ack-ack guns and search lights. Trenches, barbed-wire, and mines were placed on many eastern seaside courses such as Crail Balcombie, Elie, Dunbar, and Peterhead. On the seaward side of Leven Golf Links in Fife you can still see the cement blocks used as tank traps in the Second World War. At Tenby, the dunes on the seaward side of the fairways were fenced and mined; many playable and valuable golf balls rested just out of safe reach for the duration of the war. Much of Royal St. David's GC, sited just below impressive Harlech Castle on Wales' west coast, was torn up as a training ground for tank drivers. Nearby Pwllheli GC didn't suffer as much damage because it was only used for night training exercises by a local officer's training facility. Golfers at Fraserburgh GC in northeast

Scotland continued to play around large poles strategically placed in fairways to thwart enemy glider landings. One pole has been left on the 9-hole Rosehill course as the club's reminder of those troubled times. At St Deiniol GC in Bangor, Wales, the same type anti-glider poles were placed on fairways, which seemed to be a silly decision because when we played the hillside course, we couldn't find a level enough place to land a golf ball, let alone a troop-carrying glider. It was the RAF, though, which exacted the biggest toll when it dug up historic Turnberry and the Ladies' Course at Royal Dornoch (now rebuilt as the 18-hole Struie Course) to build aerodromes or landing fields.

Golf course land was also in heavy demand for food production. Duff House Royal on the Morayshire coast was ploughed up twice, once for each war, and rebuilt twice. The original course at Portfield Racecourse in Haverfordwest (southern Wales) was ploughed up for corn fields in World War I. Haverfordwest GC opened after the war in a new location. In World War II Balfron GC near Loch Lomand was ploughed up for agricultural use. Not much information remains about the old course, but a couple of old trophies turned up recently in a bank attic. Powfoot GC on Scotland's Solway Firth lost five holes to the plough (today those are the flattest holes on the course), while Canmore near Dunfirmline lost more land which led to a complete redesign of the course in 1946. In World War One Pwllheli was reduced to 9 holes, while the 9th and 10th holes at Baberton became known as Baberton's Patriotic Potato Patch. Many courses, such as Shiskine, Kinghorn, Muirfield, and Aboyne, avoided the plough, but were used to graze sheep and cattle. At Cruden Bay GC near Aberdeen it is said that the sheep toughened the course even more by enlarging the bunkers. At Panmure GC on Scotland's east coast, local authorities during the First World War demanded that the course be opened to sheep grazing until the shepherd reported his sheep were starving because of the sparse grass on the links course. In World War II the experiment was tried again with the same results. Panmure's a great links course, but what is good for a long drive isn't necessarily good for little lambs.

It fits with Sir Winston Churchill's words to Hitler, "You can do your worst, and we will do our best," that Clubhouses and other golf course buildings found uses in the war effort. Troops were billeted at Boat of Garden in the Highlands, Royal Troon, and Lundin Ladies' Links on Fife (the only time men have been allowed in that clubhouse). The experience at Panmure was typical. Even though more than 100 troops were billeted for much of the war, the clubhouse was returned to the club in pristine condition. Not so at Crieff GC in central Scotland. When the MOD took over the Crieff clubhouse, the club moved its historical records to an equipment shed. Those records were lost when the shed was destroyed in an accidental fire caused by troops staying there. Part of the opulent Gleneagles Resort Hotel, set to host the 2014 Ryder Cup, became headquarters for Tom Johnston, Scotland's Secretary of State, and the rest served as a convalescent hospital. In 1944, Southerndown GC in Wales became a safe haven from Hitler's V1 and V2 rocket attacks for more than 100 mothers and children from the east coast of England. The club's lounge became a dormitory and the good weather that summer allowed the children acres and acres of playground complete with sandboxes.

The golf clubs in Scotland and Wales suffered tremendous financial loses during the war years. With so many golfers enlisted in the military, club membership took a big hit. North Berwick West's membership was reduced from 87 members in 1940 to 35 in 1945. On Isle Arran, Shiskine's membership dropped from 112 to 48. In World War One Cardross GC near Loch Lomand lost 30 members to war injuries. Memberships were so depleted that at Blairgowrie GC in 1917 no quorum showed up for the annual meeting. Even worse, in the 1940s the Kinghorn Golf Club on Fife couldn't muster a quorum for a club meeting to disband the club. Records for the Aberfoyle Golf Club show that for one 5-week stretch in 1917, only 1 person had used the course. Along with a reduction of membership, of course, came a reduction in financial resources which threatened the continued existence of clubs like Kingussie GC in the Highlands. The Bangor GC in Wales was a special case. At the beginning of World War I club members felt the war would be a short engagement and went ahead with plans to build a new clubhouse. As the war dragged on and prices rose dramatically, financial disaster was imminent. The club declared bankruptcy in 1916. A reorganized St Deiniol GC opened after the war using the same Bangor course. Further financial damage was done when courses like Anstruther on Fife, Abernethy in the Highlands, Stranraer in southern Scotland, Craigentinny in Edinburgh, and the 9-hole Kingsbarns course on Fife completely shut down for the duration of the war. Nine-hole St Boswell GC in the Scottish Borders was closed from 1944 to 1947. Within a year of reopening, the River

Tweed flooded the course. It was not rebuilt until 1957. Although the St Boswell course did survive, the ultimate sacrifice was made by many courses whose names are just memories. Corriecravie on Isle Arran, Fidra in East Lothians, Falkland in Fife, Longmen GC in Inverness, and Penally in southern Wales were all closed and never reopened. Sauchhope Links, once a fine Fife golf course, is now a caravan park. Markinch GC reopened for one year after the war before succumbing to financial pressures.

For those courses which did survive, some physical scars remain. The five flat holes at Powfoot are a reminder of what war did to golf courses. More dramatic, and of more concern to today's players, are the remnants of German bombings. Stonehaven GC south of Aberdeen has a grass bunker in play off the left side of the first fairway. The bunker is the result of a bomb dropped in August of 1940 by a German plane heading home from a mission. The hazard is now named "Hitler's Bunker." Powfoot has also left bomb damage in play. The ninth hole is called "Crater" after the huge German bomb crater short of the green. Today that bunker is a reminder of how hard it is to hit that particular green. The rolling fairways of the first few holes at Forfar GC north of Dundee are the result of using the fairways in World War I for drying netted flax. In November 1940 an RAF Spitfire fighter made a forced landing at Canmore GC. The landing and the hauling away of the plane did severe damage which can still be seen to several fairways. Perhaps the most devastation was done to the Cardross and Milngavie courses along the River Clyde up from Glasgow. On May 6, 1941, the villages and golf courses were bombed when they we mistaken for the Glasgow ship works. While Milngavie suffered damage to the 18th fairway and clubhouse, the Cardross clubhouse was destroyed by incendiary devices and several members were killed in the bombing.

Besides playing around the bomb craters, avoiding the mines, and, at Scotland's Aboyne GC, having to stay out of the rough which was planted with potatoes, golfers had to contend with other special war situations. Conditioning of the courses was much affected by the wars. Many courses had to reduce their number of holes. Royal Dornoch and Boat of Garten both stopped maintenance on their farthest four holes because of the lack of grounds crew. The remaining holes at Tenby became almost unplayable as moles and rabbits took over the course. Some courses, like Tulliallan in Scotland and St Deiniol in Wales, were maintained only because members were assigned specific holes to tend. At Panmure GC there weren't enough members to keep the course playable, but the Royal Scots stationed at nearby Barry Camp helped groom the course in exchange for playing privileges. The most interesting example is that of Shiskine Golf and Tennis Club on Isle Arran. Six of the holes created by Willie Park & Sons, extending the course from nine to 18 holes, were lost during World War I. Because of the lack of maintenance staff, the six Willie Park hill holes built on the side of Drumadoon Point were left to revert to their primitive state of gorse, heather, and bracken. After the war, the club chose not to reclaim the holes. Thus was born the world's first permanent 12-hole course, a number which many visitors find to be just right. Lack of money and staff created other conditioning headaches as well. For instance, because golf courses were only allotted ten gallons of petrol per month, fairways were seldom cut and rough became very deep. We know conditions for golfers during World War I were tough when the Pyle & Kenfig GC's (southern Wales) club meeting minutes note the "admirable sacrifice of the club in giving up bacon and ham" for the duration.

Golf equipment in both wars was severely affected. In the first war importing of hickory shafts for golf clubs was banned, and club heads were often melted down for their metal. Golf balls became as valuable as gold to golfers. Since all rubber was needed for war related uses, new balls almost completely disappeared by 1940. Players used balls until they were beaten, battered and broken; then they were repainted and used some more. Searching for an hour or more was not unheard of in pursuit of a lost, playable ball. In one case early in the second war a competition was held with a fresh turkey as first prize and six new Dunlop 65 balls as second prize. Everyone played for second!

During the war years, competitions became rare or nonexistent. The Ryder Cup became the first victim of the Second World War when the 1939 matches in the US were canceled. The competitive spirit wasn't dimmed, however, as shown by the Secretary of the British PGA's cable to America: "When we have settled our differences and peace reigns, we will see that our team comes across to remove the Ryder Cup from your safekeeping." The venerated Open Championship was suspended from 1940 to 1945, as it had been during the war years of 1914 to 1919. Those local competitions which were held were often changed. The women's competitions at Grantown-on-Spey in the Highlands, for instance, donated all entry fees to the local Red Cross. During competitions or casual rounds, special war rules were in effect. One such rule said: "A player whose stroke is affected by the simultaneous explosion of a bomb or shell, or by machine-gun fire, may play another ball from the same place. Penalty, one stroke." Courses did do their part for service men and women by opening up to play by military personnel. Edzell GC in the Highlands was open to play by service personnel in the Second World War as it had been in the First and even the Boer War. Panmure, St. Deiniol, Pwllheli, Baberton, Abergele (in northern Wales) and many others allowed the military to play for free.

Not everything that happened as a result of the wars had a negative affect on the game. The war years brought more women to golf. They played more and their club status often changed from associate to full members. Powfoot GC is one of the best examples of a dramatic change to the game, which most would call positive. The Sabbatarian tradition of no golf on Sunday was well entrenched in Scotland and Wales before 1914. Because of the war, Powfoot granted workers at the munition factory in nearby Gretna the right to play for free on their only day off, Sunday. Abergele GC allowed military the right to play on Sunday in 1918. At both Tenby and Stranraer returning servicemen voted for Sunday golf, even over the objections of vociferous clergy. Other clubs followed suit and the Sunday ban slowly lifted. Examples of financial gain by clubs are difficult to find, though some do exist. A prime example is the St Deiniol GC, the former Bangor GC which went bankrupt in 1916. St Deiniol profited from the large number of evacuees from London who moved to safer Wales. When the BBC relocated to Bangor, alcohol sales in the clubhouse increased dramatically with "bar receipts in one of the war years touching a new high record level" [club minutes].

It is said that in war there are no winners, only survivors. Golf in Scotland and Wales, for the most part, proved itself a survivor. As Anne and I play one of our favorite courses in the world, Shiskine Golf and Tennis Club on Isle Arran off the Scottish Ayrshire coast, we marvel that its unique twelve hole layout is one result of the failed War-to-End-All-War.

CHAPTER 3: Scrapes, Bumps, Bruises and Beasties

With all our trips you know there have to have been some accidents or injuries. There have been, but I promised Anne that I wouldn't tell about her falling at Stonehaven, Muckhart GC, or Forrester Park GC, or about her breaking her toe in the lounge of a B&B. Not telling those stories still leaves plenty of small injuries and meetings with animals to tell about. Most of the bruising stories are painful to recall, but less painful than the actual incident. Our encounters with animals, except for the Scourge of the Highlands, have been friendly run-ins and entertaining. I'll start with a story about my stupidity in Cork, Ireland.

A Walk too Far

Sometimes we bite off too much and too often I think I'm younger than I am. Such was the case in Cork, Ireland, on our first visit.

That morning we played golf at the wonderful Cork Golf Club, known as Little Island. The course is a lovely forest or parkland track which is fairly easy to walk, but a round of eighteen holes is still an average of five miles of walking. When we got back to the B&B in the afternoon, Anne, smart person that she is, decided a little rest or nap before dinner was in order. I, being the dummy that I am, decided I would not waste the afternoon in frivolous rest, but would instead wander down to the main shopping area of Cork. A mile of pavement walking to town, at least a mile of wandering the downtown area, and a mile back to the B&B put my day's total up over eight miles.   Done yet? No. For dinner our B&B hosts suggested one of a couple of good Italian restaurants in the downtown area, but said it was best to walk since downtown parking was poor. Besides, it's only a mile to town.

By now my feet were beginning to hurt just a bit, but I was game for a walk to dinner. As I limped toward town, Anne asked what was the matter. I had to fess up that my feet were on the sore side.   What I really should have said was that my feet were absolutely killing me. Dinner was delightful, but the walk home was excruciatingly painful. Even after a good soaking, my feet throbbed all night.

By morning I could count the blisters on top of blisters with both hands. We searched the local chemist's (pharmacy) for the best blister plasters they had.   Even doctored up, at Waterford Castle Golf Club I had to take a buggy (electric golf cart) to make our round. Back in Cork for dinner I drove to downtown and to hell with the poor parking.

A Visit to a UK Emergency Room

Before we left on on our trip in the spring of 2014 our friends asked us if we had ever had to use medical facilities in the UK. Except for a visit to a dentist to repair a crown that had come loose, we told them we had never had call to visit a UK ER. That was like the announcers curse when broadcasting a golf tournament, of course it's going to happen now. And it did.

Anne noticed that she had a very red left eye.   Upon examination we could tell she'd broken a blood vessel in her eye. A search on the internet reassured us that it was nothing major, but with an artificial heart valve and taking blood thinners we were still concerned. Jacky thought it might be related to high blood pressure and convinced Anne that she should visit the local small hospital ER or urgent care.

We walked into the hospital entrance at about 6:30PM and rang the bell for the emergency nurse on duty. A sign near the bell told us to ring once and then wait. It said that a nurse on duty might be on rounds but would be with us shortly. It was a half hour before a nurse showed up who said the emergency room wasn't open--this was while she was standing next to a sign which said the ER was open until 9:00PM every day. She told us what National Health number to ring, but then said, "Oh, well. I might as well take a look at your eye."

In the care room the nurse took Anne's blood pressure and noted it was quite high, 185 over 90. She then told Anne her eye was okay and that the blood would dissipate in a few days. We were a little shocked that the high blood pressure didn't trigger any further concern. It was as if the nurse didn't want to be bothered with tourists.

Anne's eye did get slowly better and, except for a couple of instances of spots before her eyes, Anne didn't seem to be troubled with high blood pressure. Our one visit to the emergency room didn't leave us feeling great about emergency care in the UK even if it was free.

A second visit to doctors in the UK was a little better. In our fall trip Anne got to Scotland and discovered she'd brought the almost empty bottle of a necessary prescription instead of a newly filled bottle. Even though she had her prescription information, the local chemists (pharmacy) couldn't by law give her the medication-- she would have to go to a local doctor and get a new prescription.

We went to the local doctor's clinic (next to the ER we had visited before) and explained the situation to the receptionist. She put Anne in a queue to see a doctor. Thirty minutes later a doctor came out into the reception area and called for Anne. After a twenty-minute visit with the doctor--most of it spent trying to find a UK equivalent of Anne's medication--she came out with a prescription and a bill for £70 ($120 US)--the visit would have been free to UK residents. We paid our bill and went to the recommended chemist to fill our prescription. Interestingly enough, the UK prescription cost about a third of what the US prescription had cost even with insurance.

Perhaps the National Health Care System in Britain isn't so bad after all.

The Bad Knee and Grocery Shopping

Before one of our trips to Scotland I was told by my doctor that about half the cartilage in my right knee was gone and he prescribed PT to strengthen the muscles around the knee. I could golf with care, but no more carrying clubs. No problem until we got to Scotland. I had no problems on the courses or touring castles, but the first time and every time I went shopping with Anne in a grocery store the pain would flare up, my knee would start to pop, and I would walk out limping. A few minutes later I'd be fine with only a little residual tenderness. Anne and Jacky (our B&B friend) wouldn't believe me. Why only the grocery store, they'd say. I had no answers, but I swear I wasn't trying to get out of shopping--I rather enjoy seeing the differences between our stores and the Scottish stores. The next trip was the same. For the most part it doesn't happen in our Fred Meyers or Thriftway grocery stores. I've come to the conclusion that my knee is allergic to Scottish grocers and I'm trying to come up with a name for my newly discovered ailment. *Storitis-Scoticus*, perhaps.

Dunblane Zipper Club

As we played Dunblane New GC one pleasant spring day, we caught up with a threesome of members at the tenth hole. They were taking their time and decided to let us play through. As we stood around chatting I mentioned that we were on a sort of victory tour, celebrating Anne's successful heart valve replacement surgery.

The three men all applauded and one said, "Welcome to the Dunblane Zipper Club." At that all three pulled up their shirts and showed off the several inch long scars from their heart valve surgeries. Anne was tempted to do the same, but instead modestly pulled down the neck of her shirt to show a much smaller scar from her operation.

It was decided that she had been the first lady initiated into the Dunblane "Little Zipper" Club.

Attack of the Ducks

While touring the far northwest corner of Scotland, from Durness east towards Tongue, we had one of our most unusual animal encounters. We were attacked by a flock, herd, bevy, covey, gaggle, crowd, or what ever you call a gang of crazed ducks. I had gotten out of the car at an ocean overlook to photograph the view and was soon accosted by a group of local ducks, at least they all quacked with a northern Scottish brogue. They kept up their begging behavior as I walked across the road, but left me when I headed down toward the beach.

After about ten minutes of picture taking, I walked back to the car. Anne had rolled down her window and was shouting at me to come feed the ducks who had been pecking the car door under her window demanding a ransom of cracker crumbs for her release. I found some Carr's Cheese Melts (our favorite cracker) and lured away the mob who I discovered would fight each other to eat right out of my hand.

We were several miles from even a small village in the remote far northwest corner of Scotland, yet the ducks were able to eek out an existence by gang attacking tourists. Clever birds!

Attack of Ice Cream Crazed Gulls

In Llandudno (clan-DID-nu), Wales, we hit an absolutely gorgeous stretch of weather--clear skies, 80 degrees, almost no wind--in mid April. After golf one afternoon we walked from our B&B down to the waterfront and then out the Llandudno pier. It was too early in the season for most of the pier shops and attractions to be open, but the ice cream shop was doing a brisk business in the fine weather. We each bought a cone and continued to walk out toward the end of the pier making jokes about a long walk on a short pier. Without warning, a gull swooped down and hit Anne's cone holding hand, knocking the ice cream and cone to the ground. A couple of gulls pounced on the dropped cone with relish.

After seeing what happened to Anne, I guarded my cone much more closely. I saw a gull dive at me and turned to the side, but the gull hit me with a wing and knocked my glasses off. It might have been the same gull who hit Anne or a different one, I didn't get a chance to ask for identification. In trying to keep my glasses from a watery grave off the pier, I dropped my ice cream cone to the great delight of another couple of gulls.

Without ice cream cones we walked back to the beginning of the pier and noticed locals standing next to protective buildings enjoying their sweet treat. When we told our B&B hosts about the vicious attacks, they apologized for not telling us that the local birds were a "tad aggressive." Tad aggressive! Our military needs these birds!

The Birds of Glenisla GC

We arrived at Glenisla GC in Angus, Scotland, in plenty of time for our scheduled tee time. As I parked Anne noted that most of the cars had their windscreen wipers pulled out from the windscreen. We wondered if it were some kind of local superstition--good karma comes to golfers who leave the wiper blades up, or was it a local custom. Not wanting to tempt some unknown fate or offend local custom, I pulled my wiper blades off the windscreen and left them lifted up. In the golf shop talking to the club secretary who had arranged our golf, I asked about the wiper blade positioning. It isn't superstition or custom, but there is good reason to the madness. The club has two local crows, who they've named Osama and Bin Laden, who will chew on the rubber parts of wiper blades as they rest on the window. The crows won't bother the wipers if they are left in the up position. Those in the know realize that you either raise your wiper blades to the crows or be prepared to pay for their terrorism.

Heading out of the golf shop toward the first tee, the secretary gave us another warning. She said we needed to be careful as we approached the end of the walkway leading toward the course because there was a mother Oyster Catcher with a nest of eggs in the rocks by the path. She said that the previous week the Oyster Catcher had dive bombed a group of visiting American golfers and sent them sprawling. We gave a wide berth to the nesting site and gave a respectful "Good morning" to the protective momma.

I'd be tempted to say, "Glenisla GC is for the birds," if it weren't such a quality course.

Cows and Sheep on the Courses

We knew something special was going on when the first green at Narin and Portnoo GC in County Donegal, Ireland, was surrounded by electrified fencing. We discovered that the land on which the first four holes of the course are sited was leased in the winter to a local farmer. To keep the sheep and cows off the greens, the club has surrounded the greens with electric fencing. The second time we played the course a couple of years later, the fencing was gone. The farmer's lease had run out. Narin and Portnoo is not the only course where electric fencing is used to keep the animals off the greens. Brora GC, a championship track north of Royal Dornoch in Scotland, Achill Island, a beautifully sited nine-hole sheep pasture course off the west coast of Ireland, and Pennard GC in southern Wales still use the electric fencing to protect greens. It makes for an interesting round having to step over a live wire to get to the putting surface. Achill Island GC has another interesting feature. To break up the sheep droppings throughout the course, the grounds crew of one drags an old bedsprings behind a tractor. It does the job as well as fertilizes the fairways.

At Leadhills GC, the highest course in the UK at a little over 1200 feet elevation, in the southern uplands of Scotland has no fencing around the greens, but it has plenty of sheep. When we played no people were on the course except us, but there were sheep on practically every green. There were droppings from the sheep and their friends the rabbits on every green as well. At home we brush away droppings from our local oak and fir trees with our hats or hands. At Leadhills you cleared a path with your shoes or you moved the ball to an unobstructed location. It was a little difficult to play to a sheep infested green when your playing partner is saying, "Don't hit them; they're so cute." Anne eventually had to hit right at a couple of sheep, but they quickly got out of the way. The sheep must get very good at dodging golf balls on their course.

The same, evidently, wasn't true at Southerndown GC in South Wales. The club's centenary book contains a story of an early competition where a player's shot hit a sheep and lodged in the wool at the animal's posterior. The offended sheep bolted forward toward the green. The ball fell out much closer to the green than it would have had it not been carried. The argument then ensued about where the ball should be played--where it hit the sheep or where it finally came to rest. We've heard this story told at several other courses. Either sheep behinds have a magnetic attraction for golf balls in competition or it's a Celtic golfer's version of an urban myth.

The St Fillans Cow Incident

St Fillans Golf Club, a club where we are the only international members, is not a cow pasture course--most of the time. The course is a nine-hole gem in the Perthshire hills about 12 miles from our home-in-Scotland base in Crieff. St Fillans is nestled in a small valley surrounded by Highland hills and crags. Running along one side of the course is the small River Earn which flows out of Lochearn. Along the opposite side are cow and sheep pastures which butt up against the hills and an ancient walled off graveyard of

the Stewart clan. Although quite flat, the course has interesting holes highlighted by the 3rd which is the only hole with any elevation. It plays from the top of a crag down toward the green about 280 yards away. With wind behind, I've driven the green. With the wind into us, a trap and rough on the right are seriously in play. The next two holes play around the edge of the crag which affects shots considerably. The course may be short and flat, but it's definitely not easy. This sets the scene for our adventures at the sixth green.

We were playing the course one day with our American golfing friends, Helen and Grady Morgan, who spent four days traveling with us on their tour of the UK. We had all teed off on the 220-yard par 3 (par 4 for ladies) 6th and were half way to the green when the course greenskeeper jumps off of his mower and starts yelling at us to stop the bulls from trampling the green. We quickly turned around just in time to see three young bulls or steers (I didn't stop to look, but could tell they weren't Bessies) who had broken through the fence and were heading for the green and us. Neither Grady nor I are farm boys and we didn't want to start then, but we did what we could and jumped and yelled to try to turn the herd away from the green. We stalled the animals long enough for the greenskeeper to reach us with his mower and he herded them back into their field. We basked in our glory of a job sort of well done and finished our game.

Several years later Anne and I were playing the course and caught up with a couple of women on the sixth who wanted to let us through. As we waited for the group ahead to clear the green, the ladies told us a story they heard about this hole and the day the whole herd of cows got out. Anne and I looked at each other and giggled and said, "We know that story. We're the ones who corralled the herd, but it was only a herd of three young cows."

Evidently our story has a life of its own.

Dogs in Pubs

We discovered early we weren't in Kansas (or Oregon) any more when we entered an Innerleithen pub on the second day of our first trip to Scotland. There were dogs in the pubs and they were accepted by management and patron alike. Since that second day we've had numerous experiences with pub dogs.

In a restaurant in the Crown Hotel in Peebles we were having dinner in the dining room when a lady with a small Yorkshire terrier came in and was seated at the next table. She sat in one chair and pulled a second chair close, placed a pillow on it, and set the dog on the pillow. That was his/her place throughout dinner. No noise, no fuss, no food. The dog simply shared the table with its mistress.

At Skerry Brae, a pub and restaurant overlooking the 18th fairway at the fine Moray Old Golf Club, there is a sign at the entrance to the conservatory dining room, "No Dogs Beyond this Point." Dogs are allowed in the pub, the restaurant, the patio, but not in the conservatory. What is it they are trying to conserve?

At the King's Head Pub in Llandudno, Wales, we met the largest pub dog we've ever seen. The dog was a massive black Mastiff who must have weighed 250 pounds. He just lay by the fire and slobbered. We were glad he wasn't the jump-up-and-greet-you-with-licks kind of pub dog. One pub dog we sort of met we still aren't sure if he is the friendly kind or not. At the Mountain Inn in Coolaney, Ireland, near Sligo, we spent two evenings in the inn's pub. The dog never moved--not a wag, woof, or whimper. If he was stuffed, he was certainly lifelike.

Anne and I were shocked one evening at the Ship Inn in Elie, Scotland, to see a family bring their Siberian husky to dinner with them. We owned a kennel of registered Siberians for 14 years (raced them in sled dog races for 12 years). The dogs do well in the house, but knowing the friendly temperament of the husky and how they find it difficult to avoid temptation, we would have never tried to take even our calmest husky into a busy pub at dinner time. Surprisingly, the dog did fairly well. Applause to the owners and the dog.

Perhaps our favorite pub dog is the border collie we met at the Golden Arms in West Linton, Scotland. There was nothing particularly special about the dog. She very graciously accepted crisps (potato chips) from Anne until the bag was empty. Then she wandered back to her corner bed. Why we hold a special affinity with this dog is that we met her after we had finished our second round of Scottish golf at the West Linton GC, while enjoying a beer and crisps. Anne said, "This is neat. Maybe we ought to write about this." Thus was born our passion for writing about Scottish golf, pubs, and attractions. A passion that has filled our lives with great experiences for the past ten years. We owe quite a bit to that little border collie.

Kamikazi Pheasants

Except for dogs and cats, I rarely anthropomorphize animals. In the case, though, of Scottish ringneck pheasants in the autumn I make an exception. These birds are either Kamikazi trained or suicidal as a species.

When driving almost anywhere in Scotland's lovely farm country in the fall, and especially when driving in the blooming heathered Highlands, you must dodge the bodies of birds who took too seriously the saying, "Sometimes you're the bug, and sometimes you're the windscreen," then acted like the bug. Look in any parking lot and you'll find feathers on bumpers and grills of almost every auto and truck. I swear the locals often have little bird emblems on their windows indicating the season's kills. If you are successful at avoiding one bird crossing the road, the next one will fly straight at you with the attitude, "Take that, car!"

I haven't found anyone who knows why the birds have such a death wish. Perhaps it's just their way of avoiding ending up on some hunter's dinner plate. Whatever the reason, a road littered with pheasant bodies is a sure sign of autumn in Scotland.

The Golf Wildlife

One year at the Gearheart Golf Links on the Oregon coast we came upon some real wildlife. A party of businessmen had brought with them some girls in business and they were driving around the course in all manner of undress. We haven't seen that kind of wildlife on courses in the British Isles, but we have observed other wildlife.

Twice we've encountered hedgehogs in Scotland, once at Crieff and once at Tulliallan. We learned though that as cute as the hedgehog is it is probably just as full of fleas and other small critters and better left alone. Jamie Montgomery introduced us to black grouse which inhabit the Montgomery and Bruce courses in Kinross. At Boat of Garten while looking for my wayward ball I flushed a covey of ptarmigan, and I was so startled that I just pointed (Good dog, Bob!). On a recent visit to Panmure GC on Scotland's east coast I was lucky enough to get a decent picture of a harrier hawk as it fluttered above its prey. I was hoping for some special photos when I spotted a large bird at Blairgowrie's Landsdowne course in the fairway ahead of us. I took several shots and moved closer for more. I thought perhaps I'd have special photos of the rare Capricallie (a large colorful wild grouse) until I got close enough to see that it was just a colorful rooster. The pro at the shop said the bird had appeared about five weeks before and was getting quite good at dodging golf balls.

There are no serpents in Ireland; St Patrick cast them out. On Isle Arran's Corrie GC we saw a sign which said, "Beware of Snakes." It was at Pwllheli Golf Course in northern Wales that we finally heard that indeed there were snakes in the British Isles, and not just the harmless garden variety. Our golfing hosts told us that there were reports of black adders (relative to the cobra) in the area. At Milford Haven GC in southern Wales I hit a tee shot over a stone fence into an old croft orchard next to the course. Our playing companion told me to just play one from outside the stone fence. I asked if the area was Out of Bounds? He said, "No, but nobody goes in there." After my quizzical look he emphatically added, "Black adders live there!" I took my penalty and dropped a new ball well away from what the locals call "The Snake Pit."

One of our most unusual encounters was one we only heard, but never saw. As we played the St Fillans course in central Scotland on October 5 (the last round of our 2009 trip), we heard strange noises as we came up the 7th fairway. It sounded like a cow was in distress in the hills north of the club. We asked a local playing through if he'd heard anything strange, but he said he hadn't. On our second time around we could still hear the noises coming from the hills. As we stood listening the player we'd talked to earlier came over from an adjoining fairway and asked if that was the sound we'd heard before. We said it was. He then explained that it was the bellowing of red deer stags at the beginning of the rutting season. He added, though, that it was the earliest he'd ever heard their calls, which explained why we'd never heard them before since this was the time we always would end our fall trip. Anne and I played the last three holes badly because we kept looking into the hills trying to glimpse the deer.

We've had two run-ins with fox on golf courses. One was quite fleeting as a large coyote-sized red fox ran across the path in front of us just before the twelfth tee at St Andrews Duke's course. The other meeting was more interesting. At the East Clare Golf Club golf shop in Ireland the pro told us to be on the lookout for a red fox around the ninth or tenth hole. The fox was still wild but was becoming quite adept at begging for, of all things, chocolate. On the eleventh fairway the fox came trotting up towards Anne, who offered a carrot instead of chocolate (which isn't supposed to be good for canines). That offering was rejected. He came within about five feet of me (great for photos) before realizing I had nothing for him and moseying on.

We really found these kind of fox more fitting with the golf environment than the foxes we saw at Gearheart--although, they were an interesting distraction, too.

Midgies--the Scourge of Scotland

We'd heard stories, had warnings, but had never had a personal introduction to *Culicoides impunctatus*. Most of our travel has been off-season, April-May and September-October. We'd never been in the Highlands in the peak season of early June through late August. According to one book, "During the Second World War Scottish soldiers training in the Highlands branded her worse than Hitler." The "she" referred to is none other than The Midge.

Of the 34 different species of biting flies in Scotland, only five are attracted to people and 85% of the attacks are by *Culicoides impunctatus*. Midges or midgies are small biting flies that appear in mid to late summer, especially in the Highlands and around water. In the Northwest we would call them "No See 'Ems" or gnats, but ours don't bite.

September 2007 was our tenth trip to Scotland, and it was the first time for us to come face-to-face (or rather mouth-to-arm) with the midges. When we played Ullapool GC in the northwest of the Scottish Highlands it was a wind free, overcast with light showers day. We thought we were prepared with insect repellant, but I was in for a surprise. By the time we'd reached the tee at the second we knew we needed protection. We sprayed our necks and heads with *Off!* and played on. The repellant worked fairly well, except that I didn't think about the fact that I was wearing short sleeves while Anne had on long. Even though I hadn't felt a single bite, by the end of the round there were a few welts on my arms that were beginning to itch. By that evening I was putting on the only anti-itch medicine we had by the gobs. The next morning I could count more than forty bites per arm and nothing was stopping the itch. Midge bites are not like mosquito bites which sting, swell up, itch for a couple of days, and are forgotten. Midge bites itch for a month! I tried every remedy available from every chemist (pharmacy) at which we stopped. Some worked a little or for a while, some didn't work at all. We've since learned a lot more about the midges. As far as repellents go, the *Off!* worked fairly well, but we've since heard that Avon's *Skin So Soft* is the preferred repellent by locals. One description I heard said that you slathered it on good and thick, and then any midges who do land on you drown in the lotion.

Midges like the twilight and the females, who do the biting, are most voracious at dawn and dusk. Sun and wind are actually the enemies of the midge. They will never bite in the midday sun and can't fly in breezes more than seven miles per hour. If the weather is dull and overcast, as our day at Ullapool, they can bite anytime. Businesses have refused to locate in the Highlands because of the midges. Scotland loses millions of pounds in lost work-time a year at Highland outdoor employment because of the "wee beasties."

As I say, it took us ten visits to Scotland to become personally acquainted with the Scourge of Scotland. When we next travel in the Highlands in Midge Season we will be better prepared with a good repellant, protective clothing, and as much anti-itch lotion as we can carry.

Smart Aussie Dog

Some events are easily missed or overlooked happenings that you might never know you missed, but your life could be sadder for missing it. As Anne and I approached the Tourist Information Bureau in Fort Augusta, Scotland, I spied a dog in a stone-fenced and iron-gated yard across the street. Though I consider myself a dog person, having raced Siberian husky sled dogs for twelve years, what attracted my attention was the red ball in the mouth of a black and white Australian shepherd standing at the gate. As a person, probably a tourist from the bus which had recently pulled into town, walked close to the gate, the Aussie tipped her head (so coyly I was sure it was a she) and dropped the ball so it bounced outside the gate in front of the walker. He looked first at the dog, then at the ball which had rolled in front of him. He picked up the ball and threw it back over the gate and continued walking. The dog chased the ball, grabbed it, mauled it a little, then scampered back to the gate, ball in mouth, and waited for the next passerby who could be enticed into throwing the ball for her. Clever these Scottish-Aussie dogs!

The Elusive Cuckoo

The cuckoo is a medium sized slender bird which feeds on insects, insect larvae, and even wooly caterpillars that other birds won't touch. Some of the more than 150 varieties of cuckoo are brood parasites, laying their eggs in another bird's nest, but most raise their own young. The bird's distinctive call of coo-coo coo coo-coo-coo gives it its name. The species found in Scotland is bluish-grey and white. I know this not because I'd ever seen one, but through internet searches. In Scotland, and I believe in other areas as well, the cuckoo is an elusive bird.

We've heard cuckoos three times in Scotland and had yet to spot a single bird. Our first hearing was on a back road between the Glencoe Visitor's Centre and the village of Ballachulish. I stopped for a photo of a pond with a mountain backdrop. As I was snapping photos a couple walked up and asked, "Have you seen it?" "What?" was all I could reply. "The bird, the cuckoo. There's a cuckoo in those trees just beyond the pond. Didn't you hear it?" I listened, and certainly could hear my first cuckoo's call, outside of the damned clock my parents had. We looked and looked, but even with the bird watcher's help, we couldn't see the bird. We heard our second cuckoo near Rannoch Station in the Highland moors 25 miles west of Pitlochry. The small rail station is at the end of the road. The tearoom in the station serves tasty homemade soups and the usual toasted sandwiches. After a bite on one of our fall visits, we heard a cuckoo's call from the forest next to the station's car park. Again, we could hear the bird but could never spot it. Our third brush with the cuckoo was while playing Helensburgh golf course near the Clyde River north of Glasgow. Our guide, George, had us stop and listened for a moment at one hole. He said you could often hear a cuckoo from this spot. Within a few seconds we all heard the bird's unmistakable call. George said that several members had tried to find the bird's nest, but no one, including the three of us, had seen it yet.

So the score now stood at cuckoos three, visitors zip.

Fast forward several years. We since heard cuckoos numerous times in forests or on golf courses. We've also now seen at least two cuckoos. In the spring of 2016 at Carrbridge GC in the Cairngorms National Park we heard a cuckoo and then saw one fly from trees on one side of the fairway to trees on the other side. Then on the next hole there was a cuckoo rooting around at the edge of the fairway. That bird let me get within about fifteen feet before it high-tailed it to the trees. We count ourselves among the lucky ones who have actually seen the elusive cuckoo.

The Golf Round of the Flies

Anne and I played Auchterarder Golf Course on one of our trips. The course is right next to Gleneagles PGA Course where they played the Ryder Cup matches in September of 2014. The course is challenging yet fair--a good walk. This round, though, came with a new challenge. The bunkers were still there waiting to grab wayward shots, the trees which line most holes were flush with new growth, and the rough was sticky and difficult to hit out from. But an additional challenge was presented by the hordes of Dagger or Dance Flies gathered around the greens and tees. These flies are called Dagger Flies because of their long proboscis used to spear prey, and although not a danger to golfers, this crop of flies was particularly bothersome. They are agile fliers, with a sophisticated internal gyroscope, and in still air hover and twist about. They are so numerous during the few weeks of this stage that it becomes almost impossible to avoid walking into them as they float. When the wind blows they smash into you as you walk or set up your shot. Down the inside of my glasses, in my nose, in my ears, down my shirt wind-driven flies get into everything. Mouth-breathers like Anne are particularly at risk of sucking in one or two with a breath. Our round was good and Anne won our match as usual, but we will always remember this visit to Auchterarder Golf Course as the Round of the Flies.

Larks Ascending

Particularly in Ireland, but also in Scotland and Wales, we often see larks flutter and call high above the golf courses. A small to medium-sized bird, larks sing in display flight to establish territory and attract a mate. Both Chaucer in "The Knight's Tale" and Shakespeare in "Sonnet 29" mythologize the lark as standing for daybreak. In reality, the lark was often used as a fillings in meat pies. Yum! As golfers Anne and I love to see the larks flutter and sing, usually above the rough on links courses. It's not just that the lark has a lovely song or that they flutter beautifully above the course, a far stronger reason for our love is found in an Irish saying: larks only fly and sing when the weather is dry. Poets love the lark, and...

Ode to a Skylark by Percy Bysshe Shelley

Hail to thee, blithe Spirit!
Bird thou never wert -
That from Heaven or near it
Pourest thy full heart
In profuse strains of unpremeditated art.

Higher still and higher
From the earth thou springest,
Like a cloud of fire;
The blue deep thou wingest,
And singing still dost soar, and soaring ever singest.

In the golden lightning
Of the sunken sun,
O'er which clouds are bright'ning,
thou dost float and run,
Like an unbodied joy whose race is just begun.

...golfers rejoice when the lark sings.

Wee Feet

As dramatic as Edinburgh and Stirling Castle are, often the best sites in Scotland are much less known and little visited. Cairnpapple Hill cairn with its view from one side of Scotland to the other, Andrew Carnegie's birth house in Dunfermline, and the Bettyhill museum with its handwritten history of the clearances are a few examples of those special hidden jewels. Another such site is Scotland's first and oldest lending library, the Innerpeffray Library outside of Crieff.

The library is located in a small building attached to a chapel on the former Drummond estate. The chapel was the Drummond family chapel and the library was set up by Laird David Drummond in 1640 to make 400 of his family's book available for historical and research purposes. The present library building next to the chapel was completed in 1762. When first designed, the library was at a major crossroads dating back to Roman times and easily accessible. Since the collapse of the bridge over the nearby River Earn and its replacement built several miles away, the Innerpeffray Library has been a rather isolated site.

We've visited the library several times and done some research in the library's tombs for an article on the Drummonds and Murrays. Our first time to see the chapel and library, though, was in 2000 on our initial trip to Scotland. We got directions to Innerpeffray from our B&B and ventured out into the back roads of Perthshire. Though not far from Crieff, the roads were definitely not major. The closer we got to our objective, the smaller were the roads. Our final turn was onto a single-track lane with very few passing places. Both sides the road was sheltered by tall brambles. A couple hundred yards down the half-mile lane we ended up behind a car barely creeping along. Being uncomfortable on narrow lanes myself, I didn't push the driver ahead, but we did wonder why he was going so slowly--I mean two to three miles an hour slow! It took a minute for us to discern the cause for his caution. We finally saw tiny feet, many tiny feet, running as fast as they could in front of the car. It was a whole covey of baby quails who wouldn't get out of the road, and the driver certainly wasn't going to run over these babies (nor would have I). After about a hundred feet, the babies led by mama dove off the side of the road through the brambles. Both our cars then speeded on to the library (at maybe 15 miles an hour).

In recent trips we've not seen the covey again, and now the road doesn't seem quite so narrow. We will always remember that first trip to Innerpeffray Library as the trip of the Wee Feet.

They Do Exist!

Ailsa, our adopted Scottish niece (daughter of our B&B hosts), spent three days with her schoolmates at an outdoor camp near Aviemore in the Highlands. She was only thirteen and this was a big adventure--camping out, cooking out, special wildlife experiences. She returned exhausted, starving for her favorite foods, and angry. Exhausted we could understand when we heard all that she had done. Starving was also understandable, after all she had had to cook for herself on camp fires. But the anger surprised us. After a shower and at dinner she said, "We saw reindeer at the reindeer farm, and they were real. I felt so stupid. I thought they were just made up in the stories. Nobody ever told me they were real." It took several minutes for us to stop laughing.

That's Right, Ailsa, There Are Reindeer

We had never visited at the Reindeer Centre, but Ailsa had on one of her Strathallan Outdoor outings. We checked in early enough to have time to wander around the Centre before hiking up to the herd. There were displays inside the Centre, a small informative museum outside, as well as several enclosures with reindeer in each one. I took photos of the deer and several birds in the area.

The Centre represents the only reindeer in the UK. The herd originally came from Norway in the early 1950s. It now numbers about 65 individuals which are traded around with other preserves to maintain the herd's biodiversity.

We met our knowledgeable guide who gave us history and instructions about dealing with the reindeer. We then followed her in our cars (about thirteen) to a parking area from which we would begin a 20-30 minute hike up to the herd. In the parking lot we got more instruction and information, as we would a couple more times on the hike. The trail up to the deer was a good mountain path most of the way. It wasn't too steep except after we crossed the river on a bridge, then it went up steeply for about 300 yards.

After a "health and safety" lecture at the main gate into the deer enclosure, we crossed moorland on a wooden plank path. When we got into the third fenced area we met the deer. They aren't too interested in people and really don't like to be petted (especially around the head)—generally okay though on the back and rear. They were, though, interested in the special feed brought up by our guide (with help from some of our group). She spread the feed in a line on the ground and the deer (a group of about thirty) came for the feast. We could wander among the herd and take photos (trying to stay out of each other's way). Our guide then passed out special grain to hand-feed to the deer. The deer actually have gum-like plates instead of teeth. Anne fed the deer while I took photos.

We were all then free to mingle with the herd, take more pictures, or head back down the trail. Anne and I stayed a while and then hiked down to the river for more photos. The whole experience was well worth the £11 each and the three hours we spent. I'll have no trouble going up again to see the reindeer on another trip.

We've Lost the Queen

Anne and I were in the north of Scotland, getting ready the next day to return to our home base of Merlindale B&B in Crieff, when we received a phone call from Jacky our B&B host. Jacky and John were calling from Spain and they knew that we'd beat them to Crieff. Home was in a turmoil—Queenie the Cat had gone missing. Nobody (daughter Ailsa, helpers Paulette and Annie) hadn't seen her for a day. We told Jacky we'd help in the search when we got there.

Day two of the search wasn't any more successful than day one. Queenie was still missing. We'd searched the neighborhood and checked with neighbors that we could. We looked at all the bushes in case she'd been hit and crawled under one for protection. No signs of Queenie. This wasn't like her; she'd sometimes be gone overnight, but was always at the door the next morning wanting breakfast. Even the family's two Yorkshire Terriers were constantly searching the yard for the cat.

Day three still no Queenie in the morning. John and Jacky were due home in the afternoon, and by this time we were all beginning to fear the worst. After another morning search Ailsa (13 years old) was lazily bouncing on the family backyard trampoline. By chance she happened to look at the house of the neighbors behind and saw a small black figure in one of the windows. A closer look showed the figure to be Queenie locked in the neighbor's house—the neighbors were on a month-long trip. Nobody could fathom how Queenie got into the locked house. More importantly, none of us could figure how to get the captured cat out of the locked house. We called the local constabulary who couldn't help. Finally, a friend called the daughter of the vacationing couple and asked her if she could get us in to get the cat out. She came right over and let Queenie, who had been locked in the house for almost three days, free. The cat ran straight to the back fence, over the fence, and home to tears, hugs, and a full food dish.

In the end we figured out that Queenie must have snuck into the house when a cleaning person was there a couple of days ago. We never could find any cat mess in the neighbor's house. Either Queenie, with no food or water for two and a half days, had never had to make a mess or she hid it well. Missing cat trauma solved and Queenie hardly left the house for the next two weeks.

Leaving the Cat

"Good-bye, George. Be good and don't get into any fights. We'll be back in…(fill in the number of days or weeks)." "Blah, blah, blah, George, blah, blah, blah," is what he really hears. We leave for morning coffee or golf in the afternoon or dinner out, and George, our 13-year-old cat, shows no signs of care even if we wake him from one of his four or five house beds (our bed, the sewing room window, the computer room window, a dining room chair, the top of the furnace) and throw him out. Get out the suitcases and George's world turns upside down.

It was really a mutual adoption. George was abandoned by his original owners behind the house across the street. The people across the street neutered the orphan, named him George, and let him live with their other outside cats. George started spending more time in our front yard and I befriended him with Tender Vittles™ every morning. After talking to the neighbors and George finding out that we had better food and that he liked being able to come into the house, we took George to the vet for his shots and he was ours--or I should say, we were his. George really does rule the house and we live at his beck and call.

That's what makes it so hard on George when we leave. He doesn't approve or agree with our plans to leave. Oh, we take care of him. Whether we go overnight or for six weeks, we pay the neighbors to care for the house and for George. He's fed twice a day. He's let into or out of the house three or four times a day. He's played with and fussed over and cared for even when he's had to be taken to the vet because he and a neighbor cat had a disagreement.

All that doesn't change the fact that when the suitcases come up from the basement poor George doesn't know if we are leaving for a weekend, a week, or a month--and how much is six weeks in cat years, anyway? As we leave for the next trip, I'd love to be able to say we'll be gone only this long and you'll be well cared for, and have him acknowledge, "Thanks, Dad. And don't bother with the timer-programmed radio; I don't care for that station anyway." Instead, I know I'll get the sulking, the running in and out, and the cold shoulder, because all George will hear is "Blah, blah, George."

This last trip in Scotland has an interesting side note relevant to this topic. It seems that Queenie, the cat of our adopted Scottish family, began sitting outside our room's door the day before we arrived--she does enjoy coming into our room and sleeping in our suitcase when we're in residence--I say again, it was the day before we arrived. The family says she's done this with no one else. Is there a "cat hotline" and George told Queenie to take care of his family? Anne's napping on the bed as I'm writing this and Queenie is curled up next to her, just like George would be if we were at home.

George the Cat -- (?)1997 - March 20, 2013

George, named by the neighbors, was a stray abandoned by the people who lived behind the neighbors across the street from us. The neighbors neutered George and feed him, but he was just one of several outside cats the neighbors fed. I started hand feeding George Tender Vittles™ in the mornings before I went to work. He soon discovered that he liked coming into the house in the evenings, even if he had to share it with Muffy, Queen of the House. Muffy took all the best sleeping spots, but George decided that even the second best spots were better than living on the street. After talking with the neighbors and taking George to the vet for his jabs, he became our cat although weighing between twelve and fifteen pounds he freely claimed the neighborhood as his.

George was a lovey cat with us, but fairly shy among other people. He tolerated us having groups over, but relished group dinners when he'd get his own chair at the table--he was content to sit at the table and watch us eat, knowing he'd eventually get some scraps when everyone was done. Almost any meat would attract his interest and ice cream was of course his favorite.

In the twelve plus years we had George he got used to having sitters when we were away, first to debate camps and then to UK adventures. For a while we used live-in house/cat sitters, then we had neighbors who would watch over things while we were gone-- letting George in and out on a regular basis. He didn't like our traveling and started sulking as

soon as saw the suitcases come up from the basement. He never knew whether the trip was to be for a weekend, a week, or six weeks--after all, as smart as he was he never learned to read the calendar or the itinerary we always left on the table. He was almost always happy to see us return. In fact, one time we had left our car at the airport for a friend who was coming back from a trip a couple of days after we left. When Scott pulled into our carport with our car George came anxiously running until he saw it wasn't us. Scott said he looked so dejected when he left in his own car. George would punish us, though, for leaving him (even if he had been well cared for) by demanding to be let in and out at his whim for several days. Out of guilt (and fear, for George had claws which he kept very sharp) we always gave in to his demands. This was the pattern for years, until this last short trip to Eastern Oregon. When we got home George greeted us, wanted pets and a little lap time, but was far more interested in curling up in the bed we had for him in front of the heat vent. This now was the pattern for several days-- George became harder and harder to wake up. He'd get up to eat his breakfast and dinner and wait beside us for our scraps, but then it was back to sleep in front of the heater without much lap time. I had a chat with George's vet, made an appointment, and took him in for his final visit.

We hope George, good friend that he was, is now enjoying his long, permanent nap.

CHAPTER 4: Let's Eat Anything but Haggis

There is a myth about poor food in Scotland, and for the most part it is myth. We've had some bad meals and our share of fatty fried fare, but we've also had some outstanding meals in pubs as well as fine dining restaurants. I have no stories, though, about the national dish of Scotland, haggis. Haggis traditionally is sheep heart, liver, and lungs along with oats and spices boiled inside a sheep's stomach casing for several hours. In other words, it's an offal sausage, not necessarily an awful sausage. We've had good haggis and bad haggis (read cheap), but in our experience it's not been fodder for stories any more so than black puddings (blood sausage) in Ireland, Welsh Cawl (a lamb and leek soup) in Wales, or Bangers and Mash in England. Many of our stories do revolve around the restaurants or the serving of the food. You can tell by the number of stories in this chapter that golf helps works up quite an appetite.

A Tale of Two Restaurants

Helmsdale is a small, but important village along the north Scotland coast beyond Dornoch, Golspie, and Brora. Here a main road from the northwest meets the A9, the main north/south highway. Helmsdale has an interesting nine-hole course which we played one year. I think it was that year we found out about two restaurants in town, the *Bunillidh* and LaMirage. Both had great reputations for quality seafood at extraordinarily inexpensive prices. It wasn't that year that we tried the restaurants though.

In the fall of 2004 we got the opportunity to finally try a restaurant in Helmsdale. We had heard and read that both were good, but that *Bunillidh* had the more interesting decor. We decided that for our first try we'd take the more interesting *Bunillidh*. It was a great decision. The decor is pure kitsch with no theme to what was scattered on the walls--figurines, masks, toys, and other fascinations. It indeed was entertaining surroundings, but that wasn't what we discovered was best about *Bunillidh*. It was the food. The menu contained an interesting variety of offerings, from recipes dating back to the Great Clan Gatherings to Aussie specialities. The special of the night was a complete two pound boiled lobster straight out of the North Sea. The lobster was served with all the trimmings for the paltry sum of £10, equivalent to $17 at the 2004 exchange rate! The mud bug was large and delicious. The waitress was cute and engaging. The whole experience was everything we had been led to expect. What a find!

It wasn't until two years later, the fall of 2006, that we had the chance to visit Helmsdale again. After a round at Wick GC and visiting the Grey Camster cairns, we stopped at Helmsdale for dinner before heading back to our B&B in Dornoch. To our chagrin the *Bunillidh* was under new ownership, had a new menu, and seemed run down. It definitely was empty. At least we still had the LaMirage, which advertised itself as "The North's Premier Restaurant." It was crowded which should have been a good sign. We got a table right in the middle of the room--the only table available. Dinner was a disaster from the beginning. The place was too crowded and we felt squeezed in. The waitress messed up our order and what we got was not very nice. Anne's salad came on a plate hot enough to wilt the lettuce. My soup was supposed to come with a fresh roll (typical in Scotland), but mine came with a piece of plain store-bought bread. The main courses were barely edible; cold when they should have been hot, hot when they should have been cold. Our meals came out at different times. The whole evening's experience was summed up by a large painting on the wall of what looked like an ugly man in garish drag attire. We couldn't get on the road fast enough.

Helmsdale--the good, the bad, and the ugly.

A Tale of Two Restaurants, Take 2

Tralee is a good tourist town on the west coast of Ireland. The world class Tralee Golf Course, an Arnold Palmer design, is only a few miles away, the pubs are renowned for good craic and session music, and the Oyster Tavern just out of town is supposed to be one of the best in Ireland. The golf course is fantastic, one of the best we've ever played. The traditional music session at Betty's Bar was unforgettable. The Oyster Tavern was one of the most disappointing eating experiences we've ever had.

We went to the expensive (expensive as in well beyond our normal budget) Oyster Tavern because all the guidebooks gave it their highest recommendations: "Must stop dining," "super fantastic," "beyond comparison!" Boy, were they wrong. The place was beautiful and had a lovely bar even though they were playing Christmas music in May, but the food was something else. My seafood chowder was a soup with very little seafood and even less flavor. The seafood pasta was only mussels (and very few of them) in a watery sauce again with almost no flavor. My two dishes cost me about €40 or $55. We found out later that the owner was trying to sell the place and didn't care--he was selling it on the reputation. When we talked to locals at the Tralee GC the next day, they said it had really gone downhill. The lesson is … trust the locals, not the guidebooks.

We did just that, trusted the locals. The golf shop staff recommended we try The Tankard, a pub in the little village of Fenit just west of Tralee. The Tankard was as good as Oyster Tavern was bad. The staff was friendly and the pub provided quality food at reasonable prices. The Tankard may not have been spectacular, but it was far better than the Oyster Tavern. Locals do know best.

Deep Fried What?

Fish and chips is the staple Scottish fast food and chippies (fish & chip shops) are all over the place. Their menu of fried delights isn't limited to haddock and cod, either. You'd be surprised what you can find on a chippie menu. Sausages of various kinds are prevalent. Deep fried Mars bars are popular--I've tried one and it is so rich and sinful, but it is delicious. Not all things, though, are meant to be deep fried, as we found out one evening in Anstruther on Fife's Firth of Tay coast.

After golf at Crail Balcombie Links Anne and I were looking forward to trying out the Anstruther Fish Bar, reputed to be the best fish and chip shop in Scotland. On this Friday night we had difficulty finding a parking spot along the harbour, but eventually got parked. We could tell the Anstruther Fish Bar by the line of patrons extending out the door and along the store front. The Anstruther Fish Bar has enough space inside for about 20 to sit, and one line serves those eating in and one serves those taking away. We asked and found out that the wait would be about two hours for eating in or over an hour for take away. That was too long for us. We wandered down toward where we'd parked; there was another chippie down there.

There wasn't much of a line at this chip shop (that should have been a clue). We ordered one order of haddock and chips and one order of an item on the menu that caught my attention, deep fried pizza. In a couple of minutes we had our orders and went out to the harbour-side picnic table in front to eat our meals. There was nothing especially good about the fish and chips, but the deep fried cheese pizza slice we had was spectacularly awful! Imagine a slice of greasy thick crust oily cheese pizza, dipped in heavy batter, and then dropped in the deep fat fryer until it finally floats to the surface. It is then scoped up with tongs, shaken to remove 10% of the clinging fat, slid into a paper box, and served. I have no idea who was the first to try the concoction, or who thought of selling it, but whomever it was deserves to spend eternity in culinary Hades. A bite or two each was more than enough to turn our stomachs.

On another visit we did make it back to Anstruther Fish Bar and it is as good as its wall of awards attest. Oh, by the way, the menu there doesn't include deep fried pizza.

Dishwater Soup

On every trip to and from St Andrews we have passed the *Bailbie* Pub at the roundabout which connects A912 and A913, the two main routes across Fife. We've seen plenty of cars in the pub lot around mealtime and always thought that it might be a good place for a meal. In the spring of 2009 our schedule finally was correct for a dinner stop at *Bailbie*. We chalked up the mostly empty parking lot to the fact that we were fairly early for Scottish dinner crowds--we tend to eat about 6:00 and the Scots tend to start thinking about dinner at 7:30 or 8:00. That was a mistake!

The pub is very comfortable inside and the menu looked interesting. We settled upon soup of the day and a split of fish and chips. Rather safe, typical pub fare. When the soup came it looked thin and watery--Scottish soups are generally thick and pureed. After our first taste Anne and I just looked at each other. A second taste was barely required. The soup, supposedly lentil and leek, tasted like dishwater. It was absolutely inedible. We called the waiter, who happened to be the new owner, over and said he'd have to take the soup back. His response to our complaint was, "What's the matter with it? My wife just made it." We told him how bad it was, and he reluctantly took it back to the kitchen. When he returned with our fish (which was almost all batter surrounding a sardine-sized haddock) and chips (there was nothing wrong with them), he did say that the soup was "a little off" and asked if we'd like anything else. We looked at the batter and chips on our plate and said that we'd pass on anything else.

As I paid the tariff (bill) the owner asked friendly what we were doing in Scotland. When I told him we write about golf and pubs, he said, "Oh, good. We just bought this place and are excited about our future."

I guess he'd forgotten about the dishwater soup we'd sent back. We hadn't.

Don't Let Me Get Like This

With its lovely bay, fascinating Telford Bridge, and impressive castle and city walls, Conwy was a great introduction to Wales. We wandered the castle and city wall, strolled the shopping district, then popped into the Tourist Information Centre to try to wheedle a lunch recommendation out of the attendant. They are supposed to remain neutral and not give specific recommendations, but it's not too difficult to get ideas out of most of them. In this case, we heard on the sly that Anna's Victorian Tearoom above a mountain equipment store was a pleasant place for a bowl of soup and a sandwich.

We'd seen the mountain shop a couple of blocks back, so thought we'd go for lunch. We thanked the little clerk and said we'd never tell--oops, that's one promise broken.

In Anna's Victorian Tearoom we got a window table which overlooked the busy shopping street. We had just ordered our soup and sandwich when a large tour group of very senior citizens was herded in and occupied the other side of the room. Their tour guide brought everyone in and told them, "This is what we're eating and the toilets are in the back. Be sure to go!" The waitress put a large platter of sandwiches on each of the tables for the group. We watched a man at one table start grabbing sandwiches in both hands and stuffing them into his mouth without passing the plate to the rest of his table. The guide finally saw this and quickly took the sandwich plate from the gentleman and passed it to others. We decided that on this tour you had to fight for your sandwiches: survival of the fastest.

I'm certainly glad we can still travel on our own.

Impatient, Uninformed American Tourists

A favored stop in Dingle, Ireland, is a small coffee shop and bookstore just off the main shopping area. *Cafe ans Liteartha* is a *Gaeltacht* cafe, where the main language is Gaelic/Irish. The front part of the bookshop, always the kind of shop we seek out, has English books, while the back houses Gaelic tombs. In the back, also, is the small cafe section, with the wall menu in Gaelic. Gaelic language music plays in the background.

We stopped in for a light lunch one day before heading out to *Ceann Sibeal* Golf Course on the tip of the Dingle peninsula. There were a couple of tables of Gaelic speaking locals and the waitress was conversing in Gaelic at one table. I went up to the bar and ordered a toasted sandwich and two bowls of fall vegetable soup. I ordered in English and the waitress responded in English. In a short while we were eating our soups and toasty.

While eating we watched an American foursome (accents sounded like Texas) come in and sit down at a table. After they had waited a while for table service, a local took pity on them and told them to go up to the counter to order--we had easily figured it out. The couples looked at the menu board, talked in hushed tones among themselves, made some decisions, and the men waited in line to order. The waitress was talking in Gaelic with another customer in front of the men. Evidently, the Americans didn't get waited on quickly enough, and in a huff the men walked over, got their spouses, and all four walked out. It seemed they didn't like that the staff was speaking a foreign language (but after all, they were in Ireland and the staff was speaking Irish) and they didn't like having to wait beyond what they thought was reasonable.

This is a perfect example of the impatient, uninformed American tourist. I certainly think we've learned better how to live with the Irish pace.

Lamb for Dinner

Lamb is a standard item on menus in Ireland, Scotland, and Wales. We've had lamb chops, lamb shanks, lamb stew, lamb and Guinness pie, lamb liver with onions, and leg of lamb. One morning in Galway, Ireland, as we were getting ready to drive out to Connemara GC, our host Maire stopped us just before we drove out and said, "On that road you'll see plenty of free roaming sheep. Drive carefully, I don't want you bringing us a leg of lamb for dinner."

On a different trip in Scotland we had stopped for dinner at the Tormaukin Inn in Glendevon between Crieff and Dunfermline. Delicious lamb stew was the special that night. As Anne and I relished our stew we saw a farmer pull up in front of the inn and begin unloading several lambs from a small truck. Anne said, "Please tell me that's not tomorrow's dinner." She was greatly relieved to find out that the farmer was just moving the lambs to a field behind the inn. She didn't want to think about the fact that the lambs would be dinner in a week or two.

How Do I Get that Out of the Book?

In the north of Scotland, above Inverness, is a unique and very hilly golf course, Strathpeffer Spa GC. Built in the Victorian era, the course uses the land that was available. The result is a course full of short, quirky, hilly holes. Our introduction to golf at Strathpeffer was in a Couples Open competition. This means that Anne and I are a team and that we both hit our tee shots from our normal tee boxes and then select the best shot and play alternate shot from there until we hole out. In the States this would be called a Modified Texas Scramble. In effect it means that Anne gets to see and hit from parts of the course she, the straight hitter, would never normally see.

After our round we went into the clubhouse lounge for a drink, conversation, and lunch. We ordered a cheese and ham toastie to share. Everyone seemed to know we were the authors who had come to write about the course, so we got lots of visiting as well as the award for coming the farthest (6000 miles) to enter the competition--second place was a couple from about 80 miles south. Our sandwich hadn't arrived so I asked the caterer about our toastie. She gasped, "Oh, no! I forgot it. I'll get it right away," and hustled into the kitchen. When she came back with our sandwich she commented, "How can I get this out of the book?"

Here's your answer: You can't! By the way, the sandwich was quite nice.

No Cutlery in the Bar, but Tons of Cutlery

Taymouth Castle Golf Course is a fine parkland track worth the drive into the Scottish hills to find. Anne and I have played it several times. After one particular round we headed into the nearest small village of Kenmore to find some lunch. We'd visited the Byre Bistro a couple of times before, so we decided to try the Kenmore Hotel in the heart of the village.

The Kenmore Hotel is designed in hunting lodge style and has a formal dining room and a less formal pub. It was the middle of the afternoon and we only wanted to split a sandwich so opted for the pub. The waitress brought the sandwich but no fork or knife. We asked for a knife with which to cut the sandwich in half and were told by the waitress, "No cutlery is allowed in the pub." Satisfied that we'd been informed of the rules, she walked away.

We must have sat open mouthed for several seconds before either one of us could comprehend the full affect of the rule. In the pub we couldn't have even a butter knife to cut our sandwich. Were they afraid we'd try to attack the waitress with a butter knife? Did they have too many customers who would start knife duals with the cutlery? Could it be that we might try to highjack the hotel with a fork? Was the waitress worried that we'd try to gouge her eyes out with a spoon for poor service? What would they serve as a utensil if we'd ordered the soup of the day? I'd hope it would be a creamed soup so we could drink it directly from the bowl.

We tore the sandwich in half and continued our speculation. Was there a local ordinance against cutlery in the pub? A £50 fine every time you let a customer use a fork in a salad. Were the butter knives only comfortable in the restaurant or would they rebel if taken into the less formal pub?

We left shaking our heads. But then we shake our heads a lot at the cutlery customs in the British Isles. The standard is that with every course at a pub or restaurant you get new cutlery whether you used the last set or not.

It sort of makes sense when you have a starter of soup and they bring you a serviette (napkin) and a spoon for the soup and knife for buttering your roll or bread. Then they take it away when they bring you a knife and fork for your steak, potato, and veg. But why when you have a salad as a starter do they take away the fork when you're done and bring you exactly the same kind of fork for your main? Does a fork or knife which touches one course become so contaminated that it can't be used on another course? Heaven forbid you try to keep your cutlery from one course to the next. They look at you as if you've gone mad. Napkins as well are not too be cross contaminated. A three course meal means three napkins (or serviettes as they are known locally). Staff will hunt and hunt until they find your used napkin before they bring you the next course.

This all seems a bit wasteful, but maybe there is a cutlery lobby somewhere promoting the use of clean cutlery. Either that or restaurant managers live in fear that the Cutlery Police will find out you cross-contaminated a fork with pate` and haddock mornay and levy another £50 fine.

O'Grady's

Tom and Maire at Bayberry House in Galway, Ireland, suggested O'Grady's on the Pier Seafood Restaurant on our first visit to the area. We thought it was so good we had them book it ahead for us on our second visit.

O'Grady's is east of Galway in the small coastal village of Barna. Turn left at the only stoplight in the village, go 200 yards to where the road runs into the bay, and on the right will be O'Grady's on the Pier Seafood Restaurant. Dine upstairs of downstairs, it doesn't matter; you'll have a bay view from either room. The menu is all interesting seafood in large portions with equally large prices-- this is fine dining.

On our last visit, in 2005, we ventured out on quite a stormy night. We'd barely gotten our golf in before the storm hit with a vengeance. The six mile drive from Bayberry House to Barna was wipers on full speed all the way. I pulled down toward O'Grady's looking for a parking place, but found none except spots reserved for boat owners. Dropping Anne off at the restaurant door, I drove back across the main road and found a spot not too far from the stoplight. Hood of my rain jacket held down tightly, I walked quickly back to O'Grady's. As I came in shaking the water off my jacket in the foyer, Michael O'Grady, the owner, met me and said that I could have parked in the boat owner's parking, then asked if I wanted a drink. I ordered a whisky and Michael acted as bartender. He brought me over a very generous pour and said, "Don't tell the girls I didn't measure it; they give me a bad time when I do this." Now that's Irish hospitality.

Potatoes and More Potatoes

On our spring 2005 trip to Ireland, we arrived early in the day at the Dublin airport, picked up our car, and headed toward Kilkenny. Our intention was to do some sightseeing on our way to Tom and Val's Dunromin B&B. We stopped at Kildare Golf Club and talked with the golf manager, toured the Rock of Dunamase, an old castle being excavated near Port Loaise, and decided to stop for lunch in the village of Abbeyleix. The girl in the tourist office wasn't supposed to make recommendations to tourists, but by asking her where she'd go for lunch on such a fine day, we got the idea that the Abbey Gate Bar might be a good choice.

The Abbey Gate is a bright, open pub known locally for its quality pub food. When we got there several locals were already well into their lunches. We started a conversation with Colin O'Reilly, a local sculptor and teacher, who sat down near us just after we got seated. When Colin ordered the roast lamb special, he said to the waitress, "Have them put lots of potatoes with it; I'm really hungry today." The waitress said she'd tell the cook. We chatted for a while until our lunch arrived. When Colin's roast lamb

arrived, the waitress set it down and said, "I hope that's enough potatoes for you." The plate was heaped to overflowing with boiled potatoes! Colin looked satisfied.

Potatoes really are the staple of the Irish diet. In the 1800s the culture collapsed and millions starved when a blight destroyed the potato crop. Part of the problem was that the Irish didn't know anything but potatoes. There's no blight now and potatoes are plentiful in every Irish pub and restaurant. It's not an exaggeration to say that in Ireland you'll get all the potatoes you'd ever want. Sometimes meals will come with three styles of potatoes--mashed will come with the meat, boiled potatoes will come as a vegetable, and chips (fries) come with everything. At one pub in Scotland, Anne's dinner was to come with boiled potatoes and chips. She asked the waitress to please hold the chips. When her meal came it came with a side dish heaped with chips. The waitress said, "Sorry, the cook won't let anything go out of the kitchen without chips."

Red Hot Chilli and Smoked Mussels

We attended the Spirit of the West Festival in Inveraray, Scotland, in the spring of 2009, for the main purpose of hearing the Red Hot Chilli Pipers. Oh, we intended to do our fair share of whisky tasting as well, especially since 23 distilleries were presenting free tastings. We parked about a half mile away from the Inveraray Castle which was hosting the festival and joined the throngs walking in.

The first place we headed was the large performance tent from which we could hear the skirl of bagpipes and pounding of drums--the Red Hot Chilli Pipers were turned up full. The band is composed of three pipers, two percussionists, a guitarist, a bass player, and keyboards. They play both traditional Celtic tunes and their own version of rock tunes. The theme song of the Chilli Pipers is a bagpipe dominated "We Will Rock You." In a fairly small venue the pipes are loud and the drums drill through the listeners, many of whom are garbed in clan kilts. It's almost impossible not to be stirred by the music. The hour of music went far too quickly, but we were ready for some whisky tasting. It's only noon, but the free whisky was calling almost as loudly as the pipes. We tried several Islay whiskies, our favorites, and a few others before we knew we had to have something to eat.

A large tent held about two dozen food vendors around the perimeter with picnic tables in the middle. On our browse we saw haggis sellers, venison dealers, salmon in all its various presentations, shortbread bakers, and cheese makers too numerous to mention. Then we found it, the Loch Fyne Oyster Company booth. We knew the reputation of the Loch Fyne oyster as one of the best in Europe, if not the world. The sea loch is farmed for both oysters and salmon, but we didn't know about Loch Fyne smoked mussels until we tried a sample. Oily, smoky, deliciousness. We had our lunch--a couple of cups of the smoked mussels and a venison burger to share. The burger was good, but the mussels were outstanding. We went back for a second helping and then bought a couple of containers to take home to the B&B family in Crieff.

We got back to Merlindale B&B in time to share our Loch Fyne smoked mussels as an appetizer to Jacky's dinner. Can one OD on smoked mussels? We put out the mussels, some cheese, and crackers. Almost as soon as we put the mussels on the table they were gone. An absolute hit! But now we had a serious task for the rest of our stay. Find more of the smoked mussels.

It was an interesting challenge. Since we weren't planning to be back in the Loch Fyne area for the rest of the trip, our best bet for finding the mussels was at tourist shops, many of whom would have specialty food sections. Baxter's in Auchterarder didn't have them. The Perthshire Tourist Centre on the A9 outside of Perth didn't have them. We couldn't find any in the tourist shops in St Andrews. Finally, toward the end of our stay we made a trip up the A9 past Pitlochry to the House of Bruar, one of Scotland's premier merchants specializing in fine wool clothing and local produced gourmet food. Bingo! We had a source for Loch Fyne smoked mussels. How much could we carry back to the B&B? How much could we all eat in the few days we had left in our trip? The answer was about two pints.

We are already planning to make a smoked mussel run to House of Bruar early in our next trip.

Full Scottish (English, Irish, Welsh) Breakfast

When you are used to a bowl of cereal and a cup of coffee for breakfast, the B&B breakfasts in Scotland, England, Ireland, and Wales are ginormous. Even compared to an American breakfast out, the breakfast you get in a B&B is humongous. Ample, big, filling, huge are weak descriptors of how you can start a day of touring in the British Isles.

Let me describe the breakfast a guest gets at our Scotland home, Merlindale B&B in Crieff. Breakfast call comes at 8:30 with the large dining room table, which easily seats ten, set up. On a side board are about six different types of dry cereals, and on the table are two juices, a variety of fresh fruits, bowl of prunes, and several flavors of yogurt. John then comes in and presents you with breakfast options, all of which are available. The typical list includes John's special Scottish porridge, a couple of rashers of bacon (more like Canadian bacon than American bacon which is called streaky bacon), bangers or sausage, one or two eggs prepared as you want them, potatoes, fried bread, broiled tomatoes and mushrooms. On top of this is all the toast you want, served of course with a variety of

homemade jams. All this prepared by a Le Cordon Bleu trained chef. It will definitely keep you going until dinner.

While Merlindale's breakfast is perhaps the largest we've had, other B&B's serve big feasts as well. We've also had some interesting variety to breakfasts in the British Isles. One interesting selection is fish, kippers or smoked haddock, as a main course. Beware, though, sometimes you can spend more time picking out the bones than eating the breakfast. At Kilmichael's on Arran I had the most fantastically flavored kippers, but they were also the boniest. That was too much hard work just for breakfast. Many of the breakfasts will include beans (particularly in England and Wales) in place of the tomato and mushroom. To us they are just like canned Pork 'n' Beans, but they add an interesting touch. Although I love John Clifford's porridge at Merlindale B&B, at Glengolly in Durness they serve a porridge topped with caramelized sugar and whisky. Wonderfully delicious, if you like porridge and like whisky. Black pudding (blood sausage) and white pudding (without the blood) end up on breakfast platters in several B&Bs. Generally we stay away from them, but Maire in Galway, Ireland, one day said we must try the black pudding tomorrow. The next morning we had some absolutely delicious black pudding. Maria explained that the average puddings were often not nice, but she had found a producer of really good sausage. Quality of black pudding as well as haggis makes a great difference.

The breakfasts served in the B&Bs are a major reason to choose a B&B over a hotel. When you find a good one, stick with it.

The Anniversary Dinner

Noreen McGinty, our host at Arches House B&B on Lough Eske about four miles outside of Donegal, Ireland, did us a special favor. As most good B&B operators, Noreen is willing to do something extra to make sure a guest's stay is a good one. For us she called to book a table for our dinner at Dom's Pier 1 Restaurant in Donegal Town. She said we needed to book ahead because it was a busy time in town. As we left to make our 7:00 reservation at Dom's, Noreen wished us a good dinner.

Dom's is the premier restaurant and bar in Donegal Town. Nautical themed, it sits along the main street of town with pleasant views out to Donegal harbour, the priory ruins, and the Hassan Islands (where famine families were housed). The bar and restaurant were crowded, and we were surprised to be led to a prime window table. We were also surprised to see that our table was specially decorated with linen tablecloth and flowers. Anne and I talked through dinner about our luck with the table. After we had finished a fine meal, the waitress brought us a small cake with a lighted candle and wished us a happy anniversary. We now understood what Noreen had done to get us this special table. We thanked the waitress, told her it was our 37th (it wasn't), and toasted our good fortune.

In the morning Noreen asked how we had enjoyed our dinner. We told her about the table and the meal and thanked her profusely. She just smiled.

The Cook Who Left

In Duns, near the east coast of Scotland, we asked our B&B host for a recommendation for dinner. He said that the Black Swan had the best pub fare in the village. We wandered down to the pub and ordered a Guinness for Anne and a whisky for me and asked for menus. The waitress dropped off menus and hurried back into the kitchen. We heard a slight commotion in the kitchen, then a few minutes later she came out and announced, "Sorry folks, there'll be no dinners tonight--the cook has just walked out." She then turned to us and said, "If I were you, I'd go to the White Swan about two blocks over for dinner." We thanked her, finished out drinks, and in sort of a daze, left to find the other Swan.

Our meals at the White Swan were quite good--steak and ale pies for two for less than $18--and what is more important, uneventful. One cook going awry a night is enough.

The World's Busiest Tesco

Tesco is a UK grocery and department store similar to Wal-Mart or the Safeway complexes we have on the west coast. The Tesco in Aviemore, Scotland, at the base of the Cairngorm Mountains is something else.

Aviemore is a hub of outdoor activity--hiking in the summer, skiing in the winter. All year around it is a "Time Share Paradise." There are at least a half dozen different time share facilities composed of hundreds and hundreds of units in a small village of one main street, and most importantly, one grocery store. The problems come on Saturday when almost all the time share units begin their week.

Imagine a moderately sized grocery store inundated on Saturday afternoon by literally thousands of shoppers all trying to stock their units for a week of family vacation. Imagine, too, the majority of the shoppers have no idea what they really want to buy or where anything is located in the store. If you have that picture in mind, you have an accurate picture of pure, unadulterated chaos. Shoppers jostle for position in narrow aisles, grab for the last packages of bacon or sausage, argue about free range eggs versus caged eggs (What else do you call eggs when they are not free range?). The madhouse extends to the parking lot full to overflowing with drivers in rental cars with steering wheels on the wrong side.

Avoid the madness, you say. Shop on Sunday, you say. Fine idea if you want to shop an empty store! The Aviemore Tesco is picked bare by early Saturday evening, and it's not restocked until Monday. All that's left on the shelves are Branston Pickles, custard creams, and canned haggis. Locals and those lucky enough to be around before Saturday get their shopping done before the hordes arrive. The rest of us fight it out in the aisles. Mostly those in the know shop in some other village before they get to Aviemore. Although, on Saturday afternoon as we unpack in our Time Share Paradise, we inevitably find five items we forgot to pick up. So, it's off to the World's Busiest Tesco, again.

Vegetable Soup, of Course

September 12, 2001 was not a great day for sightseeing in Scotland. Not many places seemed appropriate. We did visit the Dunblane Cathedral thinking that it would be a good place to meditate and reflect on the world events. What we discovered even more depressed us. Dunblane is the village where a mass murder of kindergarden children and their teacher had occurred several years before. A memorial in the cathedral reminded us of that event and saddened us deeper.

We did find some lightness in the day in a small hotel pub, The Myrtle Inn, in a small village near Callander. We stopped for lunch of a bowl of soup and a shared toastie. Soup tends to be a specialty in the Scottish pubs--some sort of vegetable or lentil soup or a combination, usually pureed rather than a broth-type soup. The Myrtle Inn soup of the day was Fall Vegetable. We each order a bowl and then relished the delicious, greenish-yellow concoction. As we ate we tried to figure out what was in the soup. We could identify carrot for sure and probably some kind of squash. It was so good that Anne called the waitress over and asked her what was in the soup. She gave Anne a strange look, thought about how to answer for a second, and then responded, "Vegetables." Then she went about the rest of her duties, leaving us in stunned silence.

The waitress had answered what we asked. Anne took a different tact the next time the waitress was near, "I know it's vegetable soup, but what vegetables are in it?" The waitress smiled and said she'd ask the cook.

She came back in a couple of minutes and said, "The cook says it's whatever she had in back." Again leaving us in stunned silence.

Sometimes it's better to eat and enjoy than to know.

Who'd Eat Here?

Anne and I aren't in the habit of frequenting fast food joints when we're on our travels. We have stopped, though, at KFC in Scotland or Ireland on very rare occasions. One such evening occurred in the fall of 2008 when we'd been golfing all day in the Highlands and were returning to our Crieff B&B on an early Friday evening. Having had no lunch, hunger won out over our palates and we stopped at the KFC in Perth.

The line out the door as we went up to the restaurant (I use that term very loosely) should have been a warning. Instead, we interpreted the line as a sign that this KFC might exceed our expectations. Wrong! We should have gotten out of line when we saw piles of food garbage stacked on uncleared tables and rubbish bins (garbage cans) overflowing with refuse. We didn't! Perhaps it was the super bargain we discovered while reading the menu board--we could either each get a two-piece chicken dinner with chips (fries) for £9 or a ten-piece bucket with four orders of chips for £10, and take leftovers home--that addled our brains as we watched in horror the activity at the ice cream machine. A pimply faced adolescent, most likely working his first job, was pouring milk mixture into the machine. Then, oops, he dropped the whole milk mixture carton into the innards of the machine! With a quick glance at his supervisor he dipped his ungloved hand into the ice cream mixture and fished out the slippery carton. He then closed up the machine and turned it on.

We justified our purchase of the bucket of chicken and four chips by saying that he couldn't have done that with hot oil. We should have walked out of the shop for several reasons, but we didn't get sick from our chicken. None of our friends back at our B&B got sick, but we did tell them the "dipping hand" story before we shared our leftovers.

You're Charging for What?!

Most of our experiences in the British Isles have been pleasant, but the few not so good experience stand out. One such occurred in our Scottish home base of Crieff. While traveling with our Oregon friends, Marcia, Helen, and Grady, we arranged an evening meal at the Keppoch House, a guest house up the road from Merlindale B&B where most of us were staying. We started out the meal in good form talking about our favorites from the day-- we had toured Loch Leven Castle and St Andrews together. Things changed when dinners came. Helen, Grady, and Marcia all had salmon, which they said was quite dry. I had two starters, a mussels starter and soup of the day which was supposed to come with a dinner roll. When my soup didn't have the roll with it I asked. What I got was a plain piece of white diet bread with no butter. Anne had smoked haddock with cheese sauce--it was super salty, so she asked for some tap water. The waitress brought out two small pitchers of water. None of us was really thrilled with our meals, but all of us were surprised when we got the bill. The restaurant had charged each of us £1.75 ($3.50 at the then exchange rate) for the tap water. When we asked about having to pay for tap water in Scotland, we were told that the restaurant's water was metered. We found out later that wasn't true and that all Crieff's water is flat rate and dirt cheap. My £3.95 mussel starter was charged at £8.95 because it came out at the same time others had their main meals. Our drinks, cokes and beers, were about double what we'd paid anyplace else in Scotland. Needless to say, none of left happy, and Marcia was unhappiest of all because she was staying at Keppoch House.

We know the Crieff Tourist Board who rates and recommends local B&Bs and restaurants heard our complaints and the complaints of others. The restaurant closed shortly after we visited and the B&B business folded not long after that. What were they thinking--charging for tap water in Scotland!

A small aside to this story about charging for water in Scotland is the story of our first trip to the country in 2000. Anne and I had traveled extensively in the US, but neither of us had ever been out of the country. To be prepared on that first trip I went to REI (our local outdoor store) and bought the best portable water filtration system I could find. Weighing about three pounds it would be able to filter out just about every bug or germ we'd encounter in our travels. It took us about one day to discover what we should have known all along--Scotland has some of the best drinking water in the world. What were we thinking--filtering the great tap water of Scotland!

Bad Kimberley!

All day while playing golf at the wonderful Moray Old GC in Lossiemouth we'd been looking forward to our dinner at Kimberley Inn on the bay in Findhorn. When we got there we were met by an infestation of flies--really bothersome flies! The owner came into the pub area with a rolled newspaper and started swatting flies on every table. Swat… Squish…Swipe…Swat...Squish...Swipe! After killing the buggers he did make a feeble attempt at cleaning up the carnage. While this was going on our food arrived. We had ordered our usual seafood chowder and garlic cheese bread. The chowder, the specialty of the house, is usually outrageously delicious, overflowing with a variety of local seafood (including langoustines, scallops, haddock, and more). Today it was watery and lacked both seafood and flavor. It was one of the worst chowders or soups we've had anyplace. The garlic cheese bread was good, but the screaming of wounded flies was quite off-putting. Was it a new owner, a new cook, or just trying to get by on the cheap?

The Rowan Tree Restaurant and a Celebrity Dinner

We had one of the best dinners we've ever had in Scotland at the Rowan Tree Country Hotel and Restaurant just south of Aviemore in the Highlands. We'd tried several times to book in for dinner, but hadn't made it work. This time we booked early for a Wednesday night dinner. The restaurant is Highland rustic and lovely. The hotel was built in the 1700s as a coaching inn named The Lynwilg Mail. Extended in the mid-1800s, parts of the hotel served as a post office, a village store, and a local pub. Renamed The Rowan Tree in the 1990's, it has been modernized yet keeps its essential Highland lodge character. Dinner is served Continental-style--order in the lounge over drinks and then you are directed to your table when starters are ready. From start to finish the meal was absolutely fantastic, and it came with a celebrity attraction.

I noticed a gentleman who looked familiar holding court at a nearby large table--he was attracting quite a bit of attention from other diners and staff. I finally figured out that it was Scottish actor Ewan McGregor (Obi Wan Kenobi from *Star Wars I, II, and III*). McGregor actually grew up just a short ways away from our home B&B, Merlindale, in Crieff and is a frequent visitor though we had never met him. To his dinner group he was talking about upcoming projects, including being a film judge at the Cannes Festival.

Later as Anne and I were leaving I gave our waitress our business card and she was asking about our books and writing. McGregor came by us on his way to the loo and slowed down as he neared trying to figure out who "I" was to be getting the kind of attention I was getting. A slight touch of celebrity envy perhaps?

Potato Skins...Really?

In the clubhouse after our round at the famous Turnberry GC on the Ayrshire coast of Scotland we had cokes and ordered a potato skins starter off the bar menu for us to share. We know what an order of potato skins off the bar menu at our club in the States (or most pubs in the States) would be: probably four baker halves hollowed out, filled with cheese, bacon, and sour cream, then broiled. When our starter came we got five halves of fingerling potatoes hollowed out with bits of bacon and cheese. All together they amounted to about the size of one half potato skin at home. Cost was £5.50 or the equivalent of $2.00 for each half fingerling.

Upscale is one thing, rip-off is another. And this was before Trump bought the place.

Ordering Lattes in Scotland.

Anne and I arrived in Aviemore in time to stop at a local coffee shop for an afternoon latte. Here is the exchange when I went to the counter to order:

Me: I'd like two large vanilla lattes with nonfat milk for staying in, please.
Barista: That's two cappuccinos?
Me: No, two lattes.
Barista: What size?
Me: Large, please.
Barista: To go or stay in?

Me: Stay in.
Barista: Two cappuccinos to go...what size?
Me: No, two large lattes for in.
Barista: Two large lattes for staying in?
Me: Yes, with vanilla.
Barista: Two large cappuccinos with vanilla.
Me: (Loud) No, two large vanilla lattes for staying in!
Barista: Okay, do you want that for here or to go?

We eventually got our drinks, but I'm sure they were not nonfat. Some days you're the windscreen, and some days you're the bug.

The Mackerel that Fought Back

One evening in Penzance, Cornwall, we had reservations at the Bakehouse Restaurant--supposedly one of the best eateries in the area. The Bakehouse is noted for its steaks--I should have had one. Instead, I was seduced by the mackerel coated (I thought) in a red wine sauce. What I got was a whole mackerel coated with masala (a very spicy curry). At first I thought it was quite spicy, but as I ate more it got hotter and hotter. I'd finished about half the fish when I realized I had no taste left--I couldn't even taste the chips let alone any fish flavor. Anne said I was turning bright red and ordered me a glass of milk and then ordered me to drink it. I greedily slugged down the milk as well as extra Zantac tablets later. I still love mackerel, but I didn't love the one that fought back.

I Got Screwed at the Machrie Bay Tea Room on Isle of Arran

After some shopping and driving around the south end of Isle of Arran we stopped at the Machrie Bay GC Tea Room for a latte and a sweet. We've stopped here before and always enjoyed the break. This day I ordered a latte and a fruit scone with jam and wandered off to the toilet in the back room of the restaurant. On the way back into the eating area I turned the doorknob and felt a sharp pain on my knuckle--a screw was loose on the door handle and had sliced the knuckle on my index finger. I got a bandaid from Anne, went back to the toilet to clean up my bleeding finger. I did tell the waitress about the loose screw and she fixed it. After the latte and scone I went to the counter to pay the bill which came to £7.05. I gave the young girl £20.05 and expected £13.00 in change. The girl thanked me and gave me back £12.95. Do the math. I looked at her, she smiled and walked away. I thought I'd teach the girl a lesson and left no tip. In reality I walked to the car with a throbbing sliced finger having paid £7.10 for our £7.05 lattes and sweets. In other words, I got screwed twice at the Machrie Bay Tea Room.

KFC from America

Jacky, our B&B host at Merlindale, begged us and begged us to bring her some American KFC. The Scottish version is only slightly better than rubbish. For years we joked about flying KFC over to Scotland with us and poisoning the whole family. Jacky, a Le Cordon Bleu trained chef, insisted that it would be perfectly safe, especially if we vacuum packed it. Two trips ago we finally relented, bought some KFC in Canby, vacuum packed it the night before, and brought it to Scotland in Anne's carry-on. Jacky was over-the-moon with delight. She grabbed it, heated it in a very hot oven, and everyone relished the treat of American KFC. Everyone except Anne and I. We knew someone had to be well enough to rush the others to hospital when the food poisoning struck. Thankfully nobody got even the slightest ill. The next trip we packaged the KFC, but forgot and left it in the fridge. We arrived at our Scottish home in the doghouse. This trip we again brought KFC--six wings and four thighs. Again no one has gotten sick. This means we're now expected to bring KFC on every trip. We keep wondering how we'll explain the rather pathetic looking package of vacuum packed wings and thighs to an Immigration and Customs agent. Honest, sir, it's just KFC, but no, we won't eat it.

Cakes and Sandwiches to Die For

When Anne and I got back from golf at Gleneagles one day Jacky had a large plate of various sandwiches and another plate of yummy looking cakes set out on the table. She told us to help ourselves. Since we hadn't had a any lunch we dug right into both the sandwiches and the cakes. As we enjoyed the repast I asked why she'd made such a special treat. Jacky said she hadn't gone to any trouble at all. Shari from the restaurant next door had brought over both plates. The sandwiches and cakes were left over from a funeral service the restaurant had catered earlier in the day. We munched on and gave great thanks to the deceased.

Screw Top at the Winking Owl

The pub, The Winking Owl in Aviemore, has new owners and they're working hard to improve the restaurant's reputation. We'd been before and thought it wasn't worth going back to, but the new pub is brighter, friendlier, and offers decent food. We hope they make it; it will be a good addition to the town's eateries. But they still have a ways to go.

One waitress brought a screw top bottle of wine to the couple a table away. She unscrewed the top, set it next to the customer for him to smell like one would a cork, and then said, "Do you want to taste the wine tonight?" Several scenarios came to mind:

1. No, we'll wait until tomorrow at breakfast to have a taste.

2. No, I don't want to taste it. I'm just going to stare at the bottle as we eat.

3. No, I'm a tea-totaler and I just wanted to make you go through the motions of pulling the cork, which of course you didn't have to do because it's such f…ing cheap wine.

4. No, why should I taste it to see if it's "corked" since there's no cork.

The guy at the table picked up the screw top, looked at it, tasted the wine, and gave the waitress a strange look.

Steak and King Prawns

We ate twice at the Kinnneuchar Inn when we were staying in the Kilconquhar Castle estate. The food at the inn is quite good and locals are friendly. It's a kind of small village Cheers. And while the castle resort is Five Star, the bistro in the castle could use some help. We booked in for steak night in the bistro and wondered why the crowd was rather sparse. It didn't take long to find out.

I ordered steak and tiger prawns (you know the big guys). When my dinner came the steak was there (and was tasty) but there were no prawns, just a sort of cream sauce. I asked the manager about the prawns and he said, "They're in the sauce." In the cream sauce were three hard, over-cooked baby cocktail shrimps—those were my King Prawns.

We found out from a waitress that the chef had run out of prawns so they substituted shrimps in a sauce. Whether it was the manager's decision or the chef's, somebody ought to learn the difference between shrimps and prawn and when to tell the customer the truth.

The Bizarre Server

At the Moorings Hotel Restaurant in Banavie near Fort William (facing Neptune's Staircase, a series of locks) we had a nice dinner and some special service. We had menus, but were waiting for a server to take our order when a nicely dressed worker (looked like a manager) came to our table to take our menus. We stopped him saying, "We haven't ordered yet." He asked what we wanted and Anne said, "I'll have the salmon with mashed potatoes." He looked at the menu where it listed mashed as an option and said something like, "I don't know if you can have that, I'll ask one of the girls. What would you like to drink?" Anne replied that she'd like a "glass of white wine; what do you have by the glass." He showed Anne the list of bottled wine and said, "White [turned the page] and red." "I want white, but which is by the glass?" questioned Anne, a little more frustrated. "I don't know; I'll ask a girl." And he left.

A waitress did finally take our order and we got drinks and food, but after the starter the same guy came back and took our starter plates and asked us what we wanted for dessert. We worked very hard to not breaking out in hysterics. We saw him several times doing things at tables and leaving guests with perplexed looks. Our guess is that he was either an overseas owner or he was from Barcelona and "knew nuthing." [British sit-com "Fawlty Towers", check it out.]

The Whisky Train

For the first time in our Scotland adventures our stay in the Highlands coincided with the Spirit of Speyside Whisky Festival which is a week of various whisky related events at numerous local distilleries. On the day we were to book in at our timeshare unit we listened to a pipe band concert in the town square at Dufftown and did some tasting in the local whisky shop. When we arrived in Aviemore we had tickets for a Celtic rock concert by Skerryvore, a group originally from one of the smaller Scottish islands, Tiree. Then on Sunday I had booked tickets for a special Whisky Train.

The Strathspey Railway is ten miles of preserved railway from Aviemore to Broomhill (the Glenbogle Station from the BBC TV show "Monarch of the Glen") via Boat of Garten. On this particular run of the tourist train a special dining car was assigned for whisky tasting sponsored by Speyside Distillery in Kingussie. Once we had our seats in the dining car paired with a very nice couple from Holland, we were introduced to the distillery manager Pamela and her assistant. On the two hour trip (this is a very slow train) we

were served five flights of whisky for tasting as well as high tea (tea or coffee, a selection of small sandwiches, and a tray of scones and cakes). We were each given generous pours of a 10 year old single malt whisky, a 12 year old, the Chairman's Choice at 17 years old, and a 20 year old Spey Royal Choice which is exclusively served to the the Royal family in five special residences including the Tower of London. The final tasting was of a yet to be released special black whisky, sweeter than the other offerings. Anne's favorite was the 12 year old (about £40 a bottle), while I preferred the Royal Choice at £175 a bottle or about $250).

When we got off the train back in Aviemore, we wished our Holland table mates good luck with their more than two hour drive to their next destination, and we were thankful that I only had to drive about a half mile to our digs. If there's another chance to ride the Whisky train...sign me up!

A year later there was a chance to sign up again for the Whisky Train—our travel plans had us staying in Aviemore again during the Whisky Festival. There was also a chance to tour and taste at the distillery sponsoring the train, Speyside Distillery. Since this distillery is not open for touring at any other time and since we had already done the train tasting, it was easy to select the distillery tour as our festival outing—easy except for the price which was about fifty percent more than the train.

On our way from Crieff to the north we planned to take the special whisky distillery tour. Last year we had been introduced to the distillery's product on a special whisky tasting tourist train, so were anxious this year to tour the distillery.

The tour wasn't as formal as most organized tours. Instead, we got to wander the working distillery and take photos which is usually not allowed. At the end of the tour we got to taste five different Speyside Distillery products. These are very special whiskies—some of which we had tasted last year—absolutely not available in the US with only limited availability in the UK. Most of the distillery's production is sold in the Orient where it is very popular. The rest is sold in Europe. Some of the most special of the whiskies are reserved for the Royal family who serve them at State functions and in their residences, such as Balmoral Castle and Holyrood Palace. As I said, this was a special tasting.

Eilean Donan Castle

CHAPTER 5: Attractions, or Which Castle Is this?

Of the 350 or so properties managed by Historic Scotland (one of the two national trusts in Scotland) we've visited over 200. We've seen about the same percentage of attractions under the care of the National Trust for Scotland and Heritage Ireland. In England and Wales we've made a much smaller dent in the list of available attractions. Some of the attractions, like Gretna Green's Blacksmith Wedding Chapel in southern Scotland, are nothing more than tourist traps. While trusts in Scotland, Ireland, England, and Wales control a large percentage of historic properties, many others are still privately run. The properties we've visited range from castles, cathedrals, and chapels to ancient standing stones and burial chambers. A few are modern, such as Scotland's Secret Bunker (a Cold War underground command center) and the Falkirk Wheel, but the majority have some age. Tour buses, especially in Ireland, stop at many of these properties, but far more are off the beaten track. Often the attraction itself is a story, but more often it is something that happens at the attraction that leads to a story, such as the first example.

Asleep at the Castle

Our friends, Scott and Jane, believe they do best when after an overseas flight they take a nap. We, on the other hand, believe that we're better to hit the ground running and try to stay awake until at least eight in the evening. If we can do that, we wake the next morning feeling like we're really in the new time zone.

On our spring 2005 trip to Ireland, we arrived at Dublin early, picked up our car, and planned a full day of sightseeing. Our agenda included a stop at a small golf course (Kildare), a visit to the Rock of Dunamase Castle ruins, a wander around the village of Abbeyleix, and finally a tour of Kilkenny Castle before checking in at our B&B. Perhaps my planning had been too ambitious or perhaps Anne had worn herself out in the days before the trip. For sure neither of us had slept much on the airplane. So, having been awake for 30 or so hours, I shouldn't have been surprised at what happened on the tour of Kilkenny Castle. We were in the second or third room listening to the tour guide when I looked over just in time to be able to grab Anne before she hit the floor dead asleep! Only a couple of people around us noticed and we hoped that the guide didn't take offense. It was nap time when we got to our B&B.

Since the day Anne fell asleep at the castle, I have planned far less on our arrival day.

Attack of the Waterfalls Owners

Ireland advertises itself as a land of tremendous scenic beauty. It touts the Cliffs of Moher, the Burren, the Dingle peninsula, the Ring of Kerry, Galway Bay, the Aran Islands, and Croag Patrick, as well as countless other natural treasures. The scenery as you drive almost anywhere in the Republic or Northern Ireland is magnificent. Scenery alone can be a reason to visit the Emerald Isle, but there's plenty more to see as well. One of the places we had heard is filled with spots of natural beauty is the Ring of Beara, the peninsula directly south of the Ring of Kerry.

In the fall of 2005, we decided to find out for ourselves how lovely the scenery on the Ring of Beara is. Starting from our B&B in Kenmare, we drove the main perimeter road north to south around the peninsula. The Cable Car to Dursey Island at the western point of the ring road is an interesting stop and the village of Glengariff is picturesque, but the rest of the ring road is mostly through pleasant forest and farmland. Certainly the Ring of Kerry and Dingle Peninsula have far more dramatic scenery. The Ring of Beara does stand out in our minds, though, as the place where we were attacked by Irish enterprising zealots.

A sign on the main Ring road directed us down a single-track lane five miles to a "Scenic Park" with "Spectacular Waterfalls." The road itself was through some of the most beautiful countryside we saw all day--interesting rock formations, dense forests, small sparkling ponds, and in the distance, brief glimpses of a pleasant waterfall. As we pulled into the parking lot of the "Scenic Park" we noted that it was privately owned. A large sign read, "€4 per Person." We could see the falls were nice, but nothing better than typical of Oregon. We thought $10 was too much just for a pretty, but unspectacular, view.

We started to turn the car around when an Irish lady came running at us waving a clipboard and shouting, "You have to pay! You have to pay!"

We said out the car window, "Sorry, but we aren't staying."

To which she shouted, "You have to pay! You drove down our road! We paid half a million for that road. You must pay!"

Now she's trying to block our way so we couldn't leave the parking area. I pulled around her and started back down the road we'd come. She continued to shout after us, "Don't take any pictures of OUR waterfall! No pictures!" With that her husband got into a small pickup and started chasing us down the road honking and shouting. He stopped chasing us after we passed the optimum photo spot, and he pulled off to deal with another "customer" who had stopped for a picture. To their credit, when we stopped at the main road and looked again at the sign, it said in very small print at the bottom, "Fee."

The Ring of Beara may not have been the loveliest of the peninsulas in southwest Ireland, but for us it was certainly the most exciting.

The Audio Guide

On our visit to England in the fall of 2010 we noticed an interesting phenomenon in a couple of places. In Bath at the Roman Baths Anne picked up one of the audio guides, a telephone like device which plays recorded information relevant to a spot in the attraction. I usually eschew the audio guides because I'm dealing with a camera. Anne would fill me in with the information she was getting from the guide and I paid more attention to the written guides placed around the Baths. What we noticed though as we walked through the Roman Baths was that many people with the audio guides became so absorbed in the commentary that they paid little or no attention to their surroundings. People would stand in the middle of a stairway or a walkway headset to their ear staring off into space, never minding that others wanted to use the stairs or the walkway. In the crowded Baths we saw tuned-out listeners block the views of others, bump into other patrons, step on children, and generally act oblivious to everything around them except whatever their audio guide was telling them.

A day later when touring Stonehenge we saw the same behavior. People with audio guides became so wrapped up in the narration that often it seemed they didn't even look at the stones themselves. This wasn't terribly bad for us, though, since it made it easier for me get unobstructed pictures of the stone circle while other tourists wandered in audio la-la-land.

I do understand how people can fall under the spell of the audio guides. I have somewhat the same problem with audio books playing in the car. As a former speech teacher I am so audio oriented that one year while listening to a taped *Seven Habits of Highly Effective People* as I was driving back from debate camp in Durango, Colorado, my attention to the book was interrupted by a siren and flashing lights behind me. The Utah State patrol officer asked me if I knew how fast I had been going. I honestly replied that I was listening so intently that I had no idea of my speed. He said he'd clocked me at between 90 and 95 miles per hour. He kindly wrote me up for going 85 in a 75 zone, a $125 ticket.
Audio guides -- use with caution.

Badbea Clearance Village

Our tee time at Wick was one o'clock which gave Anne and I plenty of time to visit the clearance village of Badbea (BAD-bay) on Scotland's east Caithness coast five miles north of Helmsdale. I'd seen the village listed on our map, but had no idea what we'd find there. In the lay-by on the A9 near Ousdale an informative sign told us a little about the history of the village and gave a few insights into the lives of the families brought here.

The footpath is now more of a sheep trail; for about 100 yards we literally followed a sheep until she bolted off the path. We could be the only visitors this day or this week; the three-quarter mile trail was little used. As we approached the precipitous Berriedale cliffs above the North Sea, the monument, built in 1939 by David Sutherland in memory of his father and the people of Badbea, signaled we had reached the village site.

At first the monument was all we noticed; that and the quiet. Even the gulls seemed to sense the sadness in this site as they slid by in respectful silence. Then we noticed a few drystone walls and the outlines of stone longhouses and byres crofters from the straths of Ousdale, Langwell, Auchencraig, and Kildonan had built when they were evicted from their land and moved to the cliffside Badbea village. Sheep and politics had instigated the Highland Clearances and created places like Badbea, which started in 1792. Landowners like Sir John Sinclair of Ulbster evicted the crofters in preference to more profitable sheep. At its largest the village was home to 35 inhabitants, with the last leaving in 1911.

As we wandered about the site under dramatically darkening skies, we could hear in the wind the stories of families forced onto these windswept cliffs as they were uprooted from ancestral lands-- lands cleared and farmed by hand, lands which for generations had given a meager, but adequate life. Stories about men of the land forced to seek livelihood on the herring or salmon boats. Stories of many, who not knowing the ways of the ocean, did not return from the sea. Stories of children and livestock having to be tethered to rocks or posts so they would not be swept over the cliffs to the sea below by the fierce winds. Stories of a people who for more than a hundred years adapted, lived, and at times even flourished, under horrendous conditions. It didn't take long before we too were hushed like the gulls by the stories that hung heavy on the wind.

It was a quiet walk back to the car and drive on to the Wick golf course. As we played that afternoon on the lovely Wick links, every breeze brought back the stark scene and stories of the Highland Clearance village of Badbea.

Be a Volunteer

The old army mantra, "Never Volunteer," is wrong, dead wrong in so many ways. The world needs volunteers to help groups, to help other individuals, to be at the forefront. Volunteers can be the backbone of change for the better. Volunteering can also bring more rewards than just emotional rescue. Volunteering can bring tangible benefits; just look at our experience in Ireland.

As we toured the Midleton Distillery near Cork, the tour guide said, "I need a few volunteers for a special duty at the end of the tour." My hand shot up as I thought, "I'm at a great distillery, how bad can the duty be?" At the end of the tour in the tasting room our guide pulled the four of us volunteers aside and had us sit at a specially set up table. At each place at the table was a marked placemat with tastes of different whiskies. Our task was to taste and compare the varieties of Scottish, American, and Irish whisk(e)y [America and Ireland spell it with an "e," while Scotland omits the "e"]. While the rest of the tour group had one taste of Midleton or Jameson (who owns Midleton) whiskey, we four volunteers got eight small, but sufficient, samples. After we correctly stated our preference for the Midleton sample, we each received a certificate as an authorized whiskey taster.

In Northern Ireland at the Bushmills Distillery the tour guide innocently asked if anyone would volunteer for special duty at the end of the tour. This time Anne and I both quickly raised our hands. At the end of the tour we were again rewarded with eight special comparative tastings, this time the tastes were larger. One of the group quit after a couple of her samples and spread her remaining samples around to the rest of us. I could barely manage to drive the five rainy miles to our B&B for the evening.

Volunteerism is a vital duty, and it can have rewards such as golden, fiery liquid.

Button Box Blowout

Traditional music is easy to find in Ireland. Every village has one or more pubs which will feature a traditional music session sometime during the week. Often there are several pubs in the same village. Scotland is a different matter. Traditional music is available, but you must search more diligently to find it. Sandy Bell's in Edinburgh and 2 Baker Street in Stirling are music venues, but beyond those steadfast suppliers good luck.

So, when staying at our timeshare in Aviemore in the Highland we saw a traditional "Button Box" concert advertised, we jumped on the tickets. It was only after buying our reserved seats that we started to ask ourselves what a "Button Box" concert would be? It was traditional Scottish music, or at least that's what the advert said, but that still didn't give us enough information to know what we were going to hear.

On the evening of the concert we arrived at the Aviemore MacDonald's theatre with a great deal of curiosity and a little trepidation. The first act introduced was a local family--mother, father, son, and daughter--who each played the accordion, specifically the button box accordion. The evening concert was a series of family groups who all played button box accordions. Occasionally a group would add a guitar or a piano, but for the most part they would just play accordions. Not only would the groups play the same instruments, they would play the same songs. By the end of the evening everything sounded the same anyway.

Why did we stay you may ask? Because it was fun to see real families performing together and being celebrated by the audience. We started conversations with some of the audience around us and found it to be great craic. We probably would not buy tickets to another "Button Box" concert, but count our one time venture as entertaining and enlightening. Besides, how many other Americans can say that they've heard just about every button box song there is played several times in one evening.

Hello! Anybody Home?

The city park in Birr, County Tipperary, Ireland, holds a special astronomical relic I wanted to visit. We didn't have golf in the area and a trip to Birr wasn't really on our route from Kilkenny to

Killarney, but I really wanted to see the giant telescope, which was at one time the largest in the world, in the center of the park. Even after getting lost on the way (not an uncommon occurrence in Ireland) by trying to take a short cut, we arrived at the park in midmorning. Plenty of time to explore the features of the park including the telescope, pleasant gardens, and an intriguing castle. The telescope was as fascinating as I had imagined; the gardens were better than we had hoped; so, it was now time to explore the castle.

We walked through the archway leading to the castle and up to the front door. There were no signs for the hours or price of admission, but we'd often not seen those until we get into the foray of a great house like the one at Birr. We opened the door and stepped into the entryway. No one was about, no attendant, no desk with guides or brochures. A couple of pairs of wellies (Wellington boots) sat just outside the door to what we thought was the main sitting room. About the time we were getting uneasy feelings about this castle, the front door opened and a nicely dressed lady walked in carrying some shopping. She did a double-take and sharply said, "What are you doing in here!" When we sheepishly said we were looking to tour the house, she said even more sharply, "This is a private home! Didn't you see the sign?" By this time we are busy apologizing profusely and back peddling out the door as quickly as we could in flushed embarrassment. On the way back towards the car we saw a sign turned toward the wall in the archway we had passed through. When we turned it around it read "Private."

We wonder to this day what stories the Lady of Birr Castle tells about the day her home was invaded by American tourists.

It's All About Perspective

It was a dreich day when we drove up to the Scottish villages of Leadhills and Wanlockhead from the A74(M). The drive up to these high villages (Leadhills at 1295 feet is second only to Wanlockhead) is through rising pasture land and worked peat bogs. Anne and I both questioned how the peat stacks could dry in this dripping weather.

The village of Leadhills, obviously named for the nearby mining operations, was made even more picturesque by the almost fog-like mist that surrounded the hills. Quaint cottages and old pubs line the single main street. We were most attracted to the nine-hole Leadhills golf course, the highest in Britain, but the drippy weather meant we'd have to return later to try it out. We did wander in the graveyard below the golf course and found the marker for John Taylor that we looked for. Taylor, born in 1633, died at 137 years of age in 1770. Even more remarkable is that he had retired from work in the mines in 1751 when he was 117 years old. It must have been something in the air.

A couple of hundred feet higher (at 1535 feet) and six miles further is Britain highest village, Wanlockhead. It was here I was being sent by *Historic Scotland Magazine* to write about the Wanlockhead Beam Engine, a pump which used water power to pull water out of the mines. The beam engine is an interesting device which reminded me of the old grasshopper-like crude oil pumps I'd see around Los Angeles when I was growing up. The Lead Mining Museum is about the only other attraction in the village and is worth a visit as it tells the story of not only mining lead, but zinc, copper, and gold as well. What was most intriguing to us about Wanlockhead village was the sheep wandered in the yards of village cottages. A house might have a small fenced off area for a garden or have fencing to keep the sheep off the porch. Other cottages with no fencing might have a sheep resting beside the front door. Anne noticed particularly that the small one-room school had a completely fenced in playground for the children.

As we drove the 15 or so miles back to the motor-way, we talked about how isolated these villages are today, miles away from even a small store. It's almost inconceivable how isolated and self-sufficient they must have been in their glory days. We may have gone up to Leadhills and Wanlockhead looking for history, what we found though was perspective.

It's Blarney

One of the premier attractions in Ireland is also one of the worst. Blarney Castle is the quintessential Irish tourist attraction. Everybody knows about the castle, built in 1446, and the famous Blarney Stone at the top which supposedly imparts the "gift of gab" to those who kiss it. The fame of Blarney goes back to a story about its Lord, Dermott Laidhir McCarthy. When the Lord of Blarney was quizzed by Queen Elizabeth I's emissary, the Lord waxed loquacious without ever answering directly (sounds like today's politicians). The Queen is reported to have said, "This is just more Blarney!" What tourists don't realize until they get there is that the stone is up seven flights of uneven castle stairs, and that to kiss the stone you must lie on your back with an attendant holding your legs as you hang over a seven story drop so you can kiss the bottom of the stone. The tourist information also doesn't tell you what an Irish friend of ours who grew up in the area told us--at night young Irish lads sneak up to the top of the castle and urinate on the stone. I wonder who's full of blarney?

When we visited Blarney Castle we learned that the grounds surrounding the castle are lovely and interesting, containing a Druidic rock garden, a sacrificial stone, a wishing staircase, a rock with a witch's face, and two dolmens (burial chambers). The grounds are well worth the time to visit. The castle is not. The castle is an empty shell with graffiti on the walls as you climb to the top. Be warned as well that the way down is by way of the servants' staircase--narrow and winding. The day we were there a large lady got stuck on the servants' stairs (not literally stuck between the walls, but so frightened by the steep stairs that she couldn't move down) to the point that they had to bring everyone following her back up and take her down the up staircase (sounds like a movie in there somewhere) after clearing it of people trying to go up.

I must say the views from the top are fine, but not so fine that I'd ever climb it again.

It's the Wrong Kirk

The Dingle Peninsula is filled with interesting sites and grand sea vistas. It also houses one of our favorite golf courses, *Ceann Sibeal* (Dingle Golf Links) GC. We've visited the Gallarus Oratory, a 10th century stone church which looks like an upturned row boat (made without mortar, the oratory is so well constructed that it has remained dry inside for 1100 years); the Bee Hive huts, small stone houses used by farmers from at least 2000 BC; and the Blasket Visitor Centre, an interpretive center dedicated to the inhabitants of the Blasket Islands who left the islands in 1954. One site we hadn't visited was Kilmalkedar Church near the Gallarus Oratory. We'd tried unsuccessfully to find it once before. This year we were determined to find the ruined church famous for it Ogram stone, sundial, and ancient crosses.

Armed with a better map and detailed directions from an Irish antiquities website, we left the golf course on our quest for Kilmalkedar. We saw a sign pointing to the church about a mile away. A short ways down the road we spied an old ruined church. A hundred yards or so past it was a small pullout where I parked. I took several photos of the church as I approached from the road. The church was fenced and the fence was locked, but on the gate was a small sign: "Private Property: Kilmalkedar Romanesque Church and other Historic Monuments are located one kilometer up the road." In other words, "Not here stupid!"

I put the camera down, walked back to the car, and we drove down to the correct church.

Night Watchman

On a spring evening in Rothenburg ob der Tauber, Germany, we took an enlightening tour by the Night Watchman, who told us the story of Rothenburg. In Ripon, Yorkshire, England, we met a different Night Watchman.

We had talked to Neil, our B&B host in Ripon, about the Ripon Hornblower. So, at nine o'clock we wandered down to the town square and along with three other people awaited the Hornblower. Precisely at nine, the Hornblower entered the square, walked up to the town monument, and blew his horn four times, each

time facing a different direction. We learned from Charles, who has been the hornblower for a year, that this is a ritual that has been performed each night at nine o'clock for the past 1100 years! The blowing of the horn is a signal that the Night Watchman is on duty.

After he performs his ritual horn blowing, Charles like his more than 100 predecessors, goes to the mayor's house and blows once to signal his job is done for the evening. Charles said that if the mayor is not in his home, he goes to each pub in town until he finds the mayor and completes his task. Even with only a short draught at each pub, it can make for a long evening, especially if he starts looking for the mayor in the least likely pub. There is a substitute hornblower for when the official one is sick or out of town.

It's difficult to imagine that this ritualistic horn blowing was going on for more than 800 years before there ever was an America.

The Orkney Cow in Distress

We've toured the north of Scotland many times and played most of the courses there. It took until the fall of 2007, though, for us to visit the Orkney Islands off the tip of the northern mainland.

A bus tour is not our favorite way to travel. In ten years we've taken only a couple of bus tours and much prefer to drive so that we can "do our own thing." To get to the Orkneys, however, a ferry/bus tour is the easiest way to at least get a feel for the islands. We figured that if we enjoyed what we saw and wanted to see more, next time we'd plan to take the car ferry and really spend some time. For this trip, though, we caught the passenger ferry at John o'Groats, the village which is the most northerly on the British mainland. It's really not much more than a ferry terminal and tourist trap complete with a professional photographer ready to take your picture in front of the sign pointing to the Orkney Islands.

The trip over to the bus waiting on the first of the Orkney Islands is a short 40 minutes, but the crossing is rough and the weather wasn't particularly enjoyable which made it seem much longer. We were glad for landfall and the crowded comfort (sort of) of the large tour bus. The tour was a nice introduction to the features of the Orkneys including the villages of Stromness and Kirkwall, Skara Brae prehistoric village (unearthed about 100 years ago after being buried for about 4000 years), the large Ring of Brodgar stone circle, the Italian POW chapel, and the Churchill

Barriers built during World War II to block the German submarines from crossing the Scapa Flow and to allow land transport connections between the islands of South Ronaldsay, Burry, and Mainland, Orkney's largest island. As informational as the historical part of the tour was, more interesting were the stories our bus driver tour guide told about the island.

First, we saw where three locals were having a small war over flags. One flies the St Andrews Cross (the Scottish flag), a neighbor flies the Canadian flag, and the third flies a Jolly Roger pirate flag. The driver thought they were going reach a compromise and all fly the newly designed Orkney flag. Next, the driver pointed out a specially fenced yard set up with a play area for the cat who uses a tunnel to go from the house to the yard. Serious cat lovers live there. We saw the house of the first British civilian casualty of bombings in World War II. A German plane trying to reach home dumped its bombs and one landed close to a man just leaving his house. He became the first of many bombing victims. The last story we noted was about a battle fought in the 1400s between Scots from Sutherland (the Scottish mainland) and Orcadians. The Scots were routed and only one Orcadian was killed. He was a fairly young boy who found a dead Scotsman and took his clothes and shoes (never having had any of his own) and went home. His mother, thinking she was being attacked by a Scot, hid and hit the intruder with a sock with a rock in it when he came in. His was the only Orcadian death in the battle.

Most unique about the tour was when the driver pulled the bus over near a farm. We could see him looking carefully in his mirrors and finally sticking his head out the window to look back. Nobody could see what he was looking at. He said to us, "Excuse me a minute. There's a cow back there with her head stuck through the wire fence and she seems to be in some distress." With that he stepped out the door and walked back behind the bus. From where we were we couldn't see what was happening, but a couple of minutes later our driver returned and with a smile announced, "All better now." We drove on. All in a day's work for the tour bus driver--drive tourists around, tell stories, and save cows.

Seisiuns

One of the reasons to visit Ireland is for the traditional music sessions (*seisiuns* in Gaelic) which can be heard in pubs in almost every village almost every night. The sessions are open to any player who wants to sit in and is able to perform up to the standard of the evening. These session musicians are not usually paid to perform, although they would hardly ever have to buy their own beer or Guinness. They are not playing for the audience, but rather are playing for themselves. The fact that there is an audience listening and buying them drinks seems to be irrelevant. There may be long breaks between songs as the musicians talk among themselves, or

one song may blend into another and into another as the group gets it's collective shit together. We've listened in on sessions in Dublin, Limerick, Killarney, Kilkenny, Cork, Dingle, Westport, Kenmare, Doolin, Tralee, Athlone, and probably a few other places I've forgotten. Every one of those sessions has been great fun.

Our best experience with session music in Ireland was one of our first. We stayed at *Teach an Phiobaire* Guest House (the House of the Piper) run by Michael Dooley, a world renown maker of uilleann pipes (Irish small bagpipes). Michael told us he was playing that evening in a session at Betty's Bar in Tralee in the southwest. After dinner in town we drove around until we found Betty's Bar in one of the town's less desirable areas. You could tell that Betty's was a neighborhood drinking pub; people would drop in, down a pint, and head home. As it got closer to music time, which always starts late in Ireland, the smoke got lower as the night got later. [The ban on smoking in pubs in Ireland has made pub visits much more pleasant, once you get by the smokers coughing and hacking outside the front door.] Most people were standing and talking, even though a great session was in progress. We visited with a local who gave Anne his stool at the bar. We chatted about world politics and other unimportant matters until he looked at his watch and said, "Oops, time to go." With a quick good-bye he stumbled out of the bar into the darkness. We gave up our stool at the bar when Michael, who was playing guitar in the session, called us down to sit with the musicians. We listened to both the wonderful music and as much of the conversation among musicians as we could understand. We discovered that the musicians don't mind if you sit close. The fiddle player rather enjoyed explaining the songs to Anne.

In Dolan's in Limerick the music was supposed to start at 9:00. It got going a little after 10:00. This is a typical example of Irish-time--when we get around to it. When the music started it was great. The group was very lively, except for one old gentleman (octogenarian by our guess) sitting with his small drum and a glass of Guinness under a "Reserved for Musicians" sign. His glasses down on his nose, his baseball cap askew, he appeared to be sound asleep when he wasn't playing. One sign of life was that occasionally he'd sit up and sip his Guinness.

A couple of times we've watched players try to join in a session in progress with mixed results. In Dingle at *Ua Flatbeartais* (O'Flaherty's) Pub one evening we watched a young American girl (probably college age) try to sit in with the locals. She said she didn't know many Irish-Irish songs, but that she knew some Irish-American tunes. The locals told her to go ahead and that they'd keep up. She absolutely had no clue when they made a musical fool of her and left her in a dust of notes. It would have been funny if it hadn't been so sad. There was a similar instance at Matt Molloy's Pub in Westport. Matt Molloy is the flutist for the famous Irish traditional group The Chieftains and supposedly drops in to join sessions every now and again. Whenever we are in Matt Molloy's we hear top notch musicians and this one evening was no exception. The group consisted of a drummer (the bodhran, the traditional Irish drum), a couple of fiddle players, a guitarist, a player on pipes, whistles and flutes, and squeeze box player. About an hour into the session, which can go for several hours, a guy asked to join in with his flute and harmonica. The group invited him in and took off on a traditional set of reels. The new player stayed with the group for a few numbers, playing less and less each set. Finally, he quietly bowed out and blended in with the audience. The Irish musicians are open, accepting, and ruthless in their expectations.

Another visit to Matt Molloy's brought a different kind of entertaining session experience, at least for me. We were in Westport to play the great parkland Westport Golf Club on a Bank Holiday weekend. Bank Holidays are designated Mondays during the year that are proclaimed holidays. Dublin will have different Bank Holidays than Cork or Belfast, or maybe they will all have the same holiday--I still haven't discovered the pattern. Being a Dublin Bank Holiday meant that Westport was packed with revelers on a Monday night--nobody seemed to worry about Tuesday. Since Matt Molloy's is the happening place in Westport it was even more packed than usual. Holiday makers, tourists, and a wild hen party (ladies version of a bachelor party) crammed in to try to listen to the session. Anne and I slowly had worked our way into the music room like water working its way down a driveway. As one person moved or shifted, someone would fill in the void. We eventually had a fairly good seat for Anne and standing room for me not far from the session players. As we settled in the hen party migrated towards our spot. The girls, well lubricated with Guinness and well endowed by nature, moved in on our spot. For about forty-five minutes I was in some form of male nirvana with one girl after another falling, bumping, leaning, rubbing against my arms and back. I've never stood so still for so long in my life (except for toes tapping to the music), but I wasn't about to give up an inch or get out of anyone's way. I know very few men who would. Anne, aware of what was going on, sat smiling the whole time. I must say I was smiling, too.

Second only to the great golf courses, the music sessions in Irish pubs are what calls us back most strongly--Haste ye back!

Stewards or Owners?

Historic Scotland manages slightly over 300 historic sites, and we've visited more than 200 of them. The National Trust for Scotland cares for more than 150 properties, and we've visited about 90 of them. We've viewed dozens and dozens of historic sites in Ireland, Wales, and England. The most interesting common thread with all these attractions is the stewards and docents who take care of the properties and the visitors. At several of these tourist attractions we've noticed that the stewards treat the property as if it were absolutely their own.

Michael Scott, the Historic Scotland steward for Seaton Collegiate Church in East Lothian, referred to the property as "my church." The steward at Dryburgh Abbey in the Scottish Borders was another one who let you know to be careful as you toured "his abbey." Padraig O'Toole, at Aughnanure Castle in Ouchterard, Ireland, had more reason to say that the castle was "his castle." The O'Tooles were the last owners of the castle before the property was turned over to Heritage Ireland. These possessive property managers, rather than being put-offish, actually enhance a visitor's experience. You can't help feeling more appreciative of a site when your host or guide is the owner.

At other sites we've been impressed with the knowledge and enthusiasm of stewards or docents. One of our most memorable experiences was at Robert Smail's Print Shop in Innerleithen, Scotland. The property manager at this National Trust site was almost gushing as he explained what a national treasure trove Smail's Print Shop was. Smail opened the print shop in the mid-1800s and, according to the law of the time, kept a copy of each item he printed for the required six months. He went further than that and kept one copy of each item permanently. The shop's printing archives became a time capsule of small village life in Scotland. The print shop closed in the 1960s and was turned over to the National Trust, lock, stock and printed wedding invitation. The steward's enthusiasm was infectious. Then we went into the print room and met a young lady, a recent historical graphic arts graduate of Edinburgh University, who explained the workings of several vintage printing presses. Again, her love for her job spilled over onto us.

The enthusiasm of a steward can go too far, as in the case of the steward at Athenry Castle near Galway in Ireland. No golf that day, the rain was too intense.   We decided to visit Athenry Castle since we had the time.   The drive to Athenry was easy and the castle is the main attraction in the village.   We walked into the reception area and were met by the manager of the property and his young female assistant (who we think was new to the job).   We paid our entrance fees, got a little guide brochure, and started to head out on the self-guided tour.   Before we could get out the door, the steward said, "You'll want to know the history of castle before you'll be visiting it."   He then continued to give us a 20 minute condensed history of Ireland.   He was having a wonderful time showing off for the young lady assistant.   It bothered him in the least that we were seasoned Ireland travelers (this was our fourth trip) and that he wasn't giving us anything new.   As we finally got out to view the castle, you could almost see him strutting and preening for the girl.

The Athenry case of overkill aside, the stewards and docents we've met at tourist attractions have greatly added to our knowledge and enjoyment of the sites.   What a great job it must be to love where you work and get to share that love with people every day!

The Story of Twa Chapels

The story of Scotland is told in monumental movements and calamitous events, such as the Jacobite Rebellion and the Battle of Culloden.   As intriguing as is this broad sweep of history, it is the connection between small stories that I find most interesting.   For an outsider, Scottish history is like a dot-to-dot puzzle: It's only when enough dots are joined that the larger picture becomes clear.

We've spent much of our time in the British Isles exploring Scotland's history.   We've mostly based our visits to Scotland in the crossroad drover town of Crieff.   Several times we've wandered the nearby grounds of both Tullibardine and Innerpeffray Chapels. During a visit to Tullibardine in spring of 2004, I read something that suggested a connection between that chapel and the one at Innerpeffray.   With thoughts of James Burke's television series, "Connections," flashing though my mind, I determined to delve deeper into the complex relationship between the Murray's Tullibardine Chapel (near the Gleneagles Resort off A823) and the Drummond family chapel at Innerpeffray (four miles south of Crieff off B8062).

Tullibardine Chapel, also called St Savior's Tullibardine, was founded as a Collegiate Church by Sir David Murray for use of the Earls and Dukes of Atholl. Sir David died the year the church was completed, 1446, and was buried in the church yard. The chapel was rebuilt in about 1500 and today its thick walls and deep window traceries stand as one of the most complete chapels of its era.

Innerpeffray Chapel of St Mary was also founded as a Collegiate Church. A church had been on this ground as early as 1342, when the current chapel was built in 1508. Next to the chapel, the Drummonds added a school which opened in 1680 (and operated until 1947), as well as a library in 1691, which still exists as Scotland's oldest lending library. Today's simple chapel retains its altar, Laird's Loft, leper's squint (where unfortunates could view mass without entering), and part of its painted ceiling.

Several similarities between the two chapels have already been mentioned. Both were family chapels and Collegiate Churches, which means a church with a chapter of canons presided over by a provost or dean. Both exist in similar condition-- empty of all trappings, yet well preserved. Deeper connections are found by exploring

the relationship between the Murrays and the Drummonds. Both powerful central Scotland families became aligned in defense of the Jacobite Risings in 1715 and 1745. Lord George Murray, son of John Murray, the First Duke of Atholl, was active in the Jacobite cause of 1745. He was responsible for much of the rebellion's early successes, particularly at Prestopans. Murray co-commanded Prince Charlie's forces at the ill-fated Battle of Culloden. While he was on the right flank, it was Innerpeffray's James Drummond, the Third Duke of Perth, who generaled the left flank. The connection continues after the battle with the fates of the two generals. Drummond survived the battle, but died on board the French ship *La*

Bellone on his passage to France.   Lord George Murray also survived, but died in exile in France.

At Innerpeffray Library, with the help of curator Ted Powell, we traced one more connection. It seems that sometime later, probably in the early 19th Century, the Murray's Tullibardine Chapel eventually became, through marriage, the property of the Drummonds of Innerpeffray.

The ending to this story of two chapels, the last dots to be connected, is that both are linked for the foreseeable future under the care of Historic Scotland.   When visiting Scotland's historic properties our experiences can be greatly enriched by digging deeper into the plethora of stories associated with each property. We never know what picture connecting the next dot will reveal.

The Tourists

We are tourists. We hope we are good tourists. We've seen some who were not good tourists.

On an evening pub crawl in Dingle we walked into John Benny's Pub on the main street of town looking for a place to listen to the music.   In the corner a table for four was occupied by an American couple and their coats. They made it quite clear that they weren't going to share their table or the unused chairs with anyone. One person went over and asked, but the couple said the chairs were saved.   In forty-five minutes nobody came to "share" their table.   In another pub the same evening, a girl (we think American) sat on a high stool against the wall.   Her coat occupied the stool next to her.   Again it was obvious that she was protecting her privacy at the expense of the comfort of others.   With Scots or Irish there wouldn't have been a moments hesitation about sharing their table or space, but the "ugly American" syndrome still rears its head.

There is an "Ugly German" tourist as well.   In Ireland around the Ring of Kerry we had two run-ins with a group of German tourists.   The first was at Staigue Fort, a splendid round stone defensive fort dating from between 300 and 400 AD, Wandering around the fort one day taking pictures we met a small tour group of about eight Germans who were also visiting the fort and photographing.   We stayed out of each others way for a while, but as I was trying to get a photo of the interior staircase the German photographer climbed over the "Do Not Climb" sign right into the photo I wanted. We then had a short standoff as he waited for me to take my picture and I waited to take my photo until he had moved out of the way. I was going to give him the benefit of doubt thinking maybe he couldn't read the sign, but he blew that when he said to me, "Take your damned photo so I can take mine" in reasonably good English. A little later the same day we saw the same Germans stop at a Killarney Park wayside to dump their car garbage into the bushes. All American and German tourists aren't "ugly," but these examples certainly were.

Now to the typical Japanese tourist who has a camera sticking out the end of his face (I should talk!). Near John o'Groats at the far north of Scotland, Anne and I parked by the derelict lighthouse and walked the path towards Duncansby Head and the sea stacks just off shore. We stopped to watch a group of about twenty Japanese high school or college age students take a group photo with the North Sea in the background. One by one an individual would pop out of the group to take a picture of the rest of the group. Their picture taken, the student would jump back into the group and another would pop out for a photo. They were still taking turns taking group pictures when we walked past them having visited the overlook to the stacks, taken pictures, and walked back toward the lighthouse. For all we know they could still be there taking the same group photo.

What? No Free Admission!

Coming back to our Scotland home from two weeks golfing in Wales, we purposely drove through the border town of Ludlow. There was a special attraction we needed to visit.

Anne's family history can trace its roots back to Roger Ludlow who lived in Ludlow Castle. Roger came to America in the third ship after the Mayflower in 1620. Anne's connection to Ludlow Castle was a strong pull to visit the town and castle. When we went into the reception area at the castle in the heart of town, the clerk asked for our entrance fees. Anne said that her family traced back to Roger Ludlow and asked jokingly, "Shouldn't I get in free?" The clerk said in a non-joking manner, "No, that'll be £7." Pounds are evidently thicker than blood.

Young Traditional Concert

The main attractions of Carrbridge, a quaint Highland village, are the Packhorse Bridge, an attractive nine-hole golf course, and the Old Bakery Tearoom. After photographing the Packhorse Bridge and before playing the Carrbridge Golf Course, Anne and I stopped in at the tearoom for tea and a sweet. On the local activities board in the tearoom was an announcement of a special traditional music concert scheduled for Friday night. The players were all young people who were national traditional music award winners. Always on the lookout for traditional music, we paid for tickets right then.

Friday night we drove from our digs in Aviemore the twelve miles to Carrbridge for the concert which had been moved from the community centre to the local primary school multipurpose room because it was a larger venue. As we found seats in the converted gym we realized we were probably the only non-locals in the audience; everyone knew everyone else. As the lead member of the group was introduced, a young man who played guitar and Highland bagpipes, as the national outstanding young traditional music player of the year, we wondered how such a high powered concert had come to this small village. When we were told the award winner was from Carrbridge we had our answer, and we knew why the whole village had turned out.

The concert was one of the most fantastic music events we've attended any place. It was an evening of outstanding performances of traditional music, in both English and Gaelic, highlighting individual musicians playing drums, pipes, flutes, guitar, piano, accordion, and vocal performances. Since we were the outsiders and this was really a community celebration, we missed interacting with the locals, but the music more than made up for it.

Repurposing or Let's Fund the Military with a Bake Sale

It took us twenty-four trips to Crieff to find Cultybraggan Camp. It wasn't lost all that time; we just didn't know it existed until I saw a small article about it in a Scottish magazine. When I asked Jacky, our B&B host, she knew all about it and assumed we did to. Only a few miles from Comrie Village (about 6 miles from our B&B home in Crieff) is Cultybraggan Camp, a Nissan hut (we'd call them Quonset huts) World War II camp. The camp was first used as a

World War II POW camp, and then a Royal Observer Corps nuclear monitoring post. The camp was used by the MOD (Ministry of Dark Arts, no Ministry of Defense) until 2007. Finally, the camp was purchased by the Comrie Development Council. Now some huts house offices or businesses and fields are used for athletics and plantings. About 75 percent of the camp is still just abandoned buildings.

For me the camp was a good photo opportunity--abandoned buildings, interesting textures, angles and patterns. This is not the only military camp we've seen repurposed in Scotland.

Balnakeil Craft Village just a mile west of Durness in the far northwest corner of Scotland is a repurposed Cold War Early Warning base. Given (we understand for a very modest fee) to artists, crafts people, and other small businesses in the 1970s, the village is a thriving small community with several artisans, a book store, a cafe, and an outstanding chocolate shop which draws about 25,000 visitors a year; quite a lot for this far out of the way.

Wouldn't it be nice if all our military bases could be repurposed for small business, artist, and chocolate shops.

St Ives, Cornwall

On our trip down from Scotland to Cornwall in southern England we'd visited the small coastal village of Port Isaac. We didn't have much knowledge of the village having seen only one episode of the BBC series "Doc Martin," but many more people would recognize the village as Port Wenn. It was a cute, friendly village. A little later in the trip several people suggested that if we liked Port Isaac we would really like the village of St Ives--everyone said it was a "Must See."

On the day we visited St Ives we were immediately surprise to find out that you park high above the village and take a local bus down to the harbour--the village roads are so tight our bus driver hit a sign post on the way down (it was obvious that the post had been hit before). The harbour was pretty, but the town was just a tourist town with touristy junk shops and a few high class art galleries. We would have been better off spending our time somewhere else.

While in St Ives we stopped in a harbour-front tearoom for lattes. Here I had to go to the counter to order and then go back to the counter to pay. I was standing in line to order our lattes when a couple of people came up to pay. I waiting for my turn, but two other Americans behind me got tired of waiting, got their wives, and huffed out without ordering. Later, when I was waiting in line to pay, one of the Americans came back in looking for a backpack his wife had left in their haste to get out of there. The clerk who had the backpack behind the counter handed it to the man who then said he wanted a cookie to go and demanded that he get it and pay right then. A local behind me in line said to me, "Are you invisible?" To which I replied, "Americans aren't very good at queues." We both just laughed--the Ugly American strikes again.

In contrast to St Ives later that day we stopped for lunch at Heather's Coffee shop in the tin mining village of Pendeen. It was filled with locals, all friendly. We shared a table with a couple of local ladies meeting for lunch. Our stop for a sandwich and a coke in Pendeen was more enjoyable than our whole morning in St Ives.

St Michael's Mount in the Wind

One of the biggest attractions in Cornwall in southern England is St Michael's Mount, known locally as the Mount. It is a tidal island in Mounts Bay near Penzance which has a man-made granite causeway which is passable at low tide. The Mount may have served as a monastic site since between the 8th and 11th century and was also a priory and a Benedictine monastery. Currently it is the residence of Lord St Levan and under the auspices of the National Trust has several rooms open for touring,

including a chapel and embattled tower and turret. An underground rail is used to bring supplies from the mainland, because as we found out the sea route is often unreliable.

On a breezy day in May 2013, we walked out to the base of the Mount, about a quarter of a mile over a cobbled causeway open for about two hours before and after low tide. The wind, a steady twenty-five miles per hour with higher gusts, meant that the small passenger ferry from the mainland wasn't operating. By the time we walked the beach from the parking lot and then the causeway, the wind was gusting to 50 mph. We checked in at the National Trust office and started to climb up to the castle--up a long path then further up about fifty steps. The last twenty steps or so were fully exposed to the increasing wind and unprotected by railings. Anne had a bit of a problem on the last part with the wind now approaching hurricane force (80 mph by staff estimation). We both got half pulled into the entrance by NT staff who informed us that the facility would be closing two hours early so that everyone, visitors and staff, could walk in safety back off the island to the shore. The castle was an interesting tour, but getting blown off the island makes a better story.

Tomb of the Eagles

Most of our touring experiences, whether in the UK, the US, or Europe, have been very positive--we've had fun and learned. But not all have been that way. One of the worst touring experiences was visiting the Tomb of the Eagle.

We drove from Kirkwall on the main island of the Orkneys (north of the Scottish mainland) to the southern tip of South Ronaldsay island to visit the site. On the way we crossed the Churchill Barriers--a series of four causeways built in 1940 to block German submarines from access to the Scapa Flow, a main staging area for Allied ships. Very interesting. When we got to the visitor centre of the Tomb of the Eagles we paid a fairly high fee and were told we'd have to wait a few minutes for the first of two talks (5 minutes and 15 minutes) before going out to the tombs. We wandered in the display room where the fifteen minute talk would take place for twenty minutes before the steward, the owner, came in to give the talk. While we had waited we were watched intently, as if the helper thought we might steal things. One and a half hours later we completed both talks and were "released" to see the tombs. The owner rambled on about telling the story of the tombs discovery by her father and how national trusts wouldn't develop the property for touring so her father did his own research and development. On and on she went--obviously in love with her own voice.

We left without taking the one and half mile mud walk to the tombs. With some reflection we now wonder about the authenticity of what we saw in the displays and the tombs themselves. Definitely we were cheated of our time. I can't think of a poorer touring experience.

Cliffs of Moher and the Stupid People

One of the prime natural tourist attractions in the Republic of Ireland is the Cliffs of Moher (*Aillte an Mhothair* in Irish Gaelic). The cliffs are seven hundred foot sea cliffs above the Atlantic Ocean at

Hag's Head north of Lahinch in County Claire. The site draws more than a million visitors annually, and many of them are really, really stupid.

I'll start with a couple of tourist notes about the cliffs before I get to the Stupid People. The best time of day to photograph the cliffs is in the late afternoon when the setting sun highlights both the rocks and the breathtaking crashing waves. Late afternoon, after 5:00 PM, is also the best time for the budget minded to visit. Earlier in the day the tourist shop is open and there is a charge to visit the cliff's lookout and to park. After 5:00 PM both are free. We were lucky enough to take advantage of both these hints on our first visit to the cliffs. We drove out to the cliffs after a round of golf at Lahinch GC a few miles away. It had been squally all day, but the sun was out now and the wind was up significantly. We hiked up the trail to the cliff lookout for photos. It was then we saw the Stupid People.

Across from the observation area we could see a flat plateau on top of the nearest edge of the cliffs (which run in both directions several miles). Although there were steel fences and massive signs warning of the dangers of the cliffs, a number of Stupid People, mostly teen and young adults of both sexes, were on the top of the plateau. It was dumb enough that they were out on the rock with 30 to 40 mile per hour gusts and a drop of 700 feet a few feet away. But then the dumb showed they were dumber by crawling out to the edge and hanging a leg or arm or both over the edge. The really Stupid People would hang an arm and their head over the edge and wave to their friends. One of the Stupid People's hat flew off and the person made a jerking grab for it as it sailed down toward the sea. We thought for sure we were going to witness a tragic fall. No more! We headed back down to our car and left the Stupid People to their madness. We figured if anyone did fall that they probably weren't meant to breed.

A Moving History

One of the things that we like best about Scotland is how well they have cared for and displayed their antiquities. Two special trusts have responsibility for various kinds of sites--the National Trust for Scotland cares for numerous complete or fairly complete castles and gardens and Historic Scotland cares mostly for ancient sites and ruins.   Caring for these antiquities has led to some unusual preservation techniques.   One of the most unusual examples is the Cairnwell Ring Cairn in the village of Portlethen

near Aberdeen. The 4000 year old stone circle and burial cairn was first investigated in 1858.   Excavations found evidence of five cremations. The property was originally the Cairnwell Farm, but a crisis came in 1995 with plans to develop the Badentoy Industrial Park to encompass the site of the stone circle and cairn. The stone circle and cairn were moved by Scotland's AOC Archaeology Group and rebuilt (after full geographical survey) 175 meters northeast of its original location. Easy street access and parking were planned into the new location. What a great way to preserve history while at the same time accommodating progress.

Maeshowe

We knew Maeshowe, a Neolithic chambered cairn and passage grave on Mainland (the main island in the Orkneys off the north coast of Scotland), was a major site, but we had no idea how impressive it was until we toured it.   It would rival Newgrange in Ireland, but it's not quite as large.

We had booked the 4:00PM tour and were sitting in our rental car waiting for the tour guide who would lead us out to the tomb when a storm hit. At 3:40 black clouds rolled in and the sky opened up to one of the hardest rains we've seen in Scotland. Rain and wind pelted the car as we tried to wait out the downpour. At ten minutes before 4:00 we had to head out to meet the guide at the tomb about a quarter mile away. Hoods tight we walked toward the cairn and watched other tourists get their umbrellas blown inside out. About half way out to the cairn the rain stopped as quickly as it came in. Our pants were absolutely soaked, but the lovely rainbow directly over the cairn made up for it.

We stood outside the entrance to the tomb in heavy wind while the guide gave us an introduction to and history of Maeshowe. In the 15 minutes before we entered the cairn the wind almost completely dried our jackets and pants. The tour was fantastic--the informative, entertaining Historic Scotland guide made this tour one of the best we've had. The chambered cairn is approximately 115 feet in diameter and stands about 24 feet tall. We semi-crawled the 36 feet of entrance passage (only about three feet tall) to the square central chamber where we could finally stand again (it's about 12 feet tall). The cairn is aligned, similarly to Newgrange, so that light coming down the entrance passage will illuminate the back of the central chamber on about the Winter Solstice. We learned that it's believe that the central chamber was used for rituals or meetings and that side chambers were used for burials--skulls in one chamber, legs and arms in another, and other bones in yet a different chamber. Dating back to about 3000 BC, Maeshowe is, along with Skara Brae, the Ring of Brodgar, and Stenness standing stones, part of "the Heart of Neolithic Orkney" World Heritage site.

This tour was such a total contrast to the Tomb of the Eagle (in this same chapter) that it helped rid of us the bad taste of the other tour.

The Stones of Machrie Moor

It is a three mile (round trip) walk from the main Isle of Arran road to Machrie Moor and a series of Neolithic and Early Bronze Age relics. The walk up to moor is on a farm track through several fields of sheep. This particular spring the fields were full of ewes and lambs, with the curious lambs playing and almost flirting--

always under the watchful eyes of mother--with the walkers traipsing up to see the stones. The first set of stones near the path is called the Moss Farm Road burial cairn which marks the final resting place of an ancient tribal leader. The cairn itself was about 20 meters in diameter and fragments of pottery and tools have been found buried within.

The next sight is not so ancient. The ruins of Moss Farm attract less attention from visitors than does the stone circle across from it. Besides being a play area for gamboling lambs, the farm ruins at about 200 years old stand in stark contrast to ancient people's stone work still standing as much as 4000 years later. The circle across from the farm is called *Suide Choir Fhionn* (in Scottish Gaelic) or Fingal's Cauldron Seat. It is a double ring of stones.

But now we have arrived at the moor itself--a broad plain that has been inhabited for the last 8000 years or so. On the plain are numerous hut circles, cairns, stone circles, and solitary standing stones, but five sites are easily accessed and most prominent. The main attraction is site #3, a large seemingly solitary stone, which is actually a part of a large circle, the other stones of which have either been buried or removed. The other major site is circle #2 with three large stones (as tall as 18-1/2 feet) and numerous smaller stones. This circle is very much like the Stenness stones we visited earlier on the Orkney Islands off the north coast of Scotland.

All the stones of Machrie Moor have been dated to between 1800 and 1600 BC, even though evidence has been found of human occupancy much earlier. The purpose of these ancient structures can only be guessed at. Theories suggest that they may have served some astronomical purposes because of their alignments; it is likely that some served as ritualistic burial sites because of what has been found nearby; but most certainly these stones served some ritualistic purpose for the people who built them. For those of us who visit now, 4000 years later, we question, ponder, marvel, and even gambol with the innocence of the lambs as we view the mysterious Stones of Machrie Moor.

The Mull of Kintyre Lighthouse Road

From Southend (a small village at the end of Scotland's Kintyre Peninsula) it's seven or eight miles (depending upon which sign you see) to the Mull of Kintyre Lighthouse. We started up toward the lighthouse on a single-track road which got smaller and smaller. On one section we were driving along the cliff edge with a drop of about 2000 feet to the sea (Anne's side) with no verge (shoulder) or guard rails. We finally came to a driveway where we could pull off a little to take a look at the rest of our route. We still had more than four miles to go and I could see the next mile or so went straight up (straight up, no switchbacks) with no passing places. I took this opportunity to turn around.

Some attractions just aren't worth the effort.

An Opps! Phone Call

We were atop Tintagel Castle on the east coast of Cornwall, England, on a squally day in May, 2013. The castle is noted as the birthplace of legendary King Arthur.   The climb up a steep path and even steeper stone steps had been exciting in the stiff breeze, but now we were ensconced within the protective walls of the roofless castle. I said to Anne, "Wouldn't it be neat to share this with your sister Charleen back in Oregon?" Anne looked at her watch which read about 11:50 AM, did some quick calculations, and replied, "Great! She'll be just getting ready for work."

Anne clicked the speed-dial on the iPhone, then I listened to half the conversation. "Hello, Chuck, it's Anne...No, nothing's wrong, we just wanted to tell you where were are....Yes, it's noon here...Oh, 3:00 AM...I'm so sorry, go back to sleep." Anne had calculated the eight hour time difference between Oregon and the England the wrong way. We bought Charleen a nice dinner when we go home.

Buchanty Fall

Buchanty Spout is a waterfall (more a strong cascade) on the River Almond near the little hamlet of Buchanty in central Perthshire, Scotland. The falls is a favorite spot for photographers, picnickers, water watchers, and fisher folk who watch the salmon leap the falls in the autumn run. I've been down the short 200-yard hike to the falls several times for photos, but have yet to see the "spouts"--deep circular holes in the rocks are said to cause spouting when the water runs high.

The spring of 2011 was particularly rainy and all the rivers were running quite high. I decided this would be a good time to see Buchanty Spout in spate and hopefully get spectacular photos. Anne let me go alone since she knew I really did know the way to Buchanty and the falls--she kens (knows) I have basically no sense of direction and can get lost in a grocery store, so is very cautious about letting me out without a navigator. She did admonish me with the caveat, "Be careful and don't fall in." And she was correct to give me the reminder since falling into the river along the falls would indeed be life threatening.

The drive to the parking area at Buchanty was a non-event. On the short hike down to the falls I did take note of the slippery conditions on the trail. I was slightly disappointed that there was no

spouting at the falls, the water was high but not high enough. I was extremely cautious on the rocks as I took some good photos of the powerful cascade. I was not cautious enough to notice the moss around the spout hole as I backed away from the rock edge. The next thing I knew my right foot had slipped on the moss and I tumbled down with my leg mid-thigh in the hole. Instinctively I saved my camera and lens from damage, but not my leg. It took a couple of minutes to recover my senses and extricate my leg from the spout hole. I count myself as very lucky to have been able to limp back to the car with only a bruised shin bone and a major scrape, rather than a broken leg.

There was no way I could hide either my embarrassment or my bloody pant leg when I got home to the B&B. Anne was a great sport; she didn't say, "I warned you." The photos I took that day, by the way, weren't that good.

I Ain't 'Fraid of No Ghosts

Most of the tourist shops in southern England sell small books about local ghosts (i.e., the Ghosts of Dartmoor, Southern Ghost Stories, etc.). I also have a book I'd been reading at home before the trip called "Britain's Most Haunted Pubs and Inns." This led me to start asking at the pubs and inns we visited if there were any local spooks.

In Staple Fitzpaine near Taunton in Somerset we stayed at the Greyhound Inn which has been a coaching house and inn since the 1700s. While visiting with the landlord I jokingly asked if there were any local ghosts we could visit with. He said that while he'd never felt a presence, the kitchen staff say that sometimes they feel someone else is in the room with them when no one is about. He also said that a burly Irishman had stayed one night a couple years before. In the morning when he was asked how he'd slept, the Irishman replied, "I barely slept at all. I woke up in the middle of the night with hands around my neck and no one was there." The landlord didn't know if the Irishman had had a supernatural experience or just too many pints the night before.

Our next opportunity came at The Dolphin Inn in Penzance, Cornwall. We picked out this pub because of its very nice menu and reputation for food, as well as its reputation as a quite haunted inn. At least three ghosts haunt the inn: the old retired ship's captain, a young man who had committed suicide in the pub, and an elder lady who wanders amongst the upstairs rooms. We had a pint one night and a meal the next and never did see any of the resident spirits except the ones in our pints of cider.

On our exploration of Dartmoor National Park in Devon we were told by a visitor's centre docent to stop by the Warren House, the third highest inn in England. It was quite foggy on the moor, very atmospheric, so the Warren House pub was a lovely stop with its welcoming fire (which has been going for almost 200 years). The

landlord here was very chatty and when I asked about ghosts he said he wasn't sure if the inn was haunted or not. He then proceeded to tell us that there were certain places in the pub house that dogs wouldn't set foot, that the kitchen staff had seen fleeting images outside the kitchen when no was there, and that a publican had once been murdered behind the bar, but he wasn't convinced their spirits still roamed the house. Even when we went back for dinner later in the day, we still didn't find any evidence of ghosts, just friendly locals enjoying Sunday dinner.

Our last spooky place is considered the most haunted pub in England. The Red Lion in Avebury in Wiltshire is indeed special. The inn is in the middle of the largest ancient stone circle in the world. The Avebury circle, about 30 miles north of Stonehenge, is three-quarters of a mile around and consists of scores of very large stones. The Red Lion Pub has numerous eating areas as well as five resident ghosts. The staff have also reported seeing a phantom horse drawn carriage pull into the inn at night and hearing the ghostly clattering of hooves in the courtyard outside the pub. Though Prince Charles has eaten several times in the pub, not even his presence had brought out any of the spirits to seek a Royal audience.

Although we weren't successful in finding any evidence of real phantoms (now there's an oxymoron for you), we did enjoyed the search for English ghosts.

Loo of the Year or Flushing Out Britain's Best Toilets

Several times in our UK travels we've stopped at "award winning" loos. We particularly remember a loo in Lairg (Highlands) that was honored as "Loo of the Year." We thought it was nice, but we weren't sure what made it Loo of the Year. We have since found out that just like B&Bs are awarded Stars and restaurants get their rosettes, restroom facilities have a whole system of awards.

Loos are recognized for public conveniences, public toilets, cleaning staff (both in house and, pardon the pun, outhouse), baby changing facilities, and several other interesting categories. Awards are sponsored by companies such as Initial Washroom Solutions, Armitage Shanks, and the British Cleaning Council.

It's such a pleasure knowing when you enter a facility that your toilets are award winning, especially if they have received the coveted Five Star rating. We think these awards are so special that we have some suggestions for even more. How about Towel Dispenser of Magnificence. Best Bidet. Unanimously Selected Urinal. Or the Flusharama Award for Effective Disposal.

So that you can put the Loo of the Year Awards event on your calendar, the awards are given out each November--book your tickets early. The next Event is titled: Recognizing the Best Toilets for 27 Years.

Opps! Missed Opportunity.

On our first trip to the Isle of Arran, Scotland in Miniature between the Ayrshire coast and the Kintyre Peninsula, we took the tour of Isle of Arran Distillery in Lochranza in the northwest corner of the island. We were early enough in our travels that we had taken tours at only two or three other distilleries--we've now taken tours at 32 distilleries in Scotland and Ireland. The distillery tour was very interesting--Isle of Arran Distillery was quite new having opened in 1995--and we learned a great deal. At one time there were more than 50 distilleries on the small island, most of them illegal, but now Isle of Arran is the only one. As usual the distillery tour ended with a dram of the local product, in our case an eight year old Arran Single Malt. We thought the whisky tasted a little young--most single malts are bottled after ten years or more in oak casks--and decided not to buy a bottle. We also passed up on a special offer to participate in a Cask Owner's scheme: buy a cask (about 250 bottles when mature), and after ten or more years, sell the cask back to the distillery or bottle it for yourself. The cost at that time was about $1200-1500, and even after paying excise duty and storage, after ten years there should be some profit, or so the sales pitch went. We thought about it for a few moments, but decided we didn't have that kind of money to throw away on a whim.

Fast forward ten years to 2012. A cask of Arran Single Malt we could have bought for $1500 in 2002 would now bring about $15,000 when selling it back to the distillery. That's a thousand percent profit in ten years! Where else could you find that kind of return on your investment? The money may have sounded dear on that first visit, but the quality of the product and the reputation of the distillery would have turned a pretty profit. Oh, if we had only....

Can You Spell C-a-s-i-n-o?

As we drove into Bowness-on-Windermere in England's Lake District I thought I saw a sign which said "Casino." We parked and spent time wandering the shopping district in the tourist town. At the tourist information office I asked about the casino in town-- I've wanted to try British-style slots. The gal at the office said, "There's no casino here." I got the same response from another shop keeper. As Anne and I walked back towards the car I looked up and asked Anne what that sign said as I pointed to the side of a building with a large "Casino" sign on the front. We went in and played £20 in machines that weren't much fun. Either locals can't see or can't read or maybe "casino" is pronounced completely differently in Lake District English. Whichever is the case, I found out that I didn't need to look for "Casino" signs again.

Cawdor Castle and the Rude Americans

We first toured Cawdor Castle on our initial trip to Scotland in 2000. The tour has improved over the years and, even though only a few rooms were open for touring, was worth the visit. A tour group was going through the castle while we were there and the tour group was mostly Americans from Texas. They were quite rude! Several of the tour members had obviously spent too much time in the castle coffeeshop and gift shop and now had to hustle through to catch their bus. On guy shouted at another tourist (not a member of the tour) to "hurry up" when he was reading the room information. One lady said loudly, "Another bedroom. Hurumph! Who needs to see this!" Members of the tour group shoved their way past other tourists with a "I've got to catch a bus," but never an "excuse me."

It's people like these who give American tourists a bad name.

Let Me Describe a Bog

At the gate into the Callanish II stone circle on the Isle of Lewis in the Outer Hebrides islands of Scotland, I stepped into a "boggy area." I tested the stance in the mud, thankfully. My foot sank in the mud about four or five inches before I stopped—I hadn't touched anything firm. I couldn't find anyplace to get decent footing, so we went on to the next circle where I talked to a couple who thought I would have gone knee deep in the bog if I had put my full weight down.

That's what I call a bog!

The Blackhouse Village

On the Isle of Lewis in the Outer Hebrides there is a Blackhouse village called Gearrannan. It's made up of seven or eight stone, thatched roof cottages (or crofts). These double dry-stone walled cottages were built in the early 1800s and were lived in until the last resident left in 1974. Attesting to the primitive nature of these dwellings are the facts that residents used oil lamps for lighting until 1952 and that piped water didn't come into the village until the 1960s, and then it was piped to the community and not to individual houses.

We have a friend from Crieff, John Angus, who is our age (70s) and was actually born in one of the blackhouses at Gearrannan and lived there until in his late teens. Today, the village has been turned into a museum and self-catering cottages—I do believe they now have indoor plumbing.

Sunset at the Stones

One of the prime attractions of Isle Lewis and Harris in the Outer Hebrides is the Callanish Stone Circle (*Clachan Chalanais* in Gaelic), rivaling Stonehenge and Avebury for impressiveness. The stones are an arrangement of standing stones in a cross pattern with a small central stone circle and burial cairn. The Neolithic structure dates back as far as 3000 BCE and was in use for up to 1500 years.

Our first visit was on a mid-week morning. We toured the crowded Visitor Centre with bus loads of other tourists and then shouldered our way out to the stones. Even with at least two tour buses there when we wandered the stones, I still got a few photos with no people in them. We left the stones just as another two buses were pulling into the parking area.

Our second visit was later that same day. The weather was cold and windy, which made it biting cold, but the sky was cloudless. We arrived about an hour before sunset and instead of insane crowds we and six other people had the stones to ourselves. All of us were there to photograph the stones in the golden light of sunset. Except for one couple who didn't bother to keep their shadows from intruding on other's photos, everyone was respectful of the other photographers. We took turns at the various better vantage points and all eight of us stayed until the sun was well down and our fingers we well frozen. When Anne and left there was only one person staying to shoot the stones and the night sky—from the looks of his arctic-style clothing we guessed he was a local. Together Anne and I had taken about 400 pictures at the Callanish stones on this one day; crowds or no crowds, it was worth it.

Bridge to Nowhere

One of the strangest tourist attractions we've ever visited was on the east coast of the Isle of Lewis. We didn't know much about it, but were intrigued by its name, The Bridge to Nowhere. When we drove the twelve miles north from Stornoway on a small road to the bridge, we found out it was exactly what the name says. The road leads to a bridge over a substantial chasm and then stops. There's enough room to turn around (to go back over the bridge), but there's nothing on the far side at all—the bridge leads literally to nowhere.

We've looked up a little information about the bridge, but it is far more entertaining to speculate on the story of the bridge than to look up details and possible be disappointed by the truth.

Corcomroe Abbey, Tour Bus vs Car

Great bus tours are plentiful and can be a very effective mode of transport to see Ireland. But we choose to drive ourselves. It gives us more freedom and allows us to be flexible as we tour. Perhaps the best explanation of the advantages to self-touring can be summed up in one experience we had on our first tour of Ireland.

Corcomroe Abbey (*Mainstir Chorco Modhruadh* in Irish Gaelic) is a ruined 13th century Cistercian abbey in County Claire, Ireland, not far from Galway. Known as St Mary's of the Fertile Rock, the abbey is renown for its rich and ornamental carvings and was on our list of places to see on our first trip to Ireland. Set against the limestone rich hills of the Burren near the sea, the abbey is a prime tourist location.

When we visited the weather was typical of that first trip-- mist, rain, clouds, sun, wind, heavy rain, wait twenty minutes and the cycle starts over again. As we drove into the parking lot of the abbey we couldn't help but notice two things: first, the large tour bus in the lot, and second, we were in the heavy rain part of the cycle. Soon the bus horn sounded and wet tourists trundled back to their rolling cavern, which now I'm sure was steamy and smelled something like a wet puppy. Passengers from the bus were fighting with umbrellas in the wind as they struggled to get back on the dry bus. We on the other hand decided to sit in our cozy rented Toyota and wait for the rain to let up. The bus driver helped the final stragglers onto the bus, closed the door, and headed out toward whatever site was next on their itinerary. Still we sat and waited. In a couple of minutes the rain stopped, the sunshine streamed down through breaks in the clouds, steam rose off the wet stones, and we started our exploration of the now empty abbey ruins. Anne and I enjoyed our self-guided tour of the ruins--the ornate carvings, a tomb effigy, and intricate stonework.

The advantages of a car tour over a group bus tour can be numerous, but on this day waiting out the squall was a great advantage.

Merlinedale B&B in Crieff

CHAPTER 6: Bed and Breakfasts to Die For or In

Although we've stayed at the airport hotels when we've had to, our choice for lodging is the bed and breakfast or small guest house. These are more personal than hotels, and usually more comfortable. Price can be more economical or it can rival moderate price hotels. The tariffs at unique guest houses, such as Traquair House or Kilmichael House, approach or exceed five star hotels, but give great value if you value history. The other thing that bed and breakfasts offer is personality, of the house but more notably of the hosts. We've stayed in one or two bad places that you'll read about, but most of our stays have been extremely enjoyable. The following stories revolve around the lodgings, the hosts, and more often than not the guests.

The B&B from Hell

Sometimes you win, sometimes you lose. This day we lost. On our first trip to Ireland we used prepaid vouchers and the B&B and Farmhouse book to pick out our lodgings. We'd call ahead and get a reservation. All we had to go on was the description in the listing book and maybe a photo by the description. By everything we could tell *Cluain Mhuire* House in Dingle would be a good choice. It's a 50s ranch-style home with ensuite rooms and only a few blocks from the main tourist district of town. We called, they had a room, they'd take our voucher, all was set.

When we arrived at *Cluain Mhuire* in the late afternoon we rang the doorbell. The gentleman who greeted us at the door was in a welder's apron. He showed us the our room and checked us in. We threw our suitcase down and headed off to see Dingle town. The outside of the house looked quite attractive, just like the picture, but our first impression of the B&B was that it was sort of shabby with the main decoration in the living and dining rooms shelves of boxing trophies.

We forgot about our lodgings until after a full evening of sightseeing, eating, and bar hopping. When we got back to *Cluain Mhuire* and settled into our room for the night, we started looking more closely at our lodgings. Dust bunnies had taken up residence in every corner of the room and they were feeding on the dirt piled there. The blanket on the bed was dirty and we weren't too sure of the cleanliness of the linens. The ensuite toilet and shower was sort of built into a corner of the room and all the fixtures were ill-fitting. The room was cold and had a musty order as if it had been closed up for a serious while. It was an uncomfortable night, and it didn't get better in the morning.

At breakfast our fellow guests all quietly commented on the shabbiness of the rooms and overabundance of boxing trophies. Each guest was presented with a quarter bowl of cornflakes (stale we discovered), instead of the usual array of dry of cereals. For fruit, there were a few bananas on the table and some watered down orange juice. We were asked whether we wanted coffee or tea. We said coffee. We were asked again, coffee or tea? Yet a third time, coffee or tea? Each time we responded that we wanted coffee. We each got a cup of hot water with a tea bag in it. We were asked what we wanted for breakfast and handed a short menu. We made our selections and got something else. Anne had bacon, bangers, and tomato when she'd asked for no bangers. The lady across the way had asked for all bangers and got none. I had asked for a full cooked breakfast. I got one egg and a tomato. All of us asked for what we wanted, and took what we got. Boxing trophies!

We got out of there as quickly as we could.

B&B Guests from Hell

As almost permanent residents at Merlindale B&B in Crieff we've experienced almost as much as our hosts, the Cliffords. Jacky always says she could write a book about all the strange guests that have stayed at the B&B. We've seen enough to at least write a note or two about really strange guests we've met.

The strangest guest that comes to mind was a six-foot-two cross dresser who thought he had all of us fooled into believing he was a she. He and his companion booked into the B&B on a night that Jacky was serving a dinner for the guests, a real treat because it's always wonderful and she does it so seldom. As we all come down to dinner a few minutes before the appointed hour, I notice this tall guest with long blond hair, fairly short skirt, large boobs hidden under a t-neck top, with heavy makeup and a slight five o'clock stubble coming through. As dinner continues and the wine flows freely, the gal/guy's giggle gets more falsetto and the floppy wrists get floppier. At one point John Clifford pulls me into the kitchen and asks, "Is that really a man?" "I'd bet my house on it," was my reply. The evening ended with she/he wobbling up the stairs on his/her high heels. It could have been the abundance of wine at dinner, or perhaps a lack of practice. Jacky's grand meal had been overshadowed by a makeup-covered five o'clock shadow. In the morning she/he was overdressed and excessively made up, and still pretending. He and his companion probably thought they had fooled everyone, when in reality they fooled no one.

Then there was the Bastard Guest who didn't want to pay. This portly gentleman showed up at six o'clock one night, checked in, and demanded dinner. Jacky explained that dinners were only served upon prior arrangements. Mr. Bastard didn't like that answer. "Your sign out front says, 'Dinners served' and I want dinner," he said. Jacky again explained that dinners are served upon prior arrangement, and that he had made none. With that the BG said he'd report the B&B to the authorities (whoever they are) and he stormed out to find a pub. In the morning he arrived at the dining room at 7:30 and demanded breakfast, when the house rules are that breakfast is served at one 8:30 sitting. When Jacky told him full breakfast would be at 8:30 but that he was free to have cereal and fruit now, he huffed and said he was leaving. Jacky told him he was free to leave after paying his bill. He stuck out his credit card. Jacky told him that they didn't accept cards and he'd been told that when he checked in. Now he was raging mad and stormed about shouting and swearing. We all heard that rampage and the thud when he tripped over the step on the way out. As he threatened to sue, Jacky still would not let him get away without paying. He finally threw some bills at Jacky and stormed out. When John, who had been away and missed the fun, heard the story he said he would have thrown the bum out. To which Jacky responded, "Not without paying!"

Last year we had an incident in our room. Well, in our bathroom anyway. We stay in a room with a private bath across the hall--all the other rooms are ensuite. When we're staying we leave all our toiletries and extra clothes in the large bathroom. One day Anne came hustling downstairs to the kitchen where I was having tea with Jacky. Partially out of breathe she said, "There's someone in our bathroom taking a bath!" I said I'd check it out and went upstairs. Sure enough, through the bathroom door I could hear the water running and the splashing of a bather. Pounding on the door, I loudly called, "Hey, what are you doing in our bathroom?!" The splasher was quiet. "What are you doing in our bathroom?" I repeated. I heard the person get out of the bath and rustle around. Finally, the door opened and one of the other guests said, "I was just taking a bath--my room only has a shower." I let him stand there and drip while I berated him for invading our space when it was clear that our stuff was all over the room. He hurried to his room. Funny thing, he didn't show up for breakfast the next morning.

Cooking in Crieff--What Were We Thinking?

We discovered Merlindale B&B on our first Scotland trip and stayed there the last four days of that trip. The next year we booked in for 22 days, and when the attacks of 9-11 occurred we canceled a trip to London and stayed in Crieff an extra seven days. At one point in our stay our host, Jacky, asked if we would like to fix a typical American family meal for the Scottish family. We felt so much at home with the family that without hesitation we agreed.

Now came the planning. What do we fix? I do a mean spaghetti and meatball dinner at home, so we decided we'd fix an American-Italian dinner for our Scottish family. The appointed day arrived. We spent the morning shopping for all the ingredients, discovering in the process that we didn't know how grams equated to pounds. We bought what looked like the right amount of mince (ground chuck, the Scottish version of hamburger) for a dinner for ten.

I put together the spaghetti sauce and set it to simmer. Anne and I then began to make meatballs. In the middle of rolling a meatball, Anne stopped and exclaimed, "What the hell are we doing cooking dinner for Jacky and her family? She's a Le Cordon Bleu trained chef!" She was right, we were in a mess now. The family would hate our meal and we'd ruined our relationship with the family. At this point Jacky came in, looked at our pile of meatballs (over 90 in all), and said, "You've got far too many meatballs. We'd never eat all those." Then she left. Now we are absolutely devastated.

Vindication is sweet, though. At the end of the meal there wasn't a meatball left for Jesse or Jenky, the family's two Yorkshire terriers. John, who usually wants only Scottish fare, had had thirds. After dinner over tea in the kitchen, Jacky said that we could cook anytime.

Since that first cooking episode, we have cooked once or twice or more on each of our visits. Southern fried chicken (sort of northwest fried chicken) is on the menu every trip. We've now become famous for our refried bean dip to accompany the chicken. Tacos are an item we've introduced to the family--notice how all these are good old American cuisine. Beef stroganoff, barbecued hamburgers (made of mince), grilled pork chops, chocolate chip cookies, Earthquake cake (required now for family birthdays), Tolovana muffins (a specialty from an inn on the Oregon coast), and then there was the time John wanted American-style hash browns.

Anne and I often make hash browns at home for breakfast or dinner. It's so simple. Pull out a package of frozen Ore-Ida shredded potatoes, throw some of them in a pan with a little oil, spice them, fry them, and serve. Sure, John, we'll do hash browns for breakfast. Anne and I went to the local grocery store,

Somerfields, and found no frozen shredded potatoes. We drove to Stirling to Sainsbury (a bigger store) and found no shredded potatoes. To Perth to Tesco (an even larger store). No potatoes. We asked Jacky. "No, we don't have frozen shredded potatoes here." Now we're stuck. We have to make hash browns from scratch and neither Anne nor I have ever had to do that. Following an internet recipe, we shredded raw potatoes, squeezed as much water out as we could, and started frying. We planned about 15 minutes for cooking the potatoes. Wrong! Forty-five minute later the potatoes are starting to get brown. We finally served a poor batch of hash browns almost an hour late. By this time, though, everyone is so hungry that they ate them anyway. Even with the hash brown disaster, we keep getting asked to cook. I guess family is very forgiving.

The Dead Husband

We knew it would happen eventually, but we didn't know it would happen this way. In other situations we've come close to not having a place to stay when we've booked ahead. Near Lisdoonverna in Ireland one year we arrived and the B&B owners said they had no record of our reservation. When we showed them the email confirmation from them, the tune changed. At Boat House B&B in Wales, because of a change of ownership, they knew someone was coming, but they didn't know who. It was a real shock though in Mullingar, Ireland, in May 2006 when we found out we had no place to stay.

We drove through town looking for the B&B we'd booked several months earlier and had confirmed shortly before we left on our trip. We found the house on the main road fairly easily, although it looked to be closed up--no cars in the drive, no shades open. We knocked on the door and waited. Shortly after a second knock someone slowly opened the door. The young girl (late teens) just stared at us and said, "Yes?" We said we were the Joneses and had a booking for two nights. At this the girl looked startled and said, "We're closed. My father died four days ago and we told everyone that the B&B is shut." I told her we'd been traveling for three weeks and weren't anywhere to get communication. Her last comment was, "Wait a minute, I'll check with my mom." She shut the door.

We felt terrible for intruding, but we waited. About three or four minutes later the girl open the door again. She handed us a piece of paper with a name and address and said, "We're very sorry, but Malin Court B&B down the road said they could take you for the night." Again she closed the door.

We knew something like this might happen some time, but were still startled and shaken when it did. In the end it turned out all right for us. Malin Court B&B turned into a great two day stay--a return to B&B. We hope the family at the other B&B recovers well. For us that trip will always be the trip where the husband died.

Dirty Old Lady We Love You

Doolin is a small Irish community on the edge of The Burren on the west coast in County Clare. It's a village with two centers-- the port with a few shops and a pub, and a little less than a mile away two pubs, a couple of restaurants, and few houses. The port hosts a few fisher people and a passenger ferry out to nearby islands. Among the shops is a unique jewelry store (Anne found that one) and a great music shop with CDs of local artists (I found that one). None of these are the special draw to the village. Doolin's pubs are music central for Ireland. All three pubs, O'Conner's near the port, McGann's and McDermott's away from the harbour, have traditional music sessions every night, and McDermott's has some of the best pub meals in Ireland. Some people say the village is slightly commercial or touristy, but we've heard quality music every time we've visited any of the pubs. As big as is the draw of the music, we have another reason to go to Doolin--Mauve Fitzgerald and Churchfield B&B.

We discovered Churchfield B&B through a web search and have stayed there every visit to Doolin since. We fell in love with Churchfield at first sight. It's a lovely large converted house with a beautiful breakfast room and an upstairs lounge for guests. The most fascinating feature of Churchfield is its host Mauve Fitzgerald. Mauve is a character who makes sure you enjoy your stay at Churchfield. We've had great conversations with Mauve about the local area and music players in the pubs. She makes a tremendous rhubarb-ginger jam--I have to work hard to keep Anne from eating the whole jar full at breakfast. We have found out some other interesting things about Mauve.

Our friends Scott and Jane visited Doolin a couple of times and stayed with Mauve on our recommendation. Mauve seemingly has taken a shine to Scott. On each visit she has pulled him aside and quietly told him a dirty joke or story. Now Scott is about the least likely person in the world to be the target of an off-color joke. Mauve, on the other hand, has never told me even a slightly blue story and almost everyone knows I'm a dirty old man [see *Seisiuns* in Attractions]. She has also had Scott come into the kitchen to watch a horse race she had a bet on through a bookie. Gambling, dirty stories--obviously there is more to Mauve Fitzgerald than just rhubarb-ginger jam.

Doolin is a wonderful place to stay with great music available every day and Mauve Fitzgerald's Churchfield is the place to stay.

The Girls Who Broke Down

What a day! First, we attended the Morrison's Academy Harvest Assembly in which Ailsa (our adopted niece in Crieff) participated. It was a cute performance, but more Anne's thing than mine. From there we went to Gleneagle's and played the King's Course, one of the toughest courses in Scotland. The first time we played it on our second visit to Scotland, both Anne and I were very intimidate and played badly. With much more experience behind us, this time we played reasonably well.

In the evening at Merlindale B&B, our Scottish home, we were recounting all our good shots to Jacky, our B&B host and fellow golfer. At about 7:00 PM the doorbell rang, which Jacky thought was unusual because the "No Vacancy" sign was up. She went to the door and a couple minutes later came back into the kitchen and asked me if I could help with a car problem.

Three young, college age girls had been out for a day of touring when their car broke down directly in front of the B&B. When it comes to auto mechanics, even though I used to race GTIs in auto crosses and hill climbs, I'm not the snappiest pickle in the barrel--I might be able to change the oil and I can usually tell when the car isn't running, and that's about the limit of my knowledge. When I looked at the girl's car I could confirm for them that it wasn't running and that nothing we were going to do was going to get it running. With everyone's help (Jacky, Anne, Paulette, and the girls, John was at a meeting and missed all the excitement) we got the car pushed onto the street beside the B&B and off the main road. Jacky then invited the girls to come in so we could figure out how to help.

In the kitchen Paulette immediately produced a big pot of tea and plate of snacks. Jacky found a mobile phone charger so one of the girls could charge her phone. Another was lent Jacky's phone to call her father about an hour away in hopes that he could come and get them. Jacky had already come up with a plan for how to put up the girls overnight if the dad couldn't come and get them. Over tea and snacks we visited with the two Scottish lasses and one American who were all in universities in the area.

About 9:00 the father showed up and, with hugs and thanks all around, the girls were off to home. The car was to be picked up the next day. It was extremely impressive to see the openness of the Scots who were willing to make sure the three girls were safe and well cared for. I think there are many American families who would give the same aid, but I believe it would be with a great deal more reluctance and distrust.

Just one of the things we love about Scotland.

Hairy Fruit

The difficulty with writing travel guides is being fair with our evaluations and recommendations. It's a fine line between being cautious with our evaluations and being unnecessarily critical. The question we always ask ourselves is does our bias show through too much. I don't like beds with plastic mattress pads; they make the bed feel clammy to me. So, if a farmhouse B&B in Forres, Scotland, has plastic mattress pads should the B&B get a poor rating from us? A breakfast at a B&B in Falkirk is fine, but isn't quite as good as our favorite B&B in Crieff. Is that reason enough for a weaker recommendation? And what about hairy fruit?

On at least three different occasions, out of the 85 or so different B&Bs we've stayed at, fruit on the breakfast table or breakfast sideboard was furry with mold. We can see how it would happen. The fruit sits out for a couple of days and nobody takes any. The fruit on the bottom starts turning grey, but the rest of the bowl looks good. The hosts sees only the good looking fruit, but a guest wanting the orange on the bottom finds the mold. Not wanting to embarrass the host, we don't show them the fruit, but we do turn it so the hairy side is up.

Who'd have thought when we started this writing that we'd be analyzing the hairiness of breakfast fruit?   Certainly neither of us.

Hotel Hell in Wales

The name was quaint.   The internet pictures looked great. The description was fantastic.   The recommendations were outstanding.   The price was brilliant.   The reality, as the Scots would say, was shite!

We were disappointed almost immediately when we pulled up in front of the Prince of Wales Hotel in Caernarfon.   The exterior was a little shabby and a good coat of paint was in order.   The interior wasn't a whole lot better, but at first glance the room was acceptable, especially for the price.   We were booked in for two nights in a room a long way down the hall and upstairs from the main pub and reception area. That was going to be important because, as the receptionist told us there was to be an 18th birthday party that night for one of the staff. She assured us though it would be a quiet party and be done early. We parked across the street where they told us and went to tour the fabulous Caernarfon Castle and then to have dinner at Molly's Restaurant, which was a good recommendation by the hotel staff.

That was the only thing good that the staff did. When we got up to our room after dinner we looked at our digs more carefully. The dust bunnies were having a convention under the dresser and planning to attack the random bunnies scattered in other corners. The bed clothes were tattered, but at least clean.   Then the noise from the party wafted up the stairs and down the hall to our room. The noise came and the noise lasted. 11:00. 12:00. 1:00. About 1:30 AM we finally got to sleep.

Breakfast kept the staff record going.   We arrived at the breakfast room to find no juice. We got juice when we asked for it, but there were no glasses. We got cereal and then found there were no spoons. The couple at the next table leaned over and said, "Is this Fawlty Towers?" We knew exactly what they meant. We met them again at the reception desk as we were both checking out early. The staff didn't even bother to ask why we'd cut our stay short.

When we got out to our car we discovered that the lot the hotel staff had told us to park in was locked and would stay locked until five in the afternoon--the lot was not the property of the hotel. We could have gone in to complain to the hotel staff, but why bother. I climbed over a fence and found a route out of the lot over a garbage heap and down an alley (it was a rental car).

We wanted nothing more to do with the Hotel from Hell!

An Irish Sing-along

Tom and Val are magnificent hosts to guests at Dunromin B&B in Kilkenny, Ireland. We've sent many people to stay there and every one of them comes back with the same report. We didn't realize how special a stay was at Dunromin until our second stay there.

The morning we were to leave to head toward golf in Killarney was my birthday, and we discovered it was also Tom's birthday (same day, same year). We had enjoyed a grand breakfast with two Australian lady teachers when Tom said, "You all must come into the parlour for an old fashioned Irish sing-along." We'd been in about 30 Irish B&Bs and had never had one suggest a sing-along. Tom insisted. In the parlour, one of the Australian girls sat down at the piano, Val gave us all sheet music of favorite Irish tunes, and Tom brought out a homemade, foot-operated bodhran (Irish drum) and an accordion. While everyone played and/or sang, I took photos--Anne doesn't let me sing, she says I can changed keys faster than a pianist can hit notes. We ended with a fairly competent rendition of "Danny Boy." Great fun!

We told our friends Scott, Jane, and Marcia, who were staying at Dunromin after us, to expect a sing-along. We heard after that Tom and Val did give them the Irish sing-along experience.

Mistaken Identity

Excited by the prospect of what looked to be a special stay in a fantastic B&B, we pulled into Laugharne in southern Wales, drove past the castle and path down to Dylan Thomas's Boathouse (where he did much of his writing), and parked in front of the Boat House B&B. We rang the bell and introduced ourselves to Angi, who looked at us a little strangely, but showed us to the Towy Suite. When we asked about her husband George a look of recognition came over her face. Anne, not Angi, then introduced herself and her daughter Jenni who had recently bought the Boat House from Angi and George. They said Angi and George had left our reservation, but no details or contact information. We had a good laugh about the mistaken identities and a wonderful stay at a premier B&B.

The Only Guests

Our first visit to Scotland included a stay at Traquair House, the oldest inhabited house in the country. The house has been in use since sometime in the 900s, first as a hunting lodge and then as a Great House or castle. The Bear Gates, at one time the entrance

to the estate, are famous for having been closed when Bonnie Prince Charlie left in 1745 and never having been reopened. The laird of Traquair House, a Stuart, said the gates would remain closed until a Stuart regained the throne--it hasn't and will never happen. Our nephew, studying to be a travel agent, booked us in to Traquair House for a night.

When we drove up to the estate, now consisting of the main house (which has several rooms open for public touring), a brewery, and a small craft village, we checked in at the gate keeper's kiosk. She checked our name and said, "Okay, you're the guests." A strange turn of phrase we thought. We were told to pull up to the house and we'd be met there. A steward did meet us as we parked, checked her paper work, and said, "You're the guests." There it was again, "The guests." We asked and found out that indeed Traquair has only two rooms to let and no one was in the other room--we were the only guests for the evening. Our lodgings consisted of a large period decorated bedroom, wonderful full bath, and access to a lovely sitting room. Besides the two of us the only other occupants of the castle would be Lady Catherine Stuart (direct descendant of Mary Queen of Scots), her family, and a steward to care for us. Traquair House is a fantastic place to play Lord and Lady for an evening, and in the morning have a sumptuous Scottish breakfast in the Still Room filled with shelves of fine china.

Being the "only guests" was a once in a lifetime experience, but one that came back to us several years later. On another trip we took our friend Marcia out to see Traquair House. When the stewards found out that Anne and I had actually spent a night in the house, everyone treated us like long lost family. As Anne and Marcia toured the museum portion of the house, I visited the brewery in a wing of the house opposite the wing we stayed in. A wedding celebration was in progress and many of the wedding guests not involved with photos out on the lawn were tasting the local brew. When the party found out I was a visiting American who had stayed in the house, they started passing extra samples over to me. Two of the special brews made at Traquair are quite strong, 7% ABV and 8% ABV. By the time Anne and Marcia found me, I could just barely manage to drive the two miles to our dinner pub.

What a great experience, being the only guests!

Alone in the B&B

One of the great benefits to staying in a bed and breakfast is the personalized service you get from your hosts...usually. There have been a couple of times when we've stressed over a lack of personal touch. It doesn't happen often, but twice we've found ourselves alone in a B&B.

The first occasion was when we stayed at the Log House Restaurant and B&B in Ambleside in England's Lake District. On our spring trip in 2011 we had booked the Log House, actually shipped over from Norway and reassembled in Ambleside, for two nights. Our room was small, mostly because of the sloped ceiling of the large A-frame designed building, but nicely appointed and comfortable. Breakfasts both days were delicious and different than the normal B&B fare—special pastries, breads, cheeses, fruit, juices, and the full English breakfast. Our only problem with the place was that for the second night we'd be alone in the B&B from mid-afternoon on—the restaurant was closed for the evening and we were the only guests booked in for the night. That spooked us into talking about looking for a different stay for that night. We were assured that there was phone contact with the manager in an emergency and that the building would be secure. In the end, we decided we liked the room and the breakfast well enough to overcome our trepidation about being alone. We're glad we made that decision, the evening was fun being Lord and Lady of the manor.

The second incident occurred a couple of years later when we visited in the Cotswolds area of England. That day we drove from Tavistock in the Dartmoor region to Stonehenge and then to the Avebury stone circle before checking in at our B&B in Stow-on-the-Wold. Little Broom B&B is just out of the village (about a 10 minute walk) and it's a working horse farm or ranch. When we arrive the owner said she had to be away that evening to take care of a friend's horsey problem. She gave us the keys, told us we couldn't use the kitchen or have a fire in the guest lounge fireplace, though we could use the room. She also gave us the phone number of her daughter across town and said she'd come over in the morning to get our breakfast. She told us there was a family staying in a self-catering unit on the estate, but that first night we'd be alone in the house. She hooked up her horse trailer and was off. It wasn't a very comfortable night. Where the Log House in Ambleside had been in the heart of town, Little Broom B&B was out in the country and fairly isolated.

We're planning to go back to the Log House in Ambleside on our next trip to the Lake District, but we'll seek different accommodations in Stow-on-the-Wold.

Scotland's Catalina

We've stayed in some wonderful B&Bs in Scotland, Ireland, England, and Wales. Merlindale is our home-away-from home in Crieff, Scotland. Tom and Val and Barbara and Michael at Dunromin (Kilkenny) and Milestone (Dingle) are Irish family. The Boathouse B&B in Wales is a place we must get back to. The most unique of temporary homes, though, is Catalina Guest House in the far north of Scotland.

Catalina accepts only one guest (or couple) at a time--no children or pets. The accommodations are outstanding. As guests you get a suite of rooms (bedroom, sitting room, dining room, and bathroom) to yourself in a wing separated from the rest of the house. If that isn't enough privacy, the guest house is located on Strathy Point on the edge of the North Sea. The nearest neighbor is about a mile away south toward the main road (single track though it is). A lighthouse is about two miles east on the coast, and the nearest settlement west is only a little over 20 miles away. North the nearest land is probably the Orkney Islands. Catalina is the definition of isolated.

There are more unique features to Catalina Guest House. It is a nonsmoking establishment. It is so nonsmoking that guests must be nonsmokers, not just not smoking in the house. If there is a hint of smoke about you, they will cancel your reservation and they tell you that ahead of time. The B&B has won several "Clean Air" awards and intends to keep winning them. Jane and Pete strictly enforce the nonsmoker policy.

That brings me to the other unique feature of Catalina, Jane and Pete Salisbury the guest house owners. Not only are they great hosts, but they are fascinating individuals. The couple are world travelers who have competed in both long distance bicycling and canoeing. Jane, an artist in several media, sells paintings and stained glass pieces, and is a world renowned needlepoint designer. Their passion for the guest house and for life, make a stay at Catalina fascinating. Oh, they serve great scrumptious breakfasts and dinners as well.

Seven Dozen Eggs and a Rough Road

When you're adopted by a Scottish family, as we have been by the Cliffords at Merlindale B&B in Crieff, the adoption comes with some responsibilities. We've been asked to take Ailsa, the 13-year-old to hockey practice on a rainy day. We were expected to come over to Scotland for Jonathan's Speech Day (graduation awards ceremony) and 18th birthday. I've helped John unload the garage of items going to a sale. Anne has done the shopping with Jacky for the week's groceries. The most unusual request, though, was to pick up some eggs for the B&B.

As a busy bed and breakfast Merlindale goes through endless fresh eggs. On a day we were out for golf and coming home through Perth, Jacky asked us to take the old road from Perth to Crieff and stop at a particular farm to pick up some fresh free range eggs. The catch was we had to pick up seven dozen eggs!

The back road to Crieff is a narrow, bumpy road used mostly by farm implements and locals. As we bounced along the route we'd never taken, we almost went past the egg farm. With a quick backup, we pulled in by the selling shed. There was nobody

about when we went in the shed, saw the crates of eggs (firsts on one table, seconds on the other), and an honesty box for money. We picked through the crates of 30 eggs each on the seconds table to find the crinkliest shells and the largest eggs as Jacky suggested. Jacky said the crinkly shelled eggs have better flavor and the big ones are often double yoked. We picked up seconds because they were half the price of firsts and the same quality except not as pretty. Saving a little while providing quality fare is important when running a top rated B&B, besides Jacky is Jewish and married a Scot, so of course is frugal.

Now for the ride home. How do we get three crates of 30 eggs each home safely? Answer---Anne holds them in her lap and I drive as slowly and carefully as I can on a small, rough road for twelve miles. We ended up first in line behind a school bus dropping off children. Cars behind couldn't figure out why I wouldn't pass the slow moving school bus. I held my ground and let them pass us both while I thought about what hitting one bump too hard would do to the fragile cargo. Finally, as we got closer to home, Anne said weakly, "Can't you go faster; I can't hold them much longer."

We made it home without a single casualty. No Humpty Dumpty in our car.

Irish Soda Bread

B&Bs are very accommodating. If you have a special need the hosts will go out of their way to try to help. Often the thing you need is not even something you know you need.

On our second visit to Dingle we discovered Milestone B&B. It's a modern ranch-style home on the outskirts of the village. In the front yard by the driveway is a 14-foot tall, four thousand year old standing stone, the Milestone, one of a set used in ancient times for navigation. We were met at the door by Barbara Carroll, our host, who greeted us with, "Do you like good Irish music? I can get you tickets to special concert this evening and I'll get you booked into good pub before the concert." The concert was special and it is something we would have never found out about on our own. That's not the point to this story, though. It's really about Michael Carroll, Barbara's husband and cook for the B&B.

The next morning, after a wonderful concert and a peaceful night in the B&B, we went to breakfast. The breakfast was very good with some excellent homemade soda bread. We had an opportunity to visit with Barbara and Michael and talk about the B&B, the area, and about golf (they're both members at *Ceann Sibeal* Golf Club out at the end of the Dingle Peninsula, where we were going to play at noon). During the conversation we mentioned that we had some cheese and crackers (biscuits, they'd call them) that we'd have for lunch on the course. As we got ready to head out for a day of touring and golf, Barbara came out with a parcel for us. The package contained a full loaf of Michael's special soda bread. Barbara said, "Michael believes that good Irish cheese needs something better than packaged biscuits."

Just like we didn't know about the concert, we didn't know we needed the soda bread, but Barbara and Michael did.

The Spirits of the B&Bs

In Peebles, Scotland, at the first B&B we ever stayed in, Anne had some strange dreams. She would wake up as if in intense pain or as if she were hurt. This happened several times over the three visits we had to that B&B. Then at the B&B we call home in Crieff, she would wake up again with a sense of pain, although not as deep as in Peebles, and with a feeling of tremendous sadness. These feelings wouldn't last long and were easily dismissed. It wasn't until after several trips to Scotland that we began to understand a possible cause of these apprehensions.

On our second visit to Merlindale in Crieff, owner John Clifford lent me a book about our other favorite B&B, Lindores in Peebles. The book was *Leaves from the Life of a Country Doctor* by Dr. Clement Gunn. It tells the story of his career as a doctor in Peebles from the 1890s until he retired in 1933. Lindores was the house he built as his home and his doctor's office or surgery--each doctor's home would be like a small hospital where he would see outpatients and house patients too ill to let go home. A couple of years later John told me the history of Merlindale which from the 1950s to the 1980s was also a doctor's home and surgery, though the more serious patients would have been moved to hospital rather than let stay in the surgery.

We now have a good guess why Anne would have those specific feelings at those two B&Bs and no others. Somehow she would pick up on or sense the emotions that had happened in the rooms where we stayed. Rooms converted from surgeries to ensuite bedrooms in a B&B. These two B&Bs and one other where we've stayed have special histories.

Lindores was built in 1895 and occupied by Dr. Gunn and his family on August 31 of that year. For 38 years it was the local surgery. When Dr. Gunn retired, the village created a small garden area a few doors from Lindores dedicated to the doctor. A plaque still in place on the gate to the house reads:

> And one day smoke will rise, and windows in the morn
> Grow bright, through pass the founder to the tryst
> Which all must keep:--God grant his soul meet Christ!
> --From a poem by Dr. Clement Gunn

When the good doctor left, Lindores ceased to be a surgery and became a family home. In the late 1980s Carl and Kathryn Lane bought the house and refurbished it into a pleasant B&B. Lindores stayed a busy bed and breakfast until 2005 when the Lanes sold it to a local hotel and it became a specialty lodging for conventioneers. In the past year it has been sold by the hotel and converted into a B&B again. I wonder if any of the current guests have strange dreams?

Merlindale in Crieff, our Scottish B&B home, began as a family dwelling in 1867 and wasn't converted into a surgery until the 1950s. The doctor there lived and worked in the house until it was sold in the mid-1980s to a family who converted it into a B&B. The Cliffords bought the B&B, added several rooms, changed its name to Merlindale, and opened for business in 1995. Today it is one of Perthshire's best B&Bs and winner of several awards. In the Pink Room there may be some special spirits besides the whisky John and Jacky serve to guests upon arrival.

A third B&B we've stayed in with a special medical history is Craigard House Hotel in Campbeltown far south on the Kintyre Peninsula. The house was built in 1882 by local whisky distiller William McKersie who vied with his brother to see who could build the finest house. Already you can see the spirit connection. The house remained in the McKersie family until bought by the local Council for use as a maternity home from 1942 until 1973. The majority of local people in those years were born in the house. Since being converted to a guest house hotel in the late 1990s, many "Babies of Craigard" and "Mothers of Craigard," as well as several doctors and midwives, have signed in at the guest house. At least one marriage of children of Craigard has taken place in the house, with the newlyweds spending their wedding night in the room in which they were born. Now, that's the spirit!

Substitute Wait Help

We've been staying at Merlindale B&B in Crieff in central Scotland for so long that we know all the routines. That has advantages and disadvantages. If at the breakfast table one of the girls who set up the table forgot to put out a spoon for the jam, Anne knows where those are. If the table is full and John is running back and forth taking and bringing orders and coffee cups are low, I know to go into the kitchen and grab the pot and do a pour around the table. During our time in Crieff I've had fun filling in for John at breakfast a time or two.

One morning John awoke with a terrible toothache--we later found out that he had a hard seed stuck under a partial. He wasn't going to be his usual shining personality, so I volunteered to step in. I knew the routine well enough to take guests orders, bring coffee and tea, and deliver breakfasts, although I was never quite sure from which side I should serve. In another instance, John was under the weather from minor surgery the day before and I was able to fill in again. On normal days, making coffee or tea forays into the kitchen and pouring for guests is a great conversation starter and always seems to liven up the breakfast table.

When I fill in at breakfast for John, I know I am just a substitute for the day. Like a substitute teacher for me when I was teaching was just doing a temporary job, I have no illusions that I'm filling John's shoes, besides his are size 12 and mine are 10s.

Tudor House

We've stayed in expensive lodgings before--Traquair House in the Borders and Kilmichael House on Isle Arran were both in the $250 a night range. We've stayed in old places before--Traquair House has been continually inhabited for 1000 years or more. We'd never stayed in a B&B like Tudor House in Shrewsbury, England.

The B&B is right in the middle of town and almost impossible to find [see Driving: GPS]. When we did find it we were lucky to find any place to park. There were metered parking spots in the alley near Tudor House and we got one of those. Every hour until 6 p.m. and starting at 8 a.m. the next morning, we had to run out and plug the meter (buy the ticket and put it in the car window). The house, though, is as lovely as it is ancient and expensive (£120 for the night).

The black and white Tudor-style house was supposedly built in 1460, although the owner of the pub connected to Tudor House said it was more likely built in 1640. The house has a charming dining room where we had breakfast has a beautiful brick fireplace. The rooms are all decorated with period furnishings (except for the flat screen TVs which do seem slightly out of place). To get to our room at the head of the central staircase, we had to climb, at the top literally on our hands and knees, the tiniest, narrowest steps I'd ever seen. The bedroom had room for a double bed, a dresser, and enough room to squeeze in sideways between the two. The room was so small we had to leave our suitcase on the landing blocking the second bedroom--luckily we were the only guests that night. The view out one window was of the roof, but the other window looked out to the 13th century church next door. To get down the stairs was a little easier since you sort of sat down each step until you got to the first landing.

Breakfast was delicious. The pub next door, The Three Fishes, was great for dinner and visiting with locals. The shopping around the B&B was fun. Tudor House in Shrewsbury, though, was definitely a different place to stay.

Voices in the Wall

It was a lovely afternoon for watching the Lamlash Bay lap on the shore of Isle Arran. After a great round of golf at Shiskine GC, we had stopped at Arran Cheese and picked up a couple of rounds and some crisps (what we'd call crackers) for snacking. Back in our room at Lilybank B&B we had cut into one of the cheese rounds, broken out some crisps, poured two generous drams of Lochranza single malt scotch, and were sitting back enjoying the view of the bay and the Holy Isle. We were the only guests so far in the B&B, but yet we could hear voices. The closer we listened, the more the voices seemed to be coming from the wall of our room. Was it the whisky? Was our room haunted? The voices were indistinct, yet they were recognizable as voices. I walked over to the wall for a closer listen.

I couldn't tell what they were saying or where exactly the voices were coming from, but they seemed to be repeating the same refrain. I went to the door and listened outside the room. No, they seemed to be just in the wall of our room. As I moved along the wall to try to pinpoint the voices, the sound moved from the wall to my backpack which leaned against the wall.

It took me only a moment to find my mini voice recorder, the one I use for verbal notes as we play a golf course. Somehow it had turned on and was playing back the same sentence describing a hole from the previous day's golf. Mystery solved, but it might have been a better story had it been a talking mouse in the wall or the spirit of a former guest who really didn't want to leave the place.

Gaelic Coffee

On our second visit to Scotland in 2001 we met Ben and Margaret from Yorkshire who were staying at the same B&B, Merlindale in Crieff. In retirement Ben and Margaret spent quite a bit of time in Scotland, most of it at Merlindale. One evening we had a special dinner at the B&B. Special because our host Jacky is a Le Cordon Bleu trained chef and special because she didn't do these dinners often. The four course meal with wine bottles that seemed never to empty was a highlight of our trip. But poor Margaret had difficulty enjoying the evening meal. Earlier in the day Margaret had work done to a tooth and she felt the effects. She passed on the dessert, a lovely tiramisu, but she hadn't passed on the wine. Nor did Margaret turn down the Gaelic coffee offered. Gaelic coffee is a delicious combination of black coffee, Scotch whisky, raw brown sugar, and heavy cream. Margaret relished the sweet strong after-dinner drink--so much so that as she reached the bottom of the mug she held it up with both hands and licked the sides of the cup. She was smiling broadly as Ben helped her up the stairs towards bed. Not surprisingly, Margaret wasn't at breakfast the next morning.

A recipe for a great Gaelic coffee: into a warmed mug, with sugar on the rim, place a sugar cube (or equivalent) and pour a shot of your favorite Scotch or Irish whisky into the mug. Light the whisky and while burning fill to three-quarters full with black coffee. Finally, fill mug with whipped cream. Serve.

Cheating the Taxman

The IRS in the US has very few friends. We know that the taxman is just doing his necessary job, but it doesn't mean we have to like the IRS. In the UK it is the same. The feelings against the taxman in Scotland and Wales are particularly strong since all their tax money is being sent to London (at least that's the way the locals see it). In Aberystwyth, Wales, we stayed twice in a very nice B&B which would want to stay anonymous. Because we'd stayed before we were offered a great discount if we'd pay in cash for our lodging. We said that was no problem and that we'd settle up in cash in the morning. In the morning as I was getting ready to pay, our host shushed me and quickly pulled me aside. It seems the other couple who we visiting with at breakfast was a tax agent (similar to an IRS agent) and his wife, a tax lawyer. Our host said it wouldn't do for them to see her taking our cash payment, especially because when she did take my cash she put the money in her pocket--no record, no tax. I went back to the breakfast room and visited more with the other guests. No harm, no foul.

Night Noises and a Strange Animal Pen

We found a lovely B&B in the Dumfries area of southern Scotland in the isolated village of Twynholm. We had a quite nice large bedroom at Linnhope B&B, but a couple of things made the stay more unusual. First, on the menu for breakfast was "trout and scrambled eggs--when available." There was a handwritten note on the menu: "Available now." I ordered the trout because Sue, the B&B owner, is a fly fishing instructor and I figured she'd know how to do trout well. I was right. Breakfast was delicious home-smoked fresh trout and eggs. Fantastic!

The second reason Linnhope was special is stranger. In the night we heard scrabbling noises above our bedroom, but the house is only one story. We figured the noises were from some varmint in the rafters above the room; a squirrel or mouse. The noises never disturbed our sleep. In the morning we looked out to the manicured backyard and saw a strange animal pen (our guess) in the yard. It was about an eight foot square fenced in by 2x12 planks. In one corner there was what looked liked a small dog's house. We couldn't figure out what the pen was for--it wouldn't have kept in cats, small dogs, or rabbits. At breakfast we asked about the pen. Sue said, "It's for the tortoises." She explained that they have two pet tortoises who spend the day out in the pen and the nights in the house in the rafters above our room. Ah, the noises in the night explained! She went on to explain that the tortoises made great pets because in the winter when they close up the B&B the tortoises hibernate in boxes of excelsior in the attic. Then she said that right now they were overfeeding them to get ready for hibernation and then they would "purge the little guys" before putting them to bed. She left the "purging" details to our imagination.

No Power

The May storm hit with great fury. Winds to 80 miles per hour lashed at the trees around Merlindale B&B in Crieff where we spend most of our time in Scotland. Anne and I had been out and about--Sma'Glen, Aberfeldy, the Birks of Aberfeldy--and the light breeze of the morning was starting to get stronger as we drove through Perth heading home. The B&B took a hit when a large branch of a tree crashed through the back fence, but no cars were damaged in the parking area. Neighbors weren't so lucky. Up the side road from the B&B about three houses a set of four trees came down directly onto a relatively new Toyota. We were more affected by the power lines the four trees took out.

In the aftermath of the storm the B&B was mostly without power for two days. This led to some interesting scenarios. First, when we discovered we couldn't fix dinner at the B&B the family and some other guests all went to the Lounge, a nice tapas restaurant on the other side of town which still had power. The new guests, Margaret and Robin, soon became the newest family adoptees--it's a friendship we've maintained now for several years. The next crisis was how to fix breakfast for eight paying guests and the family the next morning. By candlelight Jacky planned the best cold breakfast she could under the conditions and hoped for the best. In the morning the power came on at 7:30 for two hours--just long enough to feed everyone a full Scottish breakfast and clear up after.

The storm also provided some entertainment. The whole neighborhood watched the power company hack the trees off the totaled Toyota and put up a new power pole. Later we all made a pool with our guesses for a £1 about what time the power would come back on. The power company had said it would take about two hours, which would be about 6:30 PM. Anne won the £9 pool with a guess of 11:30--the power had come on at 11:23.

We noticed other consequences of the storm over the next few days. First, the weather continued to be very unsettled. On a visit to Killin we noted that the weather changed faster than Clark Kent in a phone booth can change into Superman. One minute we were in bright sun and two minutes later grey soggy clouds. While in Killin, a Highland village at the foot of the mountains, we saw that the normally fast-flowing peaty-brown cascade known as the Falls of Dochart was a raging torrent--a mix of white and brown foam spewing into the trees beside the river. Rocks you can normally walk on for better views of the river were now completely covered. A half mile up a muddy road from Killin was the Kinnell Farm stone circle. Normally the circle is quite impressive, but it lost a little of its luster being covered in storm debris. Two days later we tried to visit one of Scotland's premier attractions, Scone Palace and the Stone of Destiny, but the attraction was closed because of storm damage. St John's kirkyard in Perth was also closed because of downed trees.

We had been in thunder storms in Scotland and played golf in really strong winds, but this storm, while not fun, was indeed interesting.

Skinny Scots Eat Everything or the Names Are Changed to Protect the Hungry

Mrs. A and Mr. D are frequent visitors to one particular B&B in Scotland where we also have been known to show up. A and D live in the far north of Scotland and have a berry farm. When they come down to the B&B they bring berries to the host for jam. Both A and D are very skinny, but they eat tons. At one dinner with the family Mr. D had three large bowls of the host's stew with boiled potatoes. I had one small bowl with one potato and was pleasantly full. At breakfast A and D ate everything on the table (the fruit, the yogurt, juices) then they had porridge and full monties (large Scottish cooked breakfasts) and ordered more toast. I've heard tales of D eating the jam straight out of the bowl of jam on the table. Their normal breakfast at home is nine raisins and five almonds each. Those of us in the B&B figure that A and D come south just to eat.

The Run on Porridge

Porridge, boiled ground, crushed or chopped cereal (in Scotland it's oats), has been a staple of the Scottish diet since Medieval times when it was eaten hot by crofters for breakfast and cold for lunch--and maybe even fried for dinner. Tradition (and superstition) says the porridge should be stirred with a wooden spoon or *spurtle* (thick wooden stick) with the right hand in a clockwise direction to ward off evil spirits. If you microwave your porridge today there is a seven step ritual performed which includes the sacrifice of a lamb in order to ward off the irradiated evil spirits. Eaten usually with milk, Scots will salt their porridge while we heathens add sugar.

Porridge is a real breakfast treat in the B&Bs in Scotland. Most of the time the porridge is very traditional, but in Durness at Glengolly B&B in the far northwest corner of Scotland I got a quite special edition. My breakfast porridge came like a brulè with burnt sugar on top and then a dram of Highland malt whisky was added. Delicious! The best porridge, though, is the porridge made by John Clifford I get almost every day at Merlindale B&B in Crieff.

Because we are oversea's family I get porridge even if it's not on the normal breakfast menu at the B&B. Every once in a while a guest or two will see my porridge and ask if it is available for them and it always is. There was one day though when the B&B was full (eight guests) and one of the guests asked about porridge before I even got mine (so nobody can blame it on me). John said, "Of course, for you my dear." Suddenly everyone wanted porridge besides the normal full cooked breakfast. There was a run on porridge! A new batch had to be started and the kitchen was kept busy with both the regular breakfasts of Scottish bacon, eggs, sausage, fried bread, potato scones, roast tomatoes, mushrooms, and toast, and the demand for John's porridge.

After breakfast John and Jacky said it had been the biggest run on porridge in 17 years of running the B&B. The next day, with a different group of guest, I was the only one to have porridge. It had been a one-day run.

The Signs Change

To get an opportunity to play the challenging links course at Silloth on Solway in Northumberland, we booked in at Wallsend House, a classy B&B at the rural village of Bowness on Solway, England. Wallsend takes it name from being at the west end of Hadrian's Wall, the Roman fortification meant to keep the savage Scotti and Picts out of Roman Britain.

To get to Wallsend House required turning off the main road near Carlisle onto a series of hedge-lined back roads following signs to Bowness on Solway. We stayed at Wallsend for three nights as we played golf and explored the Lake District. Each day we'd return to the B&B taking what seemed like a different route. We didn't question our directions much because the hedges lining the roads make them all look the same anyway. We always got back to Wallsend by following the signs.

On the last morning as we were chatting with our host Patsy Knowles we mentioned how easy it was to find our way back to the house by following the good signs. Patsy exclaimed, "What? You followed the signs!" We said that was how we got back and forth so easily each day, although, the route did seem to vary a little. At that point Patsy said, "You must lead charmed lives. The signs you've been following turn in the wind and will point a different direction every hour. You could have been driving in circles in the farmland for hours before you found your way out by the signs."

We had a great laugh, but as we followed signs to get back to the Carlisle highway we were very careful to keep track of our route on our map as well.

Holly and Claire

As soon as we arrived at Merlindale in Crieff for our spring 2014 trip Jacky told us there would be a "special" guest at the B&B, at least for the last day of our stay before heading north. She had gotten a call for a booking from Holly in Chicago who had chosen Merlindale "because of Bob's book." Holly booked in with her daughter, Claire, for four nights--her husband and son were coming for the last three nights of the booking. According to Jacky, Holly was "over the moon" when she found out we would be at the B&B for her first night. Holly, who had called several times with special requests, gushed (Jacky's term) about the stories in my travel book, *Ten Years of Travel in Scotland, Ireland, England, and Wales.*

Our last day before going north to Aviemore I heard guests arrive in the afternoon and went out into the hall to meet my fan (Holly) and her daughter. Holly is 50ish--a bubbly, exuberant pixie with short hair. Claire is about 19, had spent the year coaching Lacrosse in an English private school, and always smiles. Holly said she just loved the travel book--my "writing makes the stories come alive," she said. We visited in the hall for half an hour and then I invited them to have a drink with Anne and me in the lounge. There we spent a good hour talking about stories, helping them plan their Scotland time, and finding out about them. Later Anne told me she had overheard Holly saying to Claire, "They're just like I imagined them."

In the morning over breakfast we continued to help the two with their plans and gave them a copy of *Golf in Scotland II* (our latest golf guide) for the husband and son who were golfers.

It was great fun being a Rock Star for a few hours.

CHAPTER 7: We, the People

Of course, almost all the stories so far have involved a variety of people--golfers, B&B guests, restaurant owners, attraction stewards, etc. This chapter, though, focuses on stories about the people we've met who aren't pegged in other categories.

One-Ear

Kilfenora, Ireland is a small village on the edge of The Burren, a hundred square mile limestone area famous for its barrenness and stark beauty--an area which Cromwell called a "wild, barren, unreclaimable waste" with neither a tree to hang a man nor water enough to drown him. The village is home to The

Burren Visitor's Centre, some fantastic examples of Celtic high crosses, and the wonderful Vaughan's Pub which serves one of the best fish soups I've ever had.

We've visited Kilfenora each of the four times we've been in Ireland, but we've only seen One-Ear once. I parked the car and walked over toward the Visitor's Centre. Sitting in front of the Centre on a stone bench was a man of undeterminable, but significant age, dressed in rumpled black woolen trousers, an ancient tweed sports coat covered by a patterned vest (probably a topcoat lining), and on his head a tweed driving cap. Neither his stubbly chin nor toothless grin were his most distinct feature; that was the right ear which only had a part of the top and a piece of the bottom lobe. His blue eyes stared right into me as he pointed to my camera and held out his hand palm up. It was sign language I couldn't fail to understand. Fishing in my pocket I found and held up a one euro coin. He smiled, nodded, took the coin and then adopted a photogenic pose. I took my photo and tipped my hat to him, and he tipped his hat to me as I went into the Centre.

When we came out One-ear wasn't around. On the last visit to Kilfenora I thought I spied One-ear walking down a side street, but I couldn't be sure. I do hope he's still there and still posing for tourists, for he's as much an icon of Kilfenora as the crosses or the pub.

Our Encounters with Witches and Mystics

Travel can be spooky. Several times we've had encounters of various sorts with witches. In Kilkenny we heard the story of the Kyteler Witch. Kyteler's Pub is one of the prime entertainment venues in Kilkenny, a place to hear music almost every night. The pub was originally owned by Dame Alice le Kyteler who was born in Kilkenny in 1263. She possessed enough wiles, charms, and luck to snare four husbands, each of whom died leaving her great fortunes. Through trumped up charges of witchcraft, her local enemies managed to get Dame Alice condemned to be publicly whipped through the streets of the village and then burned at the stake, a fate which befell many a wily female. She escaped to England with the help of noble accomplices and a luckless servant who, dressed as Kyteler, suffered her fate instead. Our B&B hosts suggested we go to Kyteler's for a drink and the music, but avoid eating there.

They said the kitchen work was rather inconsistent, perhaps because the place is still bewitched.

I've had personal experience with the Witch of Crieff. In the village where we spend the most time in Scotland is a strange shop. It's a tearoom and novelty shop and always has intriguing figurines of scantly clad uniformed ladies in the windows along with butterflies, dragons, rainbows, and such. The girls who work at John and Jacky's B&B are from South Africa and are afraid of the shop. They say there's voodoo there and that the woman owner is a witch. I went in one day determined to buy one of the naughty figurines as gag gift for an Irish friend. I'm not sure I'd call the owner of the shop a witch, but she is definitely an extreme New Ager--all she wanted to talk about was the aura of Crieff and how exhilarating it was. I bought my figurine and left rather quickly.

I don't know whether to call Mazz O'Flaherty, singer, songwriter, artist, and Dingle Record Shop owner, a mystic or a magician. We found the music store one cool, windy day while prowling the shops of one of our favorite Irish towns, Dingle. Mazz introduced herself and began showing me some interesting CDs from local musicians including herself. Anne stood to the side with her arms wrapped around herself trying to get warm. Mazz noticed her and said to Anne that hers wasn't very friendly body language. Anne explained that her hands were freezing. Mazz said, "I'll take care of that." She took Anne's hands and rubbed them in her own while chanting in Irish. In about a minute Mazz said, "That should keep you warm all day." While Mazz was ministering to Anne, I had taken a couple of pictures, to which Mazz said matter of factly, "Oh, don't bother. Those won't turn out." I passed the comment off as one of those from someone who'd rather not be photographed.

We bought several CDs, thanked Mazz, and continued our shopping. The strange thing was Anne never got cold the rest of the day. Stranger still, when I got home and downloaded the 850 pictures from the trip, I got all my photos except two--the two of Mazz O'Flaherty simply weren't on the memory chip. Mystic or magician?

Our First Pub Dinner in Scotland

Our first complete day in Scotland was unbelievably full. We'd driven from Glasgow Airport to Peebles in the Borders, spent a couple of hours at our first Highland Games, played our first nine holes of golf at Innerleithen GC, and stopped in a local pub for our first pub meal. Tired, hungry, and unbelievably excited by our first day's experiences, the sign "Pub Meals Served All Day" drew us to stop at the Corner House Hotel. There was nothing fancy about this pub. Ordinary is a more fitting adjective, but "ordinary" is what we were seeking--the real Scottish experience--and, boy, did we get it here.

We sat down and waited to be serviced. After watching other patrons get served by going up to the bar to order, we figured that if we wanted to eat or drink in Scotland we'd have to take care of ourselves. A large black Labrador retriever lounged underneath an empty bar stool. That we wouldn't see at home. While sipping an ale, a young woman worked on what looked like a college term paper or business report. That we wouldn't see at home either. About the time our food arrived, fish and chips for me and beef stroganoff for Anne, we were discovered by a very inebriated Scottish lady. Even though drunk, she was so friendly to ask us about our trip and how we liked what we'd seen of her country so far, that we didn't let her state of intoxication cloud our feelings. After talking with us throughout our meal, she introduced us around to everyone else in the pub as her American friends, and they started asking us about our trip and America.

A quick stop for food had turned into almost two hours of eating and socializing. We forgot how tired we were until back on the road to our B&B in Peebles. It was good thing it was still fairly light and only a seven mile trip. The Corner House Hotel pub, its pub dog, and drunk patron still hold a special place in our memories.

The Friendly, Caring Scots

Unequivocally one of the most important reasons to visit Scotland is because of the friendliness of the Scottish people. They may have a reputation as thrifty, but I think that the Scots are thrifty for themselves so that they can give more to others. We have numerous examples of Scots going out of their way to be friendly and helpful, but the most telling example was in the aftermath of the 9-11 attack on America.

We were in the middle of our second stay at John and Jacky Clifford's Merlindale B&B in Crieff in central Scotland when the attack occurred. We came back to the B&B at about 2:00 in the afternoon after golf. Jacky met us at the door with words I'll never forget, "America's been attacked." We spent the rest of the afternoon and evening in the lounge glued to the CNN and SKY News reporting. At that point, after four days staying the year before and ten days this trip, we became a part of the family and we have remained such to this day. Concern wasn't only from our Scottish family, it was from everyone in the country. Within days American flags were hung in windows next to Scottish flags. When anyone heard our accent or saw us eat with our fork in the wrong hand, we would be asked if we were all right or did we need anything. In a small hotel pub near Callander the day after the attack, we watched an elderly lady who appeared to be mentally challenged taking her midday meal in the local pub. She heard us talk in our accents to the waitress and asked as we walked by, "Are you two okay?" Here was someone, a stranger, with her own significant problems seriously concerned with us.

The Scottish friendliness isn't only related to our American crisis, we noted many other examples. One year our plane was very late getting into London's Heathrow Airport, so we missed our connection to Glasgow and were waiting for the next plane. We were going to be hours late picking up our rental car and far later than expected by our B&B. As Anne and I sat in the waiting area discussing our plight, particularly if the B&B would hold our room, a lady seated across from us leaned over and said that she used to run a B&B and, even though she didn't run one now, if we got stranded she'd be glad to put us up for the night. As a stranger she was offering to have us stay with her. I can't see that happening so easily in the States.

In Peebles on our first trip to Scotland we decided to visit Edinburgh for the day. This was the year of the great, media-hyped petrol strike, so we planned to take the bus from Peebles to Edinburgh. Waiting at the Peebles' bus station, a large covered stop outside the small station office, we asked a gentleman waiting to put his child on a bus to boarding school a question about the bus. He answered our question and stayed with us for a half hour even after his child was well away to make sure we got on the correct bus. Certainly, a step beyond friendly.

In B&Bs, especially at Merlindale in Crieff, we've met Scots who have invited us to drop in on them when we visit in their neighborhood. A couple of ladies from the Isle of Bute have invited us to stay with them and tour their island, as have couples from Jersey and Gurnsey. The examples of small acts of kindness or friendliness are too numerous to mention, but it is certainly one reason we are drawn back to Scotland.

The Man Who Was Hiding from His Wife

Whew! What a day! After a good B&B breakfast we drove to the Park-n-Ride on the ring road around York (very reasonable, protected parking, and much easier than trying to park in the town). In the cathedral city we visited the The Shambles (market street), the grand cathedral known as the Minster, and bought special bread at Betty's Bakery. From York we toured Rievaulx Abbey about 20 miles out of town, and missed lunch at a special pub. By the time we were done at Rievaulx we were more than ready for dinner.

Our lawyer Dave Carlson, one of my former high school debaters, had suggested that we try The Crown Inn in Roecliffe for dinner, only a few miles from our B&B in Ripon. On the way we spotted The Devil's Arrows, a set of ancient standing stones. Even with light rapidly fading and hunger pangs pounding in the gut, I had to stop for a look and few pictures. The extra diversion made The Crown Inn even more welcome. We walked in, ordered a couple of halves of Guinness, and sat at a small table in the bar. Five o'clock in the afternoon on a Sunday in October, nobody was in the dining room. The bar area with one gentleman and his cane on one stool and the pub cat on another seemed more inviting than the empty dining room. We chatted with the gent who had recently had hip surgery, thus the cane. He was relishing his pint of ale as he told us he wasn't supposed to be in the pub and he definitely wasn't supposed to be drinking. He was at The Crown hiding from his wife. His justification I thought was quite sound. He told us, "What's the use of a new hip if I can't go to the pub for a pint?" Boots the Cat perked up at this, licked her paws, and curled back up on the stool again.

Not much later the man's wife came in and said to our friend, "I knowed I'd find you here. Finish that beer and get yerself right hame." She smiled at us as she walked out. About five minutes later a couple staying at the inn came down for dinner, the gentleman with the new hip got up and with soft good-byes ambled out the door. Boots never did leave her perch, and the roast beef and Yorkshire pudding was especially good in Yorkshire.

This Is Not a Joke

One spring we had arranged to play Tillicoultry's friendly nine-hole golf course near Stirling, Scotland. Anne walked the hilly course while I played with the club President, Captain, and Vice-Captain. After the round we were invited into the small clubhouse for refreshments, so Anne and I walked out to our rented Ford Focus to put my clubs away and change our shoes.

As we were tying our shoes a woman drove up in a new Mercedes sports car. She parked a little ways from us, got out and started toward the clubhouse. Perhaps twenty feet from her shiny new Merc, she hesitated and looked back towards us. After checking us out for a moment, she walked back to her convertible sports car with its top down and locked the doors. Satisfied, she headed back to the clubhouse.

This is not a joke, but you can guess what color her hair was.

Tina, the Golf Boss of Ballina

Anne and I both spent over thirty years in public school teaching. One truism we learned early is that it is the school secretary who runs the school, not the Superintendent or Principal. Whenever we wanted to get something done, we'd ask the secretary. If you knew what was good for you, you got on the good side of the school secretary and stayed there at all costs. In our careers some of the best people we ever met were those secretaries. Tina, the Golf Boss of Ballina, was like that.

We arrived at Ballina GC on the west of Ireland for our arranged round plenty early. When we met her we knew Tina ran the place. The golf pro wasn't around and the person who was to be our guide, Padraig a former club captain, would be a little late, but Tina took care of us. In her office, which was the hub of the entire club, we chatted about the course and the state of affairs in Ireland. Everyone checked in with Tina. Her language was colorful-Irish to say the least, but we never felt offended. The rough, four-letter-word laced language and easy smile were both part of her personae.

Padraig finally arrived, and with a glare from Tina for his tardiness, took us out onto the course. After nine holes of rain, Anne walked in while I continued the round with Padraig. When Padraig and I got done with our second nine we joined Anne and Tina, who had become fast friends, for lunch in the clubhouse lounge. Though she wasn't in the office, Tina continued to control the club. Everyone seemed to jump at her command.

Just like a well-run school is probably due largely to a good secretary, the Ballina GC was kept in good order by Tina the Golf Boss.

We Didn't See No Ghost

The pro at Pyle & Kenfig GC in South Wales suggested the Prince of Wales Pub as a place for a drink and a meal, but he said, "Take care now, the place is haunted."

As we pulled into the parking lot on a dark rainy afternoon (the Scots would call it *dreich,* and the Welsh would call something unpronounceable), the place looked like it could be haunted. The building is a large square inn with an ancient brick exterior and small lights in the pub windows. The interior was typical of an old pub; stone fireplace, low beam ceilings, heavy wood furniture, old photos decorating the walls, and small groups of people talking over their ales and drams. We picked out a table along the wall, sipped our Guinnesses (Or did we decide it was Guinni?), and watched the other patrons. One particular old guy garnered our attention. He was telling stories to his cronies when his daughter (we think) came in and said, "It's time to go." To which the man replied, "Not yet dearie, not until I finish my beer." She shook her head and left. About 20 minutes later she returned and said, "It's time for dinner." At this the man reluctantly left his friends and went home to dinner. We liked the pub so well that we decided to come back the next night for dinner ourselves. We left though a little disappointed because we hadn't seen the ghost.

The next day after golf at Pyle & Kenfig GC we went to the Prince of Wales Pub for dinner. The same gentleman as the day before was there telling stories to the same group of cronies--we couldn't tell if it was the same stories or not. We had a great dinner and the daughter never came to get the storyteller. Again, though, we didn't see the ghost. Maybe it only shows itself to those who have drunk significantly more than just the pint we had.

And Speaking of Pipers...

We held an interesting conversation with some guests at Merlindale B&B on a spring trip. They had stayed at the B&B overnight and where moving on to Blair Atholl where their son was entered in the solo piping competition at the Blair Castle Clan Gathering (Highland games) later that day. In the conversation they said we might have seen their son piping in Edinburgh--he's a busker who plays his pipes for coins up near the Edinburgh Castle walls. I said we'd seen several pipers in Edinburgh and, in fact... At this point I went out into the foyer and grabbed one of the photos I have there for sale. I took the photo back to the dining room and showed it to the couple. "That's our son!" was the ecstatic comment of the mother. Just as I think she was going to offer to buy the

photo, Jacky (our B&B host/ friend) said, "Bob will probably be glad to send you the original, won't you Bob?" I reluctantly nodded. Jacky later apologized as she realized she'd killed the sale--and she gets a commission on all the photos that sell.

The last day of each of our trips we spend in Edinburgh. This year we stopped in front of a piper busking near the castle. As he came to a break in his playing I asked if his name was Craig and if he came from the Isle of Bute. He said, "You're the photographer my folks met at the B&B in Crieff!" We had a nice, brief chat, took more pictures, dropped some coins in his box, and now I can put a name to my photo: "Craig, the Piper."

Craig is not the only piper we've seen in Edinburgh. St Giles Cathedral, Waverley Station, and even the Royal Mile Starbucks have had pipers busking. The very first piper we saw in Scotland was at Urquhart Castle on the western shore of Loch Ness. The haunting solo pipes set an appropriate mood as you strain to find Nessie in black waters of the loch. Buskers, whether a piper in Blair Castle, a violinist in Vienna, a flutist in Dublin, a juggler in Oxford, or a spoons player in Atlanta, add to the ambiance and entertain us all. Stop and listen or watch, and be sure to drop a few shekels into the box, especially if you are taking pictures.

Good-bye to Stephen from Canada

We met Stephen and his wife at Merlindale B&B in Crieff (our Scottish home) first in our third or fourth year of visiting Scotland. Stephen was Canadian now but had originally been from England and served with the RAF in Scotland during the war years. He had visited Crieff often during the war and was now back to renew those memories. He was a great conversationalist (but never about the war) and we enjoyed meeting the two of them.

About two years later we met Stephen again with one of his sons. His wife had passed the previous year. He was now in his eighties and wanted to show his son the country he really loved. A further two years on we met Stephen again at Merlindale. This trip he was with another son showing him his Scotland. But Stephen wasn't very well. He had been diagnosed with cancer and was going to go home to a heavy program of chemotherapy and radiation. He was still bright and witty. We wished him well, but really didn't expect that we would see him again.

The next year, though, when we arrived at Merlindale we were greeted by Stephen and his two war buddies. He was much more frail this time, but he told us how we (the whole Merlindale family) had saved his life. He related how during a particularly bad time in his cancer treatment he heard the doctors tell his family that they should gather round because Stephen didn't have much more time. He heard this and thought to himself, "No, I'm going to go back to Scotland at least once more!" He fought hard and won, if not the war, at least the battle. So here he was. This time, with his war buddies around, he did tell us stories of the Battle of Britain. He had been a fighter pilot for part of the war and then a bomber pilot who flew almost twice the normal number of missions.

When he left to go home we all wished him well--every one of us fighting back the tears of good-bye. We knew this time he wouldn't be back, but we do have an update. Just before we arrived at Merlindale for our fall 2016 stay, Stephen's family (three sons and their wives) stayed at Merlindale. They were over to spread Stephen's ashes on his old stomping grounds. It seems Stephen did return to Scotland again after all.

Celebrity Sighting

We've seen celebrities before in our travels--singer Al Jarreau in an airport, actor Ewan McGregor at dinner in a Highland restaurant, golfer Freddy Couples in a restaurant in South Carolina, rocker Rod Stewart at breakfast in a restaurant in Portland, we were passed by the Queen in her limo in the Highlands near Balmoral Castle (her Highland castle)--but in Burford in the Cotswolds we actually did a bit of celebrity stalking.

After paying for parking our rental car in the public parking lot in Burford village, I was walking to catch up with Anne when I had to step aside to let a car go by. I paid attention to the car because it was a new special edition Jaguar. I caught a glimpse of the shaggy haired driver and walked away thinking I knew him from someplace. It took a little to put the car together with the brief glimpse of the driver and come up with James May, one of the presenters on BBC's popular TV show "Top Gear." I thought that's who I'd seen, but I wasn't sure.

As we wandered through the village shops I noticed the driver I'd seen with a lady also wandering the shops. A few minutes later we saw the couple sitting at table in front of a pub, so we decided to sit as well. Over half a pint I managed to snap a couple of photos and confirm that it was indeed James May.

We found out later from our B&B hosts that May lives in the area and is often seen in the Cotswold villages. One more to add to our celebrity sightings list.

Another Celebrity Encounter

Earlier in the day Anne and I had driven through what we called Ryder Cup City, the Gleneagles golf complex near Auchterarder in central Scotland. Gleneagles three main courses and wee practice course had been turned into a city of tents (some as tall as four stories), trailers, vans, mobile media centers, and spectator stands. The Ryder Cup matches between the American and European teams were less than a week away and are a really big deal, but that's not the point of this story.

Later in the afternoon Anne went shopping in Perth with Jacky and I drove up Sma'Glen for some Highland photos. After a couple of photo stops I came upon a temporary road block. A hunting party was moving hunters, dogs, and beaters from one field across the road to another field. As I watched the process I thought I recognized the swagger of one of the hunters. Dressed in tweed hunting attire, English professional golfer Justin Rose walked past my car, smiled at me, and held up a brace of freshly killed grouse. I wouldn't have been surprised to see Ryder Cup player Rose practicing on one of the local golf courses, but I was surprised to see him in the Scottish Highlands.

Cawdor Castle and the Rude Americans

We first toured Cawdor Castle on our initial trip to Scotland in 2000. The tour has improved over the years and, even though only a few rooms were open for touring, was worth the visit. A tour group was going through the castle while we were there and the tour group was mostly Americans from the South. They were quite rude! Several of the tour members had obviously spent too much time in the castle coffee shop and gift shop and now had to hustle through to catch their bus. One guy shouted at another tourist (not a member of the tour) to "hurry up" when he was reading the room information.   One lady said loudly, "Another bedroom. Hurumph! Who needs to see this!"   Members of the tour group shoved their way past other tourists with a "I've got to catch a bus," but never an "excuse me."

It's people like these who give American tourists a bad name.

Where Are We? What Have We Seen?

We like to think that those who travel are intelligent, interesting people who seek to broaden their horizons of understanding and enrich their lives.   Then we also like to believe that someday we'll be rich beyond our wildest dreams.   Neither of these are true.   We have met some interesting travelers, but there are some we hope to never meet again, such as the couple from the Midwest we met a couple of years ago at Merlindale in Crieff.

In the kitchen over tea, Jacky asked me to visit with the American couple sitting in the lounge.   She said they weren't having a good time on their trip and Jacky wanted to see if there was anything that could help them have a better time.   I said I'd see what I could do and took my tea to the lounge.

The Midwestern couple were indeed depressed (and depressing) about their travels.   Everything they had to say about Scotland and their trip was negative.   The food was awful, beds were terrible, roads were impassable, weather was atrocious, and on and on.   I had never seen such negativism.   I asked the couple where they'd been and what they'd seen.   I was shocked at their answer, although I probably shouldn't have been.   Where had they been? They didn't know.   They thought they had been in the north of Scotland, but none of the towns or villages I named rang any bells--not surprising for these ding-dongs. I asked what they'd seen, what attractions had they visited? Neither of the couple could name one.   They knew they had spent two days in Edinburgh at the beginning of the ten day trip, but they couldn't remember if they'd seen a castle or not.   Meaningful conversation was hopeless.   The couple couldn't fathom why we'd come to Scotland more than once, let alone every year. I finished my tea and bid them good evening. In the kitchen I told Jacky I'd try again at breakfast.

In the morning Anne and I did our best, but the only response we got from the couple was a, "We can't wait to get out of this God forsaken country" and "we'll never leave home again." I guess some people weren't ever meant to travel.

The Massed Pipe Bands March

In Dornoch in the north of Scotland we learned from our B&B host that there would be a massed pipe band march through town at 7:30 that evening. Nine bands from around the area were planning to perform as a fund-raiser for Michael, a local lad of seven who had been hit by an auto when he ran out in the road without looking. At first they questioned whether he would live, and when he did they questioned whether he would walk again or talk. He is recovering slowly. Since he had been struck as he was going home from

chanter practice (beginning piping), it was appropriate to have the bands help raise funds for his medical costs. The family is well liked in the area—we never found out what his father did, but Michael's mother works in the school cafeteria.

The bands—from Tain, Wick, Dornoch, and others—massed at the top of the main street of town (about five minutes away from the famous Royal Dornoch GC). With Michael in a wheelchair and father and mother at his sides, he lead the parade for its first march down to the main stands where the mayor presided.

The bands played a set of tunes as they marched from the top of town to the officials stands and back to the top. They did this several times with different sets of tunes. All the while, volunteers sold raffle tickets and passed buckets for donations through the crowds. We didn't find out how much was raised, but it was probably quite significant. The town of 1200 had swelled to a crowd of approximately 4000, all to help a local lad. Here in the States, we set up "GoFundMe" accounts at local banks and on social media to help in emergency situations, but in Scotland whole communities make it their responsibility. We were so glad to participate.

Old Tom Morris: A Scottish Treasure, originally published in *Historic Scotland Magazine*

In looking at the big picture it can be easy to overlook the small, but significant detail. It could be easy to do just that at the spectacular Historic Scotland site of St Andrews Cathedral and St Rule's Tower. These magnificent grounds in St Andrews on Fife are so awe inspiring and full of such rich history that a unique monument tucked into a side of the Cathedral cemetery could easily be missed. And it would be such a shame to miss the golfer's shrine that contains the graves of both Old and Young Tom Morris.

Old Tom Morris is a legendary figure in the history of one of Scotland's greatest gifts to the world, golf. His son, Tom Jnr shone bright as a nova star in his short 24 years. The memorial grave site was originally the grave of Young Tom Morris who, after winning the British Open Championship four times in a row (the first time when he was only 17 years old), died of a broken heart because of the loss of his wife and child in childbirth. When Tom Jnr died in 1875, sixty golfing societies from all over Scotland contributed to his memorial stone which was erected in the St Andrews cemetery.

Tom Morris Jnr wasn't the only legacy to golf left by Old Tom. Tom Mitchell Morris, born in St Andrews in 1821, left his mark on all aspects of the game loved (and hated) by golfers the world over. As a player, a golf professional, and a course architect Old Tom will be remembered wherever golf is played.

As a player Old Tom's record is second only to his son, Tom Jnr. Old Tom won almost all major competitions of his era, including four Open titles. It was said that when partnered with his mentor and one-time business partner, Allan Robertson (who is also buried in the St Andrews cemetery), they were unbeatable. Among Old Tom's accomplishments are being the oldest to win the Open at age 46, winning by the largest margin (13 strokes in 1862), and playing in his last Open at age 75.

It is as a golf professional and golf course architect that Old Tom Morris will be remembered most. After a stint with Allan Robertson as golf ball and club maker, in 1851 Morris became the "Keeper of the Greens" at Prestwick Golf Club in Ayrshire. It was here that the first British Open Championship was played in 1860 -- Morris placed second to Willie Park who won the tidy sum of £3! In 1864 Morris moved back to St Andrews to become "Custodian of the Links and Keeper of the Greens," a position he held until 1904. While at Prestwick and St Andrews Old Tom changed the face of golf forever, literally. He was instrumental in codifying golf courses to 18 holes (St Andrews had originally been 22), planting sea grasses around bunkers to keep wind from blowing the sand away, and discovered that "top dressing" putting greens (periodically applying sand to greens) would smooth the surface and encourage new growth. As well as his work on the Old Course at St Andrews, Old Tom Morris had a major hand in the design of many of the Scotland's famous courses. Carnoustie, Crail, Muirfield, Royal Dornoch, St Andrews New, West Kilbride, Bridge of Allan, and Tain are but some of the courses where Scotland's golf visitors pay tribute to Old Tom Morris. For all his design work at courses such as Machrihanish on Kintyre (where Morris declared, "The Almighty had gowf in his e'e when he made this place.") Morris was paid the munificent sum of £1 per day plus expenses! Although many of his original designs have been altered over the years, there is still at least one course where today's golfer can play a course just as Tom Morris laid it out--the nine hole Bridge of Allan Golf Course near Stirling. Morris' influence as an architect wasn't limited to Scotland, it has been spread throughout the world by designers who studied his work (such as Alister MacKenzie of Augusta National and Pebble Beach fame) or those who grew up playing on Tom Morris' courses (such as Donald Ross who designed Pinehurst #2).

When Old Tom Morris died in 1908 after a fall down stairs at the St Andrews New course he was buried beside his beloved son in the cathedral cemetery. The memorial to Young Tom Morris and Old Tom's grave in the cemetery should remind all who visit Scotland's treasures to look closely for there are many great stories waiting to be found at Historic Scotland properties.

For more information on Old Tom Morris and his golf courses:

The Golf Courses of Old Tom Morris by Robert Kroeger
The Scrapbook of Old Tom Morris compiled by David Joy

CHAPTER 8: Everything Else, A Writer's Potpourri

When a story doesn't seem to fit anywhere else I threw it into this pot. I couldn't leave these out because they are some of my favorite stories, but they don't characterize easily. There will be a little bit of everything in these stories starting with a couple of good examples of why we love the British Isles.

A Great Day in Scotland

There have been really no bad days in Scotland, but to describe a typical month long trip I choose to tell about a great day. Monday, September 8 was our only full day on Isle Arran off the western coast of Scotland between Ayrshire and the Kintyre Peninsula.

I got up early to take a morning walk in the village of Lamlash where our B&B, Lilybank House, is located. As I walked along the road through the village (the main road around the island), I had village houses and shops on one side and Lamlash Bay on the other. Along my walk I met Colin Richardson, our B&B host, walking his dog. Colin sarcastically apologized for the weather, which was sunny and about 15°C with no wind [conversion trick: 2C° + 30 = °F, or for this day 15°C doubled plus 30 = 60°F]. In other words, fantastic! Colin had also apologized the night before for the poor view from our room--a view directly out to the bay and the Holy Island. Back from my walk having taken a couple dozen photos of the bay, the boats in the bay, the Holy Island, houses, flowers, and the local kirk (church), Anne and I went down to breakfast at 8:30.

Colin served a well-prepared typical Scottish breakfast. Various cereals, fruit, fruit juices, coffee or tea, Canadian-style bacon, bangers, eggs, potatoes, grilled mushrooms and tomatoes, and all the toast you wanted. It's your own fault if you go hungry in a Scottish B&B. After breakfast we packed our stuffed bellies into our rented Vauxhall Vector and headed for golf.

Isle Arran has a main road around the perimeter of the island (A841) and a lesser road (B880 called the "string road") which bisects the island from the main village of Brodick on the east to Blackwaterfoot on the west. It's this cross island route we took to make our tee time at Shiskine Golf and Tennis Club. The B880 afforded wonderful views as we headed up the 700 foot pass. The views of Goat Fell peak (the island's highest at 2868') and surrounding mountains was complemented with vistas of the ocean and Kintyre Peninsula beyond.

Shiskine is unique in the golfing world. It's a twelve-hole links course which plays along the Kilbrannan Sound. Built on ancient sand dunes, Shiskine has enough striking scenery to make any golfer miss shots. Besides the Sound and the peninsula, there are stunning cliffs which are home to a myriad of seabirds. Anne's golf was good, and while my swing was off, it would be hard to have bad golf in such a beautiful place.

After golf we grabbed a couple of cokes at the tearoom and headed up the coast to a beach pullout a couple of hundred yards past the Machrie Bay GC clubhouse. We sat on the shore and shared a light lunch of oatcakes (oat crackers), Arran smokey cheddar cheese, and our cokes. Refreshed by the sea air and our snacks, we went back to Machrie Bay GC to play nine more holes. This course has some interesting features: hole one plays between the main Arran road and the beach, you cross the road to play holes 2 through 8, nine crosses the road again when you shoot to the green, there's a standing stone (probably 1500 BC) in the sheep field next to #3, and from several holes you can see the Auchagallen stone circle (older than the Pyramids). Other than that it's just an average nine-hole course.

With twenty-one holes of golf complete, we continued up the coast making a couple of stops for me to take pictures (an interesting graveyard, quaint narrow roads) and for Anne to go down to the beach and collect stones which she hides in our luggage to bring home and which I pretend not to notice. At the northern tip of the island we reached Lochranza with its 15th century castle and whisky distillery. We took pictures of the castle, but we visited the distillery. Visitors to Scotland cannot live by haggis alone!

Having driven up the west side of Isle Arran, at the ferry terminal town of Lochranza at the north tip of the island the road swings east to the village of Corrie and then south toward Brodick. [I think I get bonus points for using all four compass points in one grammatically correct sentence.] Before we reached Brodick we stopped at Island Cheese Shop and Arran Aromatics where Anne stocked up on soaps, lotions, and wonderfully smelly girl goo. In Brodick I stocked up on wonderfully smelly, rich tasting sweets at Arran Chocolates. To each his/her own.

We arrived back at Lillybank House with time enough to taste some of our purchases. We sat in our room overlooking the bay sipping whisky and nibbling cheese and chocolates. At our request Colin had booked us into The Pantry--a Scottish-Mexican bistro in Whiting Bay about seven miles away. At The Pantry we enjoyed Lamb Guinness Soup and seafood enchiladas with mornay sauce. A delicious and unique meal eaten while watching the water lap at Whiting Bay.

It's 9:30 by the time we get back to Lamlash. We just had time to organize the day's souvenirs and purchases in our bags and write in journals--travel journal, golf notes, and pub notes. We both fell asleep reading--but that's okay, we needed to rest because tomorrow we were to play golf at Corrie in the morning and catch the ferry back to the terminal at Ardrossan at noon and drive on to Crieff in Central Scotland.

Another great day in Scotland.

A Great Day in Wales

The day was not going to be the weather we really wanted when playing a world class course like Royal Porthcawl in southern Wales--it was fiercely windy, spitting rain in squalls, and completely overcast. We also knew by the friendly greeting we got in the golf shop from pro Peter Evans that it was going to be a great day of golf despite the weather. We weren't disappointed.

Rain gear, including jacket, pants, gloves, hat, and bag cover on from the start, we headed to the first tee. I like it better when we can start fully prepared rather than having to interrupt play to don our gear; it's always easier to shed rain suits than to put them on during the round. The first hole, the one seen in the Wales' tourism commercial with duffers and Wee Welshman pro Ian Woosnam teeing off in glorious conditions, is a fair starting hole. A demanding drive, but not too demanding, followed by a tricky second onto an elevated green with interesting slopes. The wind, howling at a steady thirty miles an hour straight into us (measured with a portable anemometer), added character to the shotmaking. Bogeys were good on this championship start, but the score really isn't that important. Anne and I are retired after more than thirty years of teaching, we're in Wales, the land of at least my paternal ancestors (although there's English on that side as well), and we're playing golf on one of the world's great golf courses. Bogey, double-bogey, or even birdie doesn't much matter. The rest of the round was a little better than the start. The wind stiffened a little, but the rain lightened and stopped while we were still on the front. One curiosity was we kept coming into greens with the flags pulled out. The first couple of downed flags we ran into we cursed the inconsiderates in front of us. Then as we continued to find flags down and realized it was the wind blowing them out, we apologized under our breaths.

As we came off the tough 410-yard 18th with dips and hills and lush rough, we talked to the visitor who had played in front of us. He was leaning against the building catching his breath. As we approached him, he smiled and said, "The course won." But he was smiling! We told Peter about the four flags we found down on the greens. He responded, "Oh, an average day at Royal Porthcawl. Only a four flag day; we often see six or eight flags out in a round." And he was smiling!

From the golf course it's only a few miles back to the Prince of Wales Pub in Kenfig near the interesting Pyle and Kenfig GC we'd played a couple of days before. We'd heard about the pub from the golf pro at P&K who said, "It should be in your book"--a phrase we'd heard several times before referring to this pub, that restaurant, or yon attraction. After a drink in the 16th century (rebuilt in 1808) Prince of Wales Inn we knew he'd been right. This pub needed to be in the book. We enjoyed a pint, Guinness for Anne and local ale for me, heard about the ghosts, talked to a few locals who said "Good day for golf, isn't it." And they smiled! With a little adjusting of our itinerary, we planned a return trip to the pub another day for a meal, and then headed out for the hour drive to tonight's B&B in Laugharne.

Laugharne has a ruined castle and a literary heritage. It's the literary connection that gives the Boat House Bed and Breakfast its name--the Boathouse (around the corner from the castle along the water) was where poet Dylan Thomas did much of his writing. We arrived in time to take a quick peek at the castle before checking in at the B&B. We rang the bell and introduced ourselves to Angi, who looked at us a little strangely, but showed us to the Towy suite. When we asked about her husband George a look of recognition came over her face. Ann then introduced herself and her daughter Jenni who recently bought the B&B from Angi and George. They said Angi and George had left our reservation, but no details or contact information. After a good laugh we were told the dinner we had arranged would be in the dining room in about an hour.

Whenever we can we take advantage of B&Bs which do dinners--a nice change from always eating out. The dinner at Boat House was superb! A special smoked haddock appetizer started the meal for us and three other guests. The starter was followed by a main of chicken breast in special sauce served with potatoes and fresh veggies. Dinner ended with a scrumptious homemade pear pie. My Anne and I sat for an hour after dinner visiting with Jenni and Ann about the process of starting up a B&B.

Windy golf on a fantastic course. Pub ghosts and Guinness. New friends in a marvelous B&B. All in a day of touring in Wales.

Airing Out the Dirty Laundry

It is surprising how much can be said about dirty laundry and doing the laundry. When you take long trips, like our five or six week British Isle trips, doing laundry becomes an issue. On a two week train trip through Europe we did our necessary laundry in hotel room sinks and hoped it would dry over night, but on a six week trip to Scotland and Wales that's not practical. We've found some interesting ways of solving our dirty laundry problems.

Several times we've taken our dirty clothes to a cleaners in Scotland or Ireland. The cleaners will wash, dry, and sometimes even iron your load. Drop it off in the morning, pick it up in the

afternoon. All it takes is a little planning and great faith that you'll get everything back. I think we are currently on the plus side having picked up an extra sock in Inverness. Although most of the time the clothes will come back folded and paired, there was one cleaner in Ireland where we picked up our clothes stuffed into a large plastic bag. Everything was there, but we almost needed to wash again because of the wrinkles.

One year in Dingle at Milestone House Anne washed a few essentials in the bathroom sink and then asked our host, Barbara, if we could hang the clothes outside on the clothesline. Barbara almost fainted. She said that she'd been asked to do a small batch of laundry for an American guest, for a fee of course. Barbara said she'd wash the clothes and hang them out on the line to dry in the bright sun and fresh Dingle breezes. The woman was aghast. Wouldn't the sun ruin her clothes, she asked? Barbara figured Americans didn't know about clotheslines, so when Anne asked she was shocked. As it turns out, Anne hung the clothes out and we left for a golfing day. Of course, it rained most of the day. We got back to Milestone and Anne discovered that Barbara had taken our wet and getting wetter clothes off the line, dried and folded them, and had them on our bed for our return. But then Barbara Conners is like that.

Our most unique laundry experiences have been when in timeshare we tried to do laundry in the facilities provided. It was particularly troublesome at Kilconquhar Castle on Fife. Our unit had a washer and dryer in our own utility room. What a great thing, we thought, to have the freedom to do our laundry and not have to leave our room. Anne loaded the washer and an hour later had a tub full of wet clothes. She loaded the dryer, set the timer, and at the end of the cycle found she still had a tub of wet clothes. She set the timer again with the same results, wet clothes. We could tell that after three cycles the clothes were a little less wet, but only a little. After looking through instruction books, that could have just well been written in Gaelic, and talking to housekeeping we learned that normal UK dryers could only handle tiny loads and took a long time. As Anne started a tiny batch of the most needed socks and underwear, we began hanging damp clothes everywhere we could in the unit. For the next three days we came home to our apartment draped with drying clothes. The only positive thing about the experience was that we had started early in the week. I don't know what we'd have done with a whole load of wet clothes if we had started on Friday and had to leave the timeshare on Saturday.

Our best solution to the laundry conundrum has been to pay the helpers at Merlindale B&B to do the laundry. It costs a little, but Annie, Paulette, or Tertia do such a fantastic job that we plan our trips away from the B&B around bringing dirty laundry back for the girls to do. This next year we'll make sure we have everything clean before we leave Merlindale for a sojourn to England and Wales, and after three weeks down south we'll bring back a fresh load of dirty laundry.

Futzing

Futze - verb. Anne's definition: to organize. Bob's definition: to mess about with things or obsessively organize.

Anne is a *futzer* (one who futzes). When we leave on a trip she must spend many hours futzing (organizing) all the items we're taking in the car. For example, water bottles have to fit under her seat, books under mine, spare bags (the main tool of a futzer) just so between the water and books, etc. There are some real advantages to being married to a world class (I don't believe anyone else is even in her league) futzer. If I need a paper clip, Anne has them and knows where they are. If we have a leftover quarter of a sandwich, Anne has the proper sized baggy and knows where it is. If I need first aid cream Anne knows it's still in the car in the first aid kit underneath the books on the driver's side back seat floor.

There are also several disadvantages to having a world renown futzer in the family. At times on the golf course Anne will fall behind because she stopped to reorganize everything in her golf bag. Every morning when we leave to play a new golf course for our writing, we must carry out six or seven different bags full of items for that day--one of which is my camera case. The others are our traveling maps and papers, extra clothes for the day if we get too wet, enough snacks to feed a small third world country, and some mysterious bags that I dare not ask the contents.

The one major drawback to being the champion of futzing is that it's a catastrophe if something is out of place. If Anne can't find something, she will search and search until it either turns up or she remembers where she re-filed it in the last futz-a-rama. In one instance on Narin and Portnoo Golf Course in Ireland, as the rain started Anne began looking desperately in her golf bag, which she had re-futzed the night before, for her rain hat. By the time she found it most of the contents of her bag were scattered on the fairway and the rain had stopped. For me, the disorganized, bumbling non-futzer, when I can't find something, I either give up with a "It'll turn up," or more likely, I ask Anne; after all, she knows where everything is.

I've learned to live with and love having the Futzing Queen always around. I almost never go wanting because Anne has everything. Need a rubber band on the golf course? Anne will have several sizes in her golf bag. I don't have to do the packing. Anne sends me away because she'd just have to repack what I did anyway. I am glad, though, there's only one futzer in the family--can you imagine the fights with two futzers competing!

Irish Time

Time is different in Ireland. I don't mean that the Irish are in a special time zone, although it may seem that way. I don't refer to time seeming to go more quickly or more slowly when you vacation in Ireland. I mean that the Irish people have their own sense of time.

A well-known Irish saying is, "When God made time, he made lots of it." The Irish live by this saying. Except for the high powered business district of Dublin, they don't hurry. It's not the slow down you see in the southern states of the US where everything moves at a snail's pace because of the heat and the humidity. The Irish pace is just unhurried.

We've seen examples of the Irish pace in the grocery stores. As a customer comes through the check out line, the clerk and customer have a conversation. It makes no matter that there are no other clerks working or that the line behind the clerk is five deep. The conversation goes on until the conversation is over. On a single-track road in the west one year we waited for five minutes as the mail carrier blocked the road in both directions as she had a conversation with the resident. We could begin to understand Irish Time as we sat in the car on a pleasant day with beautiful scenery around us. Why hurry, indeed.

Irish Time can be frustrating though. In Donegal's tourist office Anne wanted to buy a small book. She was second in line behind a lady arranging a B&B for the night. The clerk, a sweet young thing, gave full attention to the lady's booking, as well she should. When the girl had to wait for a callback on a lodging, she still gave her attention to the lodgee. After ten minutes of waiting in line to pay for a two euro book, we decided Irish Time has its drawbacks.

Enjoy Ireland on Irish Time and try not to get frustrated.

L-L-O-Y-D

I find the Welsh language spoken by a native beautiful, slightly guttural, and exotic. It's one of Europe's oldest languages. For the visitor, though, the language presents some difficulties. For i n s t a n c e ,   h o w   d o   y o u   p r o n o u n c e LLanfairwllgwyngyllgogerychwyrndrobwllllandysiliogogogoch? It's the name of a small village on the Isle of Anglesey and there's nothing to the village except a church, an old railway station, a tourist shop, and the name.   In point of fact no one tries to pronounce the full name (except for special effect); instead, the locals refer to the village as Llanfair PG.

Of more practical concern is the pronunciation of villages you might stay in, such as LLandudno, Pwllheli, and Aberystwyth. To try to earn points with the Welsh golfers we'd be playing with, I tried to learn a little of the Welsh pronunciation.   For instance, Pwllheli sounds sort of like "puh-CLU-hell-ee" and Llandudno is "clan-DID-nu."
Notice that the double "L" is pronounced as a sort of guttural "CL."

This made me interested in the pronunciation of my Welsh middle name, Lloyd. In Caernarfron we met a native Welsh speaker in the Tourist Information Office. She booked us into a B&B near Porthmadog, a name I never did get correct. Taking the opportunity I asked the young lady how she would say my middle name, and I spelled out L-L-O-Y-D. She looked at the paper, back at me, and said, "Lloyd."

"What?" I exclaimed, "You just pronounced the double 'L' in Llandudno as "CL."

She smiled, "Yes, that's a place name and it's pronounced with a 'CL' sound, but yours is a person's name and it's pronounced with an 'L' sound."

I will keep trying to say the Welsh names the best I can, but I know it will be a long time before I understand the beautiful language of my ancestors.

No Visa Card

The next to last day of our first Ireland trip was traumatic. We wandered around downtown Dublin doing a little shopping and stopped at the first ATM machine we found so that we could top up on euros for our last couple of days. The machine wouldn't take the card. I tried several times, but the card was refused each time. We figured something was wrong with the machine. We tried a different machine at a different bank. Same results. Now we started to get worried. We were down to our last €20 and had a Visa card that didn't work. Luckily we found a Thomas Cook travel store who let us get €50 for an outrageous fee. At least we could still use the card for shopping, but at this point our day in Dublin was fairly well ruined.

The next day, our last in Ireland for that trip, we had golf planned before flying home. We got to the course in plenty of time to check in, but now the card wouldn't work at all. The club even tried calling the credit card company for approval, but we were out of luck. We used almost the last of our cash for greens fees and planned to deal with the credit card company when we got home.

Back at home I worked on sorting out the credit card mess. We had used the card at ATMs, shops, and restaurants for three weeks with no problem. It was using the card to make a €2 phone call to book a B&B that sent red flags flying at the credit card company. We could buy whatever we wanted for three weeks, but making a simple phone call indicated that our card might be stolen. So what does the credit card company do? They sent us a letter in Oregon, saying call or they'd cut off our card. That would have been fine if we'd been home instead of using the card in Ireland.   Of course, we didn't get the letter, didn't make the call, and did get our card shut off.

We have since learned to call the credit card companies before we travel and let them know we will be using our card out of the country. In the seventeen trips since that Ireland trip we have had credit card problems only once, and at that it wasn't a serious problem. It was frustrating, though, walking around Dublin worrying about money instead of enjoying the vibrant city.

Scottish Pounds--Not in England

Ireland uses the euro for its economy, but Great Britain has remained true to the Pound Sterling. It might have something to do with a rebellion against the European Union, or perhaps the fact that the British couldn't put the Queen's image on a euro note or coin. Regardless, when we travel in the UK (England, Scotland, Wales, and Northern Ireland) we use the Pound Sterling. At least that's how the system is supposed to work.

During the summer of 2010 Anne traveled to Scotland to meet up with our Scottish family and then the girls (Anne, Jacky, Ailsa, and Paulette) got the train to spend a long weekend in London. Talk about your JetSet crowd. In Scotland Anne hit an ATM and drew out some Pounds for the trip. In London, though, she found that many of the businesses refused to take her Pounds because they had been issued by the Royal Bank of Scotland. In the UK monetary system each bank will issue their own paper money; it's all Pounds Sterling, but would be issued by RBS, Clydebank, Barclays, or others. Businesses would look at the Royal Bank issued notes and say, "That's Scottish money, we want English money."

It's all the same money: Pounds Sterling!

When in the fall we visited the Wales, a pub in Caernarfon refused to take my £20 bill because, as the barkeep said, "That's Scottish funny-money and we don't take it." I scrounged in my changed to find coins enough to pay for our two halves of Guinness. Our B&B gave us the strategy to use when our Scottish Pounds were refused. It didn't happen again until Anne and I were boarding a bus to go from Corsham to Bath in England. I handed the Scottish note to the bus driver and he said, "I'm sorry, we don't accept foreign money." I simply turned the bill over and pointed to the inscription which read, "Pounds Sterling." He looked at that, turned the note over, and said, "That will be fine."

We now have the clue and traveling from Scotland to England has just gotten easier for us.

The Trouble with *Reader's Digest* Is You Have to Buy One

As a debate coach I always called *Reader's Digest* "Reader's Disgust." It just isn't quality information. If one's sitting on the table I'm liable to pick it up to read the humor sections, and I've even been known to send them an item or two of humor. They've never bought one of my submissions, that might have something to do with my feelings toward the publication. In Ireland one year, though, Anne wanted a *Reader's Digest* for some light reading material (for when her mystery novels get too heavy). Thus began the Irish quest for the *Reader's Digest*.

We first tried at the Dunne's store in Kilkenny. They had the latest issue, so Anne picked it up and took it to the register. After a couple of attempts, the clerk said it wouldn't ring up. A manager was called over and even she couldn't get it to ring up. They couldn't find a price code anywhere on the magazine. My suggestion that it may be free was met with frowns. I even said I'd just pay the usual price, but they said they couldn't sell us the magazine without ringing it up and they couldn't ring it up without the price code. Anne had to watch as her magazine was carried off to the inner bowels of the store, probably never to be seen again. Unsold and unread.

The next day we were in Waterford town after playing golf at the Waterford Castle course. We were walking the mostly closed downtown looking for a place to eat when Anne spied a book/magazine store with the lights on and the door unlocked. We walked in and easily found Anne's cherished *Reader's Digest*, cousin to the one she couldn't buy in Kilkenny. Anne took it to the register, but nobody was about. We waited a minute or so before a clerk came up from the back of the store and stared incredulously at us.

"What are you doing in here?" she aggressively asked.

"We just want to buy this *Reader's Digest*," Anne responded.

"But we're closed," was the clerk's reply.

We told her that the door was open and the lights were on and that we saw no sign of the store being closed, and besides, we really just want to pay for the magazine. The clerk's attitude softened a little when she realized we weren't the dreaded *Reader's Digest* hijackers that must have been in the news recently.

With that she tried to sell us the *Reader's Digest,* but her till was shut down and she couldn't open it back up for one small sale. We agreed on a quick €2 under-the-table in exchange for the magazine.

All that for "Reader's Disgust." Oh, well, Anne was happy and I did enjoy the humor sections.

Whisky A-Go-Go, Whisky A-Went-Went

We usually try to bring home four bottles (our legal limit) of single malt whisky on each of our trips. The whisky is always special, something we can't get easily in the States. It is packed very carefully in bubble wrap and placed strategically in our luggage to be checked. Since 2001 we haven't been able to carry-on liquids. In seventeen trips since 2000 we have had only one bottle break and I suspect the bottle was defective. We have, though, lost one bottle and it was my fault.

In 2006 we were coming home after six weeks in Scotland and were traveling under very strict UK travel guidelines. We each were allowed only one small personal item as carry-on, but Continental Airlines allowed us to check our second carry-on as a third piece of checked luggage with no charge. Check-in went fine. The flight to Newark was fine, except that it was late and we missed our connection to Portland. Now the story gets tricky.

Continental arrange for us to stay the night and fly out the next morning at 5:00. With several flights having been delayed, picking up our luggage and getting to our lodging was a disaster of epic proportions and took well into the night. After a four-hour sleep over we returned to the airport to check-in for our flight. Now comes the tragedy. We were now under US flight rules and could carry on one piece of carry-on and one personal item. We checked our two each large pieces of luggage, and moved to TSA security screening. As my bag went through the screening machine--the bag that came from Edinburgh as the extra checked bag--the TSA agent says, "Whoa, what's this?" He pulls my bag out, has me come over to a special table, and reaches into the bag. He pulls his hand out holding a $150 bottle of special Ardbeg whisky. "You can't take this on board."

I had put the bottle in the carry-on bag knowing it was going to be checked. In my sleep deprive and hassled stage the night before and in the early morning, I had forgotten all about the bottle now being in a carry-on. To his credit the agent was very sympathetic. He suggested I go back and put the bag through as extra checked luggage. It was too close to our flight time to do that. He asked if there was anyone I could give it to. Alas, no. He asked if I wanted to drink it, but at 5:00 AM even $150 whisky is out of my league. With tears in my eyes, I watched as he carefully placed the bottle in garbage bin. I do hope someone later retrieved the bottle and did justice to the fine whisky it contained. On that trip, though, it wasn't me.

A Celebration of Dance

We had played golf at Powfoot GC in Annan on Scotland's Solway Firth in the morning and were to play in a competition at Colvend GC the next day. So we took the opportunity to spend the afternoon wandering in the shopping area of Dumfries. When we walked into town from parking the car near our B&B we heard a band playing an interesting jazz/reggae mix--they were very good. While we listened to the street concert several costumed dancers, male and female, came out and began dancing to the music.

The costumes were interesting--several looked like animal costumes including heads and antlers, others were dressed in what might be medieval garb, and another set wore makeup and costumes reminiscent of Japanese Kabuki dancers. The dancers kept inviting spectators to join in the dancing--of course most of the children did. I wasn't interested in dancing, but I did get out into the middle of the dancers with my camera and took a ton of photos. I finally asked one of the dancers what was the occasion? The dancer told me it was just a celebration of dance in Scotland, a street festival to encourage people to dance. It was one of those magic moments of travel when something unexpected becomes unforgettable.

Collecting a Taste of Scotland

Haggis and black pudding may not be our favorite dishes, but another taste of Scotland is not only worth having while in Scotland, it's also worth taking home and collecting. *Uisge Beatha*, The Water of Life, Scotch Whisky. I had always like Scotch whisky, although in college it was whiskey and 7 Up or whiskey and soda-- always the blended stuff (Johnnie Walker, Vat 69, Teachers). It wasn't until we started traveling to Scotland that I really discovered my taste for Single Malt Whisky. In 2000 we brought a couple of bottles home, then went to the local liquor store and bought more. Not that I'm a heavy drinker--a couple of fingers a night is my usual limit--but I do enjoy the collecting of various whiskies and having

several bottles to choose from when I want a dram or offer a dram to guests.

Visiting the distilleries is always an entertaining enterprise and so far we've visited more than 30 in Scotland. There have also been a few adventures in my whisky collecting experience, especially when trying to bring home whiskies I can't get in my local store.

Once, early in our travels, I was almost caught by US Customs in violation of our quota which is four and half bottles of spirit. I was carrying five and listed "whisky" on our customs declaration without specifying the number of bottles. The agent saw that I had declared whisky and asked, "How much?" I lied, "Five bottles, but one is a half." She said, "Okay. This time." That was the last time we tried to bring more than four bottles back.

There was once when I tried to bring back an unusually shaped bottle, sort of like a crock-style large flask (if that makes any sense) of special Caol Ila (Islay) whisky. It's the only bottle we've ever had that leaked. We lost about a quarter of the contents, but thankfully it was sealed up well in bubble wrap and plastic bags (Anne does a great job of packing) and no whisky got on anything else in the suitcase. No, I didn't lick the bubble wrap.

On a recent trip we brought home just three bottles: a Pittyvaich (closed distillery) 18 Year Old by Rare Malts, a 20 Year Old Braes of Glenlivit whisky, and a special bottle I just bought the day before we left of Mackinlay's Rare Old Highland Malt Whisky, a commemorative recreation of the whisky from the British Antarctica Expedition of 1907. The Nimrod Expedition (named for his ship) was the first of three Antarctica expeditions lead by Ernest Shackleton. The whisky was found almost a hundred years later buried under Shackleton's McMurdo Sound cabin. After 18 months of analysis the whisky is reported to be an exact match for the Shackleton whisky and "sheer heaven" to drink. I hope so, but we'll see.

A last note on whisky collecting. While staying at the Neidpath Inn in Peebles we saw two display cases of old rare miniatures. The owner didn't name a value, but I'd estimate from the age and rarity of some of the wee bottles several thousands of pounds Sterling were mounted on the wall. Anne won't let my collection approach anything near that. Damn!

Innerpeffray Library, Chapel, School, and Concert

Early in September (2013) we made our fourth visit to Innerpeffray Library and Chapel about seven miles out of Crieff. The library, the oldest lending library in Scotland, was the Drummond family estate library and is still a treasure trove of information about Scottish history. The chapel adjacent to the library was the family chapel and is relatively intact considering it was built in the 1500s. The downstairs of the library has been newly renovated to be an office and a library showcase. They have recently acquired a new set of Robert Burns' manuscripts willed to the library by an American lady--the set includes a copy of the Kilmarnock edition of Burns' poetry, his first book. We had a look around and then had a special tour of the "modern" books (after 1850) by the curator of that section. We also found out about a concert in the chapel the day we get back from our trip north. We bought our tickets on the spot and arranged for a couple more tickets for anyone in our Scottish family who was interested.

Three weeks later we came back to Crieff from timeshare in the north in time to get ready to go to the Innerpeffray Chapel concert. Sally from Dubai and her daughter Cindy who lives in Crieff took our extra tickets and together we drove over to the Chapel. First on the agenda was a tea and cake social hour in the classroom of the Innerpeffray School fifty yards from the Chapel. The school's teacher's quarters are now used by caretakers of the property and the classroom is a function room. We visited with several locals, many who wanted to know about the Welch kilt I was wearing. The concert was held in the chapel where about 200 seats had been set up. Performing was a small community choir and trio (two ladies who sang and a gentleman who played harp). Songs were a mix of classical and traditional Scottish, particularly songs of Robert Burns.

The only downside to the whole evening was that the chapel was not heated and the October air was cool. It was especially cool for me as I was sitting next to the stone wall in a light-weight summer kilt. Chilly!

The Return of the Lost Lace

On several of our trips to either Scotland or Ireland we've acted as tour guides for friends. It's always been fun, but it is a bit nerve wracking--it's difficult taking on responsibility for someone else's trip, even for a couple of days. On this particular trip, fall of 2010, we arrived back at Merlindale B&B in Crieff, Scotland, on Monday, September 20 from a ten day sojourn to Wales and the Yorkshire Dales and our friends, Dave and Susi Gordon arrived for the beginning of their first trip to Scotland the next day. We planned to be tour guides for a day and a half before they took off on their own travels.

They got to Crieff late in the afternoon on Tuesday. We all visited at the B&B with hosts John and Jacky and then took a walking tour of the local village. The tour of town is a great introduction to Scotland--it's very eye-opening to see how locals live, work, and play. But the real treat of the Gordon's first day was a paella dinner that Jacky fixed for eleven friends (some local and some B&B guests like us). Dave and Susi were made welcome and the food, wine, and craic (conversation) flowed freely.

Our next day was filled with touristy things including a drive down a Scottish glen (Glendevon), a museum (the Andrew Carnegie Birthhouse Museum), a cathedral and abbey (Dunfermline), a major castle (Stirling Castle), and fine dining at Yann's French/Scottish bistro next to our B&B. The most enlightening highlight among many highlights of the day happened at lunch. After a tour of Dunfermline Abbey and Cathedral and a little shopping in the gift shop, we stopped next door at the Abbot's House tearoom for a typical Scottish lunch of soup and scones. While sitting in the restaurant eating lunch the clerk from the cathedral gift shop came up to our table and asked, "Did either of you ladies buy some lace in the shop and leave it in a pew in the cathedral?" Anne looked up and said, "That would be me." The girl handed Anne the package and went back to work. We were all impressed that the clerk would work so hard to find the owner of the lost lace, but Anne and I weren't surprised. We know how caring and thoughtful the Scots are. The Gordons really got a quick education about the people and the culture they were about to explore.

The day and a half of touring with friends ended as spectacularly as it began. At the end of dinner at Yann's Restaurant where we'd been seated in the conservatory room we were treated to a dramatic rain storm, complete with lightning and thunder. The storm was so intense that we got thoroughly soaked walking next door to the B&B. I wish we could plan that kind of touring for all our visiting friends coming to Scotland.

Will You Have Your Roast Bishop with or without B-B-Q Sauce?

In 2002 after touring Culzean (Cull-een) Castle in Ayrshire we visited the much ruined 15th century Dunure Castle not far away. The ruin and doocot (a dwelling for housing doves or doos often called a "Scottish refrigerator") sited along the cliffs above the crashing waves is very picturesque, but what was most entertaining is the story we read about the "roasting" of a bishop. It seems that in 1570 a dispute over land arose between Earl Gilbert Kennedy of Dunure and Allen Stewart the Bishop of Crossraguel Abbey nearby. To force a concession by Stewart, Gilbert Kennedy roasted him over a spit while basting his feet, not once but twice two days apart. The Bishop finally consented to sign over the land to Kennedy and was then rescued by his own men. The Kennedys never did get the disputed land, but Allen Stewart, the roasted Bishop, never walked again. I'll take small claims court any day over the Clan Kennedy form of dispute resolution.

The Day of the Wedding

Anne told me we had to arrange our trip to Scotland in the spring of 2011 to either be at home or at our Scotland home (Merlindale B&B in Crieff) on April 29; we couldn't be in transit. The reason for the exact schedule was that the wedding of Prince William and Kate Middleton was on that day and Anne wanted to be able to watch the whole thing. We actually arrived a couple of days ahead of the wedding day so Anne and Jacky could watch the spectacle in depth and in real time. They watched from start to finish and taped some of it so they wouldn't miss anything when they had to break for lunch.

The Royal wedding was quite a big deal in the UK with most women glued to their televisions and most men played golf. John and I played 18 at St Fillans, the course Anne and I belong to, and it was busy with men--I saw only one woman at the course and that was after most of the wedding to do was over. A guest at breakfast a few days later said he went to play his club (in England) on the wedding day and it was packed. The wedding was a real lady thing.

When John and I played St Fillans on the wedding day we ran into an unusual situation beside the fact that there were no

ladies on the course. There were deer on the course--I mean really on the course. We've seen red deer run across a fairway or two a couple of times, but this day the deer had set up camp on the seventh tee box. I saw them first when I was on the fourth green; two red deer laying on the tee with a group of four guys trying to tee off over or around the deer. I got several good photos from the fifth tee. When we got to the seventh tee the deer were still in the vicinity; in fact, I practically hit one as I teed off over its hind end as it was standing twenty yards down the fairway (more photos). The Glasgow paper the next day had pictures of the wedding and of deer on the tees at St Fillans.

As a follow up note, Anne and I played St Fillans two days later and one of the deer was still on the course (still more photos). The other was nowhere to be seen--either road kill or in someone's larder.

A Scottish Tradition I Don't Buy Into

I've celebrated my birthday several times in Scotland—Jacky usually fixes a great dinner of my choosing. She has asked at times if I really wouldn't rather go out for dinner. What, and pass up one of her Cordon Bleu meals? Never!

On one recent trip we were in Scotland on her birthday and she chose dinner at Yann's, the fancy Scottish-French restaurant next to the B&B. Yann's is the best restaurant in the area and one of the best in Scotland. Good choice for a birthday dinner party of twelve. But now I know why Jacky suggests going out for my birthday. In Scotland there is a tradition of the birthday celebrant picking up all or most of the bill. Our birthday dinner for Jacky cost her several hundred pounds. It's a Scottish tradition I rather enjoyed, but I just can't seem to buy into it.

The Converter

We take far too many electrical gadgets in our travels to the UK, but we haven't yet figured out how to leave it all at home. We have phones, computers, iPads, iPods, portable speaker systems, noise reduction headphones for the airplanes, and I have tons of photo batteries which need to be charged—I'm sure I've left out a couple of dozen electrical devices that we can't do without. We have converter plugs for many of our items, particularly our Apple products. For the rest I still need a converter to plug into which will change the current from American 110-volt to UK 220-volt. On a recent trip our Brookstone electrical converter gave up the ghost—things started to come loose inside and there was no way I was going to plug it into a 220-volt outlet; that stuff's dangerous!

When the converter died we were on the Orkney islands staying at Avalon B&B in Kirkwall. Marina, our hostess, was considerate enough to loan us a converter until we could find another one to buy. We went shopping in Kirkwall that morning looking for a converter for 220 to 110—not an adapter for the plugs, but an actual electrical converter. Four stores, no luck. None had converters. Each store sent us to another store with the hopeful send off, "Surely such-and-such store will have a converter." They all had adapters, but without a converter the adapters would fry our electronics. Marina told us to keep the converter until we could find one on the mainland, then send hers back if we could.

On the mainland, it took us several stores to find a good converter. I packaged Marina's loaned converter and mailed it with a note that I had enclosed £5 for her or a favorite charity. I took the package to the post and mailed it to Orkney. When I got back to the B&B I found the £5 note still sitting on the desk. The next day I mailed the money with an apology for not getting it into the package with her converter. Thinking about it that evening I figured out that the note and money would probably arrive before the package with the converter. Made a royal mess of that, didn't I.

The Turkish Barber

In Crieff I needed a beard trim and my normal barber (Neismiths) was closed because he was having knee surgery. I decided to try the Turkish Barber new to town. It was a very interesting, entertaining, and frightening experience.

The barber, who always called me "Boss," trimmed my beard first with an electric razor, then a straight razor. Next, he lighted on fire an implement (ball of some kind on a hard wire) and started hitting my face with it. Wow! Before I knew what he was doing he was hitting my beard with the flaming ball and whisking the flames away with his hand—I think this was to burn off the frizz left from the trimming. Finally, he wrapped my face with a hot, wet towel (to put out the fire?) while he messaged my shoulders and arms. Oh, that felt good! The whole thing cost me £7 and I gave him a £2 tip. I'm going to do this again.

Be Careful What You Say…

We were having a cuppa at the Corrie GC tearoom on the Isle of Arran and doing some writing. The tearoom manager was friendly and chatty with those of us in the room. She commented about a group of young people who had just left saying, "They startled me. I hadn't heard them come in and when I came from the kitchen they were there quietly fiddling with their mobile devices not saying a word. Just think, they're the ones who will be in charge of us when we're all in those special homes."

She notice me writing and asked what I was doing. When I told her that I was working on my notes for the golf guides we write she said, "Oh, I've got to watch what I say when I don't know who's in the room." She laughed and went into the kitchen.

A couple of minutes later she came out and told us a story of another time she should have held her tongue. She and one of her regulars were talking about fireworks for Hogmanay, the

Scottish New Year's celebration. The customer was bemoaning the fact that you couldn't bring fireworks over to the island on the Caledonian MacBryne ferries from the mainland. The tearoom manager said loudly enough for the whole room to hear, "I just go over to Ardrossan, buy about £400 of fireworks, cover them with a blanket in the back of my car, and drive right on the ferry—to hell with CalMac rules." One visitor said sort of quietly to her, "Young lady, you ought to be careful what you say in front of strangers."

She gasped and said, "Oh my God, you work for Calmac ferries don't you!"

"Yes, I'm a ship's Captain."

She said he wrote down her car registration (license plate number) and that her car now gets regularly checked.

The History of the Kilt

There's no more iconic Scottish symbol than the kilt--the bagpipes are a close second with the wild Highland haggis a distant third. Kilts have been the traditional dress of men and boys in Scotland since the 16th century. The kilt has also received wider association with celtic heritage (Welsh, Irish, Cornish) in the late 19th century. Today's kilt, though, isn't what the Highland Scot wore several hundred years ago; that would be the Great Kilt, Big Kilt, or *Breacan* (Gaelic). Originally Norse, the Great Kilt was a full length garment with the upper half worn as a cloak draped over the shoulder or brought up over the head. The wearer had to actually lay down on the garment, made of several yards of wool cloth, and wrap it around himself. The Great Kilt was a full function wrap which could serve as a blanket when snuggling down in the heather and had enough material left at the top to be able to make a pouch in which to carry your essentials. After the Battle of Culloden (1746), when the English Duke of Cumberland defeated the Highlanders fighting to return Bonnie Prince Charles Edward Stewart to the throne, tartan attire, along with weapons and bagpipes, were banned in Scotland. Non-Jacobite lowland Scots didn't really mind the banning of the tartan kilt which many condemned as a barbarous form of apparel. It took Queen Victoria's fascination with her Scottish roots and her display of enormous pride in her Stewart ancestry (1860s) to bring the kilt back into vogue for all Scots--Highland and lowland.

The modern kilt, short kilt, walking kilt, or little kilt (*Feilreadh Beg* in Gaelic) was invented by English Quaker (to the Scots' chagrin) Thomas Rawlinson in 1720 for use of working Highlanders. Today's kilts are usually 18-22 ounce wool for formal heavy weight models and 10-11 ounce weight for lighter kilts. Most common are the kilts in the 13-16 ounce range which equals about six to eight yards of material for an adult. Although you will see utility kilts made of cotton or canvas in solid colors, the traditional kilt will be of a tartan (patterned) material called a sett. Setts are associated with particular families or clans. These patterns began to be formalized in the Victorian era and are now registered with the International Tartan Index. Besides family or clan tartans, setts have been registered for districts (such as the counties of Ireland), countries, corps, and schools as well as numerous generic patterns. For instance, the tartan Welsh National is a pattern of green, red, and white--the colors of the flag of Wales. Since the modern kilt isn't long enough to provide material for a pouch, one had to be invented. The sporran (Gaelic for pouch or purse) is a small leather or fur bag worn by chain in front of the groin of a kilt wearer. The sporran, serving as a wallet (and from experience I can tell you that it carries little more than a wallet), comes in various styles from the a simple pouch for day wear to a highly decorated formal sporran worn by pipe band members.

Whether a kilt is utilitarian or formal, a family tartan or a generic, there is a level of truth to the Scottish saying, "A man in a kilt is a man and a half!"

The Wearing of the Kilt

I don't know if I should share this secret or keep it all to myself, but it's a shame for all other males who have Scottish, Irish, Cornish, or Welsh heritage not to know the advantages of wearing a kilt (in Welsh it's a cilt because the Welsh language doesn't have a "k").

Many advantages have been written about including freedom of movement and ventilation, but I have yet to see anyone discuss the positive attention factor. The wearing of a kilt definitely attracts much attention from both females and males. From the ladies I always get very appreciative looks, more than my naturally attractive legs would garner. I often get comments like, "I think kilts are so sexy," and "a man always looks sexy in a kilt." Considering I'd get those comments at no other time, except from my adorable wife, I find it a little embarrassing and a great thrill to hear those type of compliments.

Women, also, are constantly asking "The Question." Is it true about what men wear under a kilt? I have been known to "Go Commando," as they say, on occasion--all right, most of the time--and I have developed a stock answer: "They say if a Scotsman wears a kilt, he wears nothing under it. If he wears something under it, he's wearing a skirt. I wear a kilt, but I'm a Welshman, so make your own guess." It leaves some room for their imagination, which may or may not be better than the real thing. I have had a couple of women joke about reaching under my kilt to find out. I always invite exploration in the name of discovery, but have yet to have anyone be bold enough to find out for themselves. Though, we were on an Alaskan cruise one year and I wore my kilt for dress-up evening.  After dinner while sitting in the bar a lady came over admiring my kilt. She was quite drunk and kept asking what I wore under my kilt. I gave her all my stock answers, such as "My socks," but she kept reaching her hand higher. The only thing that stopped her was her husband standing behind her along with her two sons. He smiled and said, "Honey, do you really want to do that?" She thought and then pulled her hand back.

Once at a birthday dinner for our Scottish sister Jacky a friend of hers said she'd find out what I wore under my kilt by taking a picture. It was probably the alcohol making her brave enough stick the camera under my kilt, and it was definitely the alcohol that made her hit the off button on the camera instead of the shutter button. After two attempts I said, "Nope, two is your limit." Since I had been willing to let her grab a photo, the lack of a photo still left her guessing. While all this banter is going back and forth, the lady in question is often snuggling close and rubbing her female charms about. It's a hell of a position to put a man in, but I'm man enough to take it.

The reaction from men is interesting as well. Only a couple of times have I been asked what I wear under my kilt. More often my wearing of the kilt is acknowledged with a "way to go," a thumbs up, or a high-five. I think other men realize and recognize that to wear a kilt an individual has to be a little bit of a performer and very self-confident.

One other advantage to wearing a kilt is that it makes me feel dressy in a way that a business suit never did. There's a flair associated with wearing a beautiful and meaningful tartan, accessorized with a striking sporran, hose, flashes, and bonnet. It just makes one feel good.

I know there won't be many out there who will jump on the kilt band wagon, but if you've got balls enough there are definite advantages.